BRIGHT
PARTICULAR
STARS

Also by David McKie

Jabez: The Rise and Fall of a Victorian Rogue
Great British Bus Journeys: Travels Through Unfamous Places
McKie's Gazetteer: A Local History of Britain

BRIGHT PARTICULAR STARS

A
GALLERY OF GLORIOUS
BRITISH ECCENTRICS

DAVID McKIE

ATLANTIC BOOKS
LONDON

First published in Great Britain in 2011 by Atlantic Books,
an imprint of Atlantic Books Ltd.

Copyright © David McKie 2011

The moral right of David McKie to be identified as the author of this work has
been asserted by him in accordance with the Copyright,
Designs and Patents Acts of 1988.

Lines from *What's It All About* by Michael Caine, published by Century.
Reprinted by permission of The Random House Group Ltd.

1 2 3 4 5 6 7 8 9

A CIP catalogue record for this book is available from the British Library.

ISBN: 978 184887 248 6

Designed in Bembo by Geoff Green Book Design, Cambridge
Printed in Great Britain by the MPG Books Group

Atlantic Books
An Imprint of Atlantic Books Ltd
Ormond House
26–27 Boswell Street
London
WC1N 3JZ

www.atlantic-books.co.uk

For Gordon, Annabel and Jeff

CONTENTS

CONTENTS

CONTENTS

PREFACE

ARIBALDI, military and revolutionary hero, arrives in London and so enthuses the populace that Victoria becomes alarmed and her ministers persuade him to hurry back to Italy. The dreamily romantic Archibald, 13th Earl of Eglinton, sets out to recreate historic glories and succeeds in engineering one of the great nineteenth-century fiascos, which leaves thousands of those who flock to see it historically drenched and miserable. Mary Macarthur first mesmerizes and then liberates the oppressed chain-maker women of Cradley Heath. A civil servant in a blue double-breasted blazer called Scott-Piggott bestows an unexpected moment of fame on unprepossessing Trowell in Nottinghamshire. This is a book about people who through some two centuries excited, enthralled, intrigued, shocked or scandalized otherwise ordinary places and lit up the lives of those who lived there – about men and women who became for a time, in Milton's phrase, 'the cynosure of neighbouring eyes'; or in the formulation that Shakespeare's Helena uses in *All's Well That Ends Well*, bright paticular stars.

Some, like Garibaldi, were already famous. The story of his visit to Britain in 1864 has been told in many biographies, but to read the reports of local newspapermen coming fresh and excited from the ecstatic clamour that greeted him – the 'Garibaldi sentiment' as one of them called it – gives it a new immediacy. Others slipped long ago into obscurity, like Mary Elizabeth Smith, the country girl who took on the fearsome might of the Ferrers dynasty in a trial for breach of promise of marriage in Westminster Hall. What became of her thereafter I cannot discover: yet the record of the proceedings, which I found on Google Books while looking for something else, still sizzles on the page.

Some of my people are good, almost to the point of saintliness, like Adelaide Anne Procter, a poet once second only to Tennyson in the esteem of Victorian England, now remembered, if at all, for having written the words for the song by Sir Arthur Sullivan sung in every middle-class parlour – 'The Lost Chord'. But my test for writing biography clearly differs from that of the Victorian moralist Samuel Smiles, who taught that 'the chief use of biography consists in the noble models of character in which it abounds.' Some of my subjects are scoundrels, like Barnard Gregory, newspaper editor, ace dabbler in sleaze and reputed blackmailer, whose eventual public humiliation delighted Dickens – and whose more salubrious second career as an actor was ruined by the fall-out from his first.

Still others mix the admirable with the deplorable. Ralph Ward Jackson created a prosperous town but, failing to impose his imperious will on a priest and a congregation, was ready to wall them up in their church. Philip Heseltine, refurbished as Peter Warlock, briefly installed at Eynsford, Kent, composed his gentle and sensitive song cycle, *The Curlew*, but set net curtains twitching and tongues affrontedly wagging by the roistering life he led there with his equally unbuttoned friends. He has not, as I discovered, been entirely forgiven yet.

Many of this contingent seemed to me to fall into a category that falls short of justifying a full-scale book but deserves rather more than the limited space that the *Oxford Dictionary of National Biography* can provide. There's a persistent story that the 2004 edition of the *ODNB* contains a hoax entry. A friend sent me its account of Dame Lucy Houston and said this must surely be it – but read the accounts of her life by her besotted admirers or the incendiary pieces she wrote for the weekly paper she owned and edited, and she comes out as even more wildly extraordinary than the *ODNB* makes her.

Houston is one of those who lit up the sky for a while but left little mark behind her. You can wander today through the spotless avenues of Shoreham Beach on the Sussex coast without discovering even the slightest trace of the joyous Bohemian world that flourished there in the days of Marie Loftus and Sidney Morgan. But William Gilpin, measuring up the River Wye to see how far it satisfied his demanding definitions of what deserved to be called picturesque, inspired a new kind of topographical tourism. Sydney Yates of Blackburn, hardly remembered now outside the town or even (to judge by the slightness of his commemoration in the pub where it all began) within it, set off the trend that brought professionalism into football by breaking the aristocratic monopoly on the FA Cup.

Some of these stories are commemorated in writings that most readers might well never come across. But for the Shakesperean scholar Marvin Spevack and his publisher in Hildesheim, Germany, I would never have encountered the enchanting Henrietta, daughter of the tyrannical bibliomaniac Sir Thomas Phillipps, whose diaries he selected and edited in his book *A Victorian Chronicle*, available in far fewer libraries than it deserves to be. Ward Jackson's story is told in a book by the former town clerk of Hartlepool and published by Hartlepool corporation – hardly the recipe for a bestseller, but the book is exemplary. The history of the Jezreelites of Gillingham and their tower is recorded in a book long out of print by the fine Kent historian P. G. Rogers, whom I discovered while researching for a previous book the tale of the crazed sect leader whose life and death he described in *Battle in Bossenden Wood: The Strange Story of Sir William Courtenay*.

Much else has been dug out of libraries, especially the London Library and the British Library's newspaper base at Colindale, and the Guildhall library, London and also from that glorious boon for writers of this kind of history, Google Books. The Medway Archives at Strood, the Wiltshire and Swindon History Centre at Chippenham were especially helpful. Eton College Library kindly invited me in to read past issues of their College Chronicle. Comparisons between monetary values of former times and those of 2010 are based on the National Archives on-line currency converter. Among other conspicuous benefactors, Jim Muir and Jim Miller introduced me to Kilwinning, Victor Keegan illuminated a visit to the Wye Valley, Mark Whyman and David Walsh showed me around the territory described in the chapter on Boosbeck, Cleveland and Audrey Gillan took me on an instructive tour of Spitalfields. June Wyndham Davies, now living in retirement in Spain, sent me a long and generous account of her happy and hectic days in the poor doomed theatre in Horsham.

My thanks are also due as ever to Toby Mundy and my editor Sarah Norman at Atlantic, my agent Jonathan Pegg, and my tirelessly alert and perceptive copy-editor, Jane Robertson. Judy Goodman and my wife Beryl worked through the text, pounced on errors and offered much constructive advice.

I have been to all the places I have written about, walked their streets, examined their principal buildings, their streets broad and narrow, their monuments and statues, and have sensed why in towns from plain industrial Blackburn to lovely Cromarty on Scotland's east coast, in unglamorous suburbs such as Nine Elms, in rural villages like Bishops Cannings in Wiltshire, and in so many places throughout the land, people might look about them and say to themselves, even now, with some feeling of pride: 'It happened here.' These visits have necessarily been brief, and to those who feel I have failed to understand and appreciate the deeper merits of their communities, I would echo this apology, written in 1658 at the start of an address on the Epistle to the Galatians by one of his predecessors, James Fergusson, which I found in the local history by Mr Lee Ker, quoted in my chapter on Kilwinning:

> What humane frailties you may discerne in this piece of mine (which doubtless are not a few) pitie them, and so much the more pray for me that I may discerne and amend them, and if any will be so faithful and free to advertise me immediately, or by causing others to acquaint me with them, I shall (God willing) be humbly thankfull, and endeavour to make the best use I can of their freedom, knowing that such reproofs will not break my head but be as precious ointment...

BRIGHT
PARTICULAR
STARS

I

LOWER LYDBROOK, GLOUCESTERSHIRE

WILLIAM GILPIN EXAMINES THE RIVER WYE
AND THOUGH FINDING IT ON THE WHOLE
SATISFACTORY THINKS THE RUINS OF TINTERN
COULD BE IMPROVED BY AMENDMENT.

&

*Had they known who he was and what he was up to, the
more aesthetically sensitive of Lydbrook's villagers might
have witnessed with some trepidation the progress of the
scholarly, sharp-chinned gentleman who was training his
critical eye on their waterfront...*

THERE ARE CARS FROM Bristol and Birmingham, from
Leeds and Sheffield, from Caerphilly and Laugharne in
South Wales, parked on the forecourt of the Courtfield
Arms. Across the road where the wharf used to be – today it's replaced
by a couple of car parks and a prim little garden – a Roma-home
caravette has arrived and settled alongside a little saloon from
Evesham. A rather bigger number from Newton Abbot, Devon, has
a canoe strapped to the top which will soon be down in the water,
alongside a host of already active canoes out on the Wye on this
warm June morning as it flows peaceably west towards Monmouth
and thence to the Severn Estuary and the sea. It's too early for the
holiday coaches of high summer, but they too will be thronging
this valley a few weeks from now.

Tucked away in the trees a little way down the road towards English Bicknor, where a railway junction and a mighty viaduct used
to be, there is still an industrial site, patrolled by a security man who,

if you peer through the fencing, will ask a little suspiciously if he can help. But it's derelict and abandoned, with a comprehensive array of shattered windows and, despite the hopeful advertisements proclaiming the availability of an industrial warehouse site, it looks set to remain that way. Up the hill past the Forge Hammer Inn, on a road where a company tramway used to bring coals from the Forest of Dean down to the waterfront, there is still a sense of industrial Britain; but even here, it's unlikely that anyone stopping to take a break before climbing back on a Wallace Arnold would find this scene reminiscent of Sheffield.

Yet that was a comparison quite solemnly advanced in the early years of the nineteenth century. Here, as along much of the river from Ross to Monmouth and on to Chepstow, there were forges, blast furnaces and foundries, collieries and copper works, paper mills and shipbuilding yards and throngs of busy boats on the river – a world at work to command the eye and assault the ear. This area could claim to be as much the birthplace of the Industrial Revolution as Ironbridge on the Severn, where those times are so vividly and proudly commemorated. But that was all before the Reverend William Gilpin paid the Wye a visit which would help to create for it an image of an utterly different kind.

Had they known who he was and what he was up to, the more aesthetically sensitive of Lydbrook's villagers might have witnessed with some trepidation on that warm summer day in 1770 the progress of the scholarly, sharp-chinned gentleman who, comfortably ensconced in a boat propelled by three sweating plebeians, was training his critical eye on their waterfront. And what in fact was he up to? We now know, from the book he later produced – *Observations on the River Wye, and several parts of South Wales, &c. relative chiefly to Picturesque Beauty; made in the summer of the year 1770, by William Gilpin, M.A.* – that Gilpin was grading the river and countryside, mile by mile, field by field, to measure its picturesqueness against a set of scholarly rules devised by himself.

The Reverend Mr Gilpin was a pedagogue (once headmaster of

Cheam School in Surrey) and a pedant. He would come on both counts to be gently mocked by Jane Austen in *Northanger Abbey* and gleefully ridiculed by the cartoonist Thomas Rowlandson and the satirist William Combe, who portrayed him as 'Dr Syntax', sketching a lake from the back of his scrawny horse while a yokel with a fishing rod gawps at this curious spectacle, or so obsessed with the detail of the ruin that he is drawing that he tumbles backwards into the water: a man simply out of touch with the way that most of us live and behave. Even so, this journey along the Wye, and the various excursions with which he followed it, changed the way that people looked at the landscape and responded to what they saw; and one day would bring thousands by sightseeing car and coach to places like Lower Lydbrook.

The notion of the picturesque that he sought to define has since been degraded to mean nothing more than pretty. Jocular coves in saloon bars, puffing on sturdy pipes, used to say of some chocolate box scene: 'very pictureskew!' Recognizing the picturesque in the Gilpin sense, however, demanded something more than a glow in one's heart and a pleasing sense of one's aesthetic sensitivity. Once a schoolmaster, always a schoolmaster. The landscape, he teaches, must be assessed on a series of tests which appear to depend on science as much as on art. As he surveys the woods and the rocks and the craggy cliffs and the waterside villages on his journey, Gilpin seems compulsively set on giving them marks out of ten – or, more likely in his case, on a scale from alpha to gamma. Despite his love and respect for nature, he cannot conceal the unfortunate truth that it does not always live up to Gilpinesque standards. Where it falls short, it has to be warned of its failings. Nature, he says at one point, 'is an admirable colourist... and harmonizes tints with infinite variety and beauty; but this is seldom so correct in composition, as to produce a harmonious whole'. 'Could do better,' he seems to be saying.

The most perfect river views, he asserts at the start of the book, depend on the area: the river itself; two side-screens (the banks of the river); and the front screen, which points out the winding of the river. As readers in Lydbrook must have been delighted to hear when his book was eventually published in 1782, for the contrast of its screens, and the fading of side-screens over each other, the Wye scores well in this context. Additional marks are awarded by these criteria for what he calls ornaments, such as the ground, the woods, the rocks and the buildings in the vicinity; these last, as he stipulates, should be abbeys, castles, villages, spires, forges, mills and bridges – 'venerable vestiges of the past or cheerful habitations of present times'. None of them, though, is essential: 'In pursuing the beauties of nature, we can be amused without them.' Trees down to the water's edge are commendable, but not mandatory, since as a man accustomed to travel by boat he has to accept that they may constitute a danger to navigation. Marks are deducted where corn-fields run right down to the river, since a riverside pasturage is more picturesque, and bonus points accrue where cattle are 'laving them-selves' in the river.

Ross-on-Wye, where he starts his journey, fails to meet his re-quirements. He accepts that the view from the churchyard is much admired, and indeed, is 'amusing', but it doesn't deserve to be called picturesque. 'It is marked by no characteristic objects; it is broken into too many parts; and it is seen from too high a point.' But Goodrich, a little down river, with its rugged ruined castle, is a different matter entirely. 'A grand view', he says, 'presented itself; and we rested on our oars [though that seems to imply that Gilpin was rowing himself, which is unlikely] to examine it. This view, which is one of the grandest on the river, I should not scruple to call correctly picturesque'. A straight alpha for Goodrich, I think. Unfortunately it was raining so hard at this point that Gilpin's hopes of climbing out to explore were thwarted.

The highlight of the journey, one tends to assume, must surely be the historic, romantic, melancholy ruined abbey at Tintern. But that is to underestimate this traveller's rigour. There is quite a lot wrong with Tintern. Though he's not a believer in neatness for neatness' sake, he finds the huddle of hovel houses around the abbey offensive – and not just to aesthetic taste. He deplores the poverty and wretchedness of inhabitants in little huts clustered about the ruins who have no employment but begging. To his admitted surprise, Gilpin is moved and disturbed by what he sees. 'One poor woman we followed, who had engaged to shew us the monks' library. She could scarcely crawl; shuffling along her palsied limbs and meagre contracted body by the help of two sticks. She led us through an old gate into a place overspread with nettles and briars; and pointing to the remnant of a shattered cloister, told us that was the place. It was her own mansion. All indeed she meant to tell us was the story of her own wretchedness; and all she had to shew us was her own miserable habitation… I never saw so loathsome a human dwelling. It was a cavern loftily vaulted between two ruined walls, which streamed with various coloured stains of unwholesome dews. The floor was earth, yielding through moisture to the tread. Not the merest utensil or furniture of any kind appeared, but a wretched bedstead, spread with a few rags, and drawn into the middle of the cell to prevent its receiving the damp which trickled down the walls. At one end was an aperture, which served just to let in light enough to discover the wretchedness within…'

Still, surely the abbey ruin cannot fail to give satisfaction? Not so. 'The abbey does not make that appearance as a distant object which we expected… Though the parts are beautiful, the whole is ill-shaped… a number of gable-ends hurt the eye with regularity and disgust it by the vulgarity of their shape.' At which point he unleashes perhaps the most famous sentence he ever produced: 'A mallet judiciously used (but who durst use it?) might be of service in fracturing some of them; particularly those of the cross aisles, which are both disagreeable in themselves, and confound the perspective.' He does, however, give high marks to the ivy that has gathered over the structure, while parts of the abbey's interior are praised as 'perfection'.

The Reverend Mr Gilpin, as this sequence establishes, can be a hard man to satisfy. Yet the fact that this is a place not just of abbeys and castles but of forges and mills pleases him more than his reputation might have suggested. Some sensitive visitors seem to have edited that out of their consciousness. William Wordsworth, returning to the valley in 1798 after a five-year absence, marvelling as before at the beauty of sounding cataract, mountain, and steep and gloomy wood, was at this point aware in this place, as he had not been in his younger more impulsive and passionate days, of the 'still, sad music of humanity'. Yet even now, the natural business of humanity has little place in his picture. Though it is sometimes portrayed as a meditation brought on by the prospect of Tintern, the title of Wordsworth's poem says otherwise: these are 'Lines composed a few miles above Tintern Abbey' – possibly, modern research suggests, as far upriver as Symonds Yat. So he may have been right when he attributes 'wreaths of smoke sent up, in silence, from among the trees' to vagrants camped out in the woods or even a hermit's cave. Yet along the valley generally, the abundant wreaths of smoke which greeted the visitor may have had rather more to do with ugly old manufacturing. Tintern itself in those times had forges and wireworks and mills and blast furnaces – relics of that can still be seen on roads that run west into Monmouthshire. Gilpin, free from the selective myopia that affected some of those who followed him into this territory, acknowledges their presence, not with bursting enthusiasm, certainly, but with none of the repugnance that the huddled houses bred in him.

As for the busy, even clamorous scenes he surveyed from his boat at Lydbrook – the forge, the cornmills, the tinplate works and the working boats on the Wye – they positively delighted him. 'At Lidbroke is a large wharf, where coals are shipped to Hereford and other places. Here the scene is new and pleasing. All has thus far been grandeur and tranquillity. It continues so yet; but mixed with life and bustle. A road runs diagonally along the bank; and houses and carts appear passing to the small vessels which lie against the wharf to receive their burdens. Close behind, a rich woody hill hangs sloping over the wharf; and forms a grand background to the whole. The contrast of all this business, the engines used in lading and unlading, together with the variety of the scene, produce altogether, a picturesque assemblage. The sloping hill is the front screen; the two side-screens are low. But soon the front screen becomes a lofty side-screen on the left; and sweeping round the eye at Welsh Bicknor, forms a noble amphitheatre…' This is man and nature combining to earn the master's ultimate accolade: a rating as truly, fully paid-up, picturesque.

It's at moments like this that one sees how inclusive and unpedantic is Gilpin's sense of the picturesque, how far it transcends the merely pretty, how fundamentally it differs from the common unthinking assumption that unless the sun is high in a cloudless sky, beauty is dimmed. The rain that fell on our traveller at Goodrich may have been inconvenient – 'yet the picturesque eye… in quest of beauty, finds it almost in every incident and under every appearance.' Though it hid greater beauties, causing the loss of broad lights and deep shadows, 'it gave a gloomy grandeur to many of the scenes.' Even the sightseer's ancient enemy, fog, qualifies in certain contexts for a nod of approval.

Other subsequent compilers of guides to the Wye took the same liberal line. Here is Charles Heath: 'On the right side of the river, the bank forms a woody amphitheatre, following the course of the stream round the promontory. Its lower skirts are adorned with a hamlet, in the midst of which volumes of thick smoke, thrown up at intervals from an iron forge, as its fires receive fresh fuel, add a double grandeur to the scene.' Or Thomas Whately (sometimes spelled Wheatley) at New Weir, lauding the operation of engines: 'machinery, especially, when its powers are stupendous, or its effects formidable, is an effort of art which may be accommodated to the extravagancies of nature'. The mood of this and other zetetic reflections is nicely caught in a paper by C. S. Matheson, *Enchanting Ruin: Tintern Abbey and Romantic Tourism in Wales*, which I found on a University of Michigan website: 'It was common', she says, 'for tourists to visit the natural, industrial and archaeological sites of

Tintern in sequence. The industrial sublime thus qualified the architectural sublime of the Abbey and the picturesque features of its setting. Tintern's industrial patrimony (reaching back, in fact, to the ancient iron works in the hills around the village) is a crucial element in the valuation and experience of the Abbey in the period. To Romantic viewers, the contrast between the frantic activity and clamor of the foundries, and the old silences of the Abbey was just the touch needed to push poignancy into better-grade melancholy.'

Below Tintern, Gilpin lost his taste for the Wye. He found the river 'ouzy'. He admired the estate created by a local Croesus, Valentine Morris, at Chepstow – Piercefield, where the racecourse is today – for he had a taste for landscape that was designed as well as for that which was natural and unpremeditated; though Morris's shrubberies were not to his taste. He hurried back through Monmouth and on into deeper Wales, which he found decreasingly praiseworthy as he hurried westward.

Gilpin was not the first to discover the Wye Valley and analyse and chronicle its romantic attractions. In 1750 Dr Egerton, then Rector of Ross, later bishop of Durham, and his wife used to entertain guests with boat trips along the river, while James Evans, a basketmaker of Ross, hired out boats from 1760 onwards. Even so, it was Gilpin who made it a classic home excursion, especially when the Napoleonic Wars forbade the Grand Tour, teaching travellers to look for beauty at home as well as across the Channel. As the younger Pliny says: '*ea sub oculis posita neglegimus, seu quia ita natura comparatum, ut proximorum incuriosi longinqua sectemur*', which M. Willett, author of yet another Wye Valley travelogue, *The Strangers' Guide to the Banks of the Wye,* handily translates as follows: 'Abroad to see the world the traveller goes, / And neglects the fine things which lie under his nose' – a judgement as true today as the day it was written. That the valley draws the world as it does today, as a place to enjoy an alpha-class landscape while luxuriously succumbing to better-grade melancholy among the unmalleted ruins at Tintern, is very much Gilpin's legacy.

LLANDEILO,
CARMARTHENSHIRE

WILLIAM PAXTON SEEKS TO FULFIL A
LONG-HELD AMBITION THROUGH THE TACTICAL
DEPLOYMENT OF DINNERS.

*Voting took place in four booths in the churchyard. In one
election here, the Reverend Edward Picton, the first man
to vote for the Tory candidate, was assured by a shoemaker called Morgan that because of what he had done,
his soul was destined for Hell...*

DAVIESES, HUGHESES, HARRIESES, JONESES and
the occasional Price throng the graveyard of St Teilo's,
the principal church of Llandeilo, Carmarthenshire, in
Welsh-speaking south Wales. The Davieses are perhaps the most
numerous, though given the history of this place one would never
dare say that aloud, for fear that the Hugheses and Joneses and occasional Prices would rise from their graves as one and demand a
recount. A road bisects the graveyard, with the church to the south
and up the hill to the north a handsome parade of houses, giving
the place the sense of an unpremeditated square. Which is what, in
effect, it was; for this was the heart of the town. Fairs and markets
were held here, with the flat surfaces of box tombs serving as coun-
ters for buying and selling. Here, too, in what might nowadays be
regarded as too sacred a spot for such an occasion, the electors of
Carmarthenshire, in days when the business of voting was conducted in full public gaze, assembled to decide who should represent
them in London: most famously in what was later talked of as

Lecsiwn Fawr (the Great Election) of July 1802, which inhabitants remembered long afterwards as one of the most exciting times of their lives.

Though others threatened to stand, just two did battle: an indisputable Welshman, James Hamlyn Williams, and a very rich, but not in the slightest degree Welsh, incomer called William Paxton. Born in Edinburgh, the son of a clerk in a wine merchant's store, he had lived most of his early life in London, before joining the navy at twelve, becoming a midshipman at sixteen, and then leaving to join a merchant company operating in India. Giving up the sea for the safety and greater potential riches to be made on the land, he had risen by 1778, when he was thirty-four, to be Master of the Mint for Bengal; an office which, like so many in the Raj in those days, could be usefully supplemented by lucrative opportunities on the side. By acting as agent for ambitious moneymakers back home, he made himself a rich man, and when he returned to London in 1785 he must have felt that the world lay before him.

In the event, the segment of the world in which he chose to seek the status and recognition he believed that he deserved proved to be Wales. A Welshman he met on the boat back to England convinced him that he'd have a better chance of making a splash in Wales than he would in more competitive London. At the end of the 1780s he purchased an estate called Middleton Hall near the village of Llanarthne, Carmarthenshire. Here he called in the architect Samuel Pepys Cockerell to demolish the hall and build him a grander house. He enlarged the grounds, had them expertly landscaped, and even hoped at one point to establish a spa, as a kind of Welsh rejoinder to Tunbridge Wells.

Today, the Paxton estate is the National Botanic Garden of Wales. Of Cockerell's mansion, only the stables survive: the great house, like so many, was lost to fire, on the final day of October 1931. But if you look out eastward from the top of the gardens, you can see another emblem of the Paxton inheritance: a curious triangular tower, officially known as the Nelson Tower but locally famous as

Paxton's Folly, created, also very probably by Cockerell, on the top of a hill across a green valley. Inscriptions in Welsh, English and Latin declare its ostensible purpose: 'To the invincible Commander, Viscount Nelson, in commemoration of deeds most brilliantly achieved at the mouths of the Nile, before the walls of Copenhagen, and on the shores of Spain; of the empire everywhere maintained by him over the seas; and in the death which in the fullness of his own glory, though ultimately for his country and for Europe, conquering, he died; this tower was erected by William Paxton.'

To the glory of Nelson certainly; but also, one can't help suspecting, to the glory of Paxton. Other motives were attributed in the inns of Carmarthen. Paxton had built the tower, it was said, as a place from whose high windows he might watch through field glasses his two cherished pairs of white horses thundering up from Tenby, down on the coast – a town he had rescued from derelict days – over the thirty-six miles to his private palace. Or, he was taking revenge for the failure of Carmarthen borough to let him erect a new bridge over the Towy: denied the chance to deploy his riches to the benefit of his adopted county, he would spend it on a personal indulgence. Or, perhaps this was another kind of revenge: his riposte to what had befallen him at the general election for the county of Carmarthen in 1802.

He had tried to get to Westminster on an earlier occasion, putting up unsuccessfully at Newark in 1790, and topping the poll, only for the mayor to disqualify so many votes in his favour that his rivals surpassed him. Paxton protested to Parliament, but Parliament supported the mayor. This later contest, however, mattered far more. Already installed as a burgess of Carmarthen, he wanted to add the much more glorious achievement of being the county's choice for Parliament.

The history of the constituency was against him. True, he had the support of the formidable Cawdor family, but James Hamlyn Williams was backed by an even mightier local aristocrat: Lord Dynevor, who for many years had seen his choices elected to

Parliament with scarcely a challenge. And where Williams was impeccably Welsh, Paxton, a Scot from London, was an undisguisable interloper. Although much of his time was now spent in Wales, he still had extensive business interests in London where he owned a fine collection of properties, especially in Piccadilly. Moreover, he had lived and worked and made his money in India – making him one of the 'nabob' class, as their detractors called them, who liked to deploy the gains they had made in their Indian days (not always, but often, ill-gotten) to have their ways with communities with which they had no established connection. This election of 1802 was the time when their parliamentary presence reached its highest level so far: thirty such 'nabobs' won seats at Westminster. And possibly, in God-fearing Wales, another offence stood against him. Paxton was a director of the Gas Light and Coke Company, regarded by some as seriously impious because it traded on Sundays.

The dominance of the Dynevors ensured that such that elections were rare. Across much of Wales, the results were stitched up well in advance of polling day by aristocratic masters. Carmarthenshire had not seen a contest since 1754, and now that William Paxton had provided it with a chance, Llandeilo was determined to make the most of it. 'This contest was a very remarkable one,' wrote local historian, Edwin Poole, at the end of the century, 'and may be taken as a fair specimen of the "spirit and life" (and shall we say bribery and corruption) which characterised the election battles of our forefathers.' Supporters of the candidates – many of whom, since the right to vote was still so restricted, would themselves have been voteless – marched around the town, bands paraded, favours and ribbons were aggressively displayed, drunkenness and ribaldry flourished. Voting took place in four booths in the churchyard. Because the process was open (the secret ballot would not be achieved for a further seventy years), the choices electors made were subject to public view, and cheered and jeered accordingly. In one election here, it is recorded, the Reverend Edward Picton, the first man to vote for the Tory candidate, was assured by a shoemaker called Morgan that because of what he had done, his soul was destined for Hell.

Officially this encounter was Whigs against Tories; in reality, it was more – almost as if this were football rather than politics – the Blues versus the Reds. Even the official records categorize the contest as Blue against Red. The Reds were the Tories, or Lord Dynevor's people; the Blues were the Whigs, supporters of Lord Cawdor and Paxton. But their party labels were minor aspects of their campaign identities.

One reason why elections were usually settled by private deals between the aristocrats and their managers was that they were hugely costly; and this one would prove substantially more costly than most. Before long, the county seemed to be sinking in a sea of calculated benevolence. 'The voters,' wrote the Llandeilo poet, novelist and historian Anne Beale – too young by fourteen years to have been there to see it, but fed full of it by her elders' recollections – used to 'make their ways to the different ale houses… After allowing sufficient time to elapse for digestion, dinner parties assemble at different inns where meat and drink, those external rousers and calmers of John Bull's excitable feelings, are again the order of the day. Speeches are either made or spoilt in the making, healths drunk and jollity kept up. All are merry as a successful party and plenty of wine can make them.' The bills for all this merriment were spectacular. In one of the ripest electoral statistics ever recorded, to be found in the 1896 report of the Royal Commission on Land in Wales and Monmouthshire, Paxton was shown to have run up expenses of £15,690 4s 2d (the equivalent today of just over half a million pounds). Items included payments to innkeepers for 11,070 breakfasts, 36,901 dinners, 684 suppers, 25,275 gallons of ale, 11,068 bottles of spirits, 8,879 bottles of porter, 460 bottles of sherry, 509 bottles of cider, and eighteen guineas for milk punch. The charge for ribbons was £786, and the number of separate charges for horse hire was £4,521. No figure for equivalent damage to the Dynevor/Williams finances survives, but as inquiries into the election would later reveal, austerity was hardly the rule on their side either.

In documents in the Carmarthenshire Record Office one can track the process of the election, recorded by an official in a cramped academic hand. On day one, the Reds went romping into the lead, with 227 votes for Williams against 87 for Paxton. By day five, Williams was leading Paxton by 901 to 754. Then the margin began to erode. On day ten, Paxton's forces outvoted Williams's, and the Cawdor camp may even have hoped their man might succeed. The numbers of those turning out were dwindling day by day: on day twelve, it was 16 for Williams but 42 for his challenger; on day fourteen, 8 for Williams, 19 for Paxton; and on day fifteen, when the sheriff ordered the booths to close at 3 p.m., it appeared that Williams had won the seat by just 46 votes – 1,267 against 1,221.

There was never the slightest chance that these numbers would go unchallenged. Carmarthen town and the surrounding county had a tradition of rioting, sometimes against the price of corn, sometimes in protest against the conscription of men for the militia, but especially in the borough elections, where shots had been fired on occasion. Now Paxton's Blues were swiftly in turbulent action, convinced that they had been robbed. Three petitions were raised for consideration by Parliament: one by Paxton against the victorious Williams, a second by Williams against his defeated opponent, and a third by a voter called Mansel Philips, who alleged offences of bribery and treating by both candidates.

In all, Williams objected to 557 of Paxton's votes and Paxton to 688 of Williams's, which meant, remarkably, that the number of votes subject to objections exceeded, by two, the number of votes uncomplained of. A panel of parliamentarians was convened to deal with these protests. But Williams survived. Paxton was told that to have any chance of making his charges stick, he would have to assemble in London a larger contingent of witnesses than could ever have been persuaded to travel there. He withdrew his charges of bribery and treating, cutting his objections to one, which was that the sheriff had closed the poll too early; and even that was rejected.

It may have been some compensation that the following year

Carmarthen borough made him its mayor. It would no doubt have been still more rewarding that the member for the borough constituency, John George Philipps, resigned his seat in the following year, making way for Paxton to find a seat at Westminster. Significantly, one of the reasons stated for Philipps's departure was that his success at Carmarthen had cost him so much of his money that he seemed on the verge of bankruptcy. Still, in those days, representing your county outranked representing your borough, so Paxton returned to the county hustings. In 1806, now past sixty, he at last attained what he'd missed four years earlier: victory at Llandeilo. No candidate was put up against him. Yet he did not have long to savour this belated success. In a further election the following year, he fared so badly in the first few days of the poll that he conceded the contest to his Red opponent – thus precluding any repeat of the juicy public spectacle, epic gorging and other shenanigans that had run for over two weeks in 1802.

From then on, Paxton – Sir William now: he was knighted in 1803 – abandoned politics, and concentrated his activities on the provision of public works for Carmarthen and on shaping Tenby into a first-class resort. 'The town', *Leigh's Guide to Wales and Monmouthshire* recorded 'is… indebted to Sir W. Paxton for having furnished it with a supply of excellent water, and this removed the inconvenience under which it long laboured for want of this essential article.' He also built public baths, on whose wall he had inscribed the legend (in Greek): 'The sea washes away all the ills of mankind.' And though his campaign had failed to leave the town of Llandeilo with an untarnished name for ethical conduct, its townspeople no doubt reflected that the Cawdor/Paxton mode of campaigning had contributed far more to the sum of local happiness than had been the case when, as more often happened, determined aristocrats and their agents simply inflicted their preferences on communities.

Paxton died, in London, in 1824 at the age of eighty and was buried at St Martin in the Fields. It's a cruel reflection on the eternal reputation he hoped to achieve – and a symbol of the way that communities can swiftly forget those who were once local heroes – that when the house he'd created was burned down in 1931, one local paper informed its readers that Middleton Hall had been built by Edwin Adams MP (who in fact had succeeded Paxton), with the help of the famous architect, Joseph Paxton (in fact, the one who created the Crystal Palace). *Sic transit gloria mundi.*

3

BISHOPS CANNINGS,
WILTSHIRE

THE BRETHREN THAT AGREE ARE FORTIFIED BY
THE SOUND OF A DISTANT DRUM.

❧

*'When, henceforth, the members of the Friendly Society
"walked the village", he would hurry to the Crown and,
standing beside the open window of the upper room,
hammer the drum with all his might…'*

I N AN UPSTAIRS ROOM in the museum in the Wiltshire
market town of Devizes there's a brightly coloured barrel-
shaped drum decorated with patriotic slogans (*Dieu et mon droit,
honi soit qui mal y pense*) and emblazoned with the legend: 'Lo, what
an entertaining sight are brethren that agree; Brethren whose
cheerful hearts unite in bands of piety. May the Friendly Society of
Bishops Cannings ever flourish! 1820.' You sense as soon as you see
it the pride with which it must have been paraded through the
streets of this downland village a mile or so outside the present
boundaries of the town, and the swaggering joy with which it was
beaten by the men entrusted with the honour of carrying it. You
may possibly wonder, however, why it was needed. 'Friendly society:' says *Chambers Dictionary*, 'a benefit society, an association for
relief in sickness, old age, widowhood, by provident insurance.' Why
should a welfare organization have had need of a drum?

The church in Bishops Cannings, St Mary's – three stars in
Simon Jenkins's *England's Thousand Best Churches* and sometimes
compared by enthusiasts, though not by Jenkins, to Salisbury
Cathedral – is still much as it was in those days, but the village itself

is irrevocably altered. Some of the statelier houses survive, but none of the squalid ones that used to infest the area known as Pip Lane. In the century after the 1831 census, the population halved (from 1,365 to a mere 665) though late twentieth-century building, some of it fairly unlovely, has taken it back to its former level. Yet the old Bishops Cannings survives in the writings of Ida Gandy, daughter of the Reverend Charles Hony, vicar and principal bee-keeper here from 1873 to 1907 – books which admirably mix warm nostalgic affection with meticulous scholarly footnotes. In *A Wiltshire Childhood*, she wrote: 'All round the church was scattered the village. There was no concentration of houses in any particular place; they just gathered in little groups along the roads and by-lanes, like friendly neighbours met for a gossip. Some, of a less sociable nature, had set themselves right in the heart of the fields.' As she accepts, the village had a reputation for daffiness. She recounts a favourite story in which a cooper ordered his son to get into a cask he was making to hold up the lid as he hammered it on; and then had to prise it off because his son could not get out.

Though she knows all about the drum, Ida Gandy has disappointingly little to say about the friendly society, the records of which are lost. Bishops Cannings in 1820 was responding to a tide of opinion which had spurred other villages in this sector of Wiltshire into action years before. From the late eighteenth century onwards, they were springing up everywhere, creating a kind of localized proto-welfare state and providing a new sense of security for unprivileged England. The essential principle was simple: all members paid into a fund; those who fell ill claimed benefits, which were also paid to the widows of those who had died; those who remained well and working drew no benefit but no doubt rejoiced in their own good fortune. In England in 1803, according to P. H. J. H. Gosden, the historian of the movement, there were more than 9,000 societies with some 704,000 members. By 1872, there were 32,000 societies, with four million members – four times as many as the trade unions had.

Seven years after the public debut of the Bishops Cannings drum, a different kind of friendly society was founded in Wiltshire. This was a county society, which grew to be the second biggest in England: one of a network whose origins were grander and more worldly-wise than the ones that had grown up in villages. Its list of patrons and committee members included a seething throng of marquesses, earls and viscounts, a batch of bishops and many inferior clergy – a guarantee, this, of a stability that was not always to be found in local societies staffed by people of limited education and experience. Here and there, sometimes through cupidity but often simply from incompetence and confusion, such local officials ruined their societies and left their members bereft of any further hope of assistance. 'Lloyd George', wrote the journalist A. G. Gardiner, having discussed with the great man his authorship of the first tentative welfare state, 'will tell you how, when he was a boy, he used to take his uncle's shilling a week to the friendly society. And when he fell ill, the society had failed. Out of that memory largely came the Insurance Act.'

Yet despite their weight and authority the county societies failed to catch on. Because of their top-down nature they did not seem friendly enough. Although the founder of the Wiltshire Society, the Conservative MP Thomas Sotheron Estcourt, was the lord of the local manor, Bishops Cannings remained uninvolved until the first local committee was established in 1844 and Silas Dyke became county member number 1422. The first woman to join enlisted in 1848. Even by 1870, the registered membership in Bishops Cannings mustered fewer than forty. And long before then, articles of agreement for a 'society of tradesmen and others' were signed at a meeting in the Crown public house in June 1836.

Happily, this one's rule book, unlike the one instituted by the society that commissioned the drum, survives. It begins with this aspiration: 'May God for every bless, / And crown each member with success; / That they may never disagree, / But live in love and unity.' Practical requirements follow:

1. That no person shall be admitted into this Society who is a profane swearer, drunkard, sabbath breaker, thief, murderer, or otherwise notoriously wicked; and that no one shall be admitted that exceeds the age of 30 years, or is a cripple, or otherwise infirm...

2. That this Society shall meet once every six weeks at 7 o'clock and leave by 10, from Michaelmas to Lady-day; and at 8 o'clock, and leave by 10, from Lady-day to Michaelmas; but the meeting hours may be prolonged on any night, if there be an actual necessity for it. Each member shall then contribute One Shilling, to be laid up in stock for the better support and maintenance of each other when rendered incapable of labour, and Threepence to be spent in company.

The funds, says the rulebook, are to be kept in a box with three locks and three keys, one each for the two stewards and the third for the book-keeper. Then:

4. That if any member, after having paid to this Society eighteen weeks, shall be rendered incapable of work, or be sick or lame (unless caused by drinking, quarrelling or fighting), he shall receive Three Shillings per week for three months; but if, at the expiration of three months, he shall be adjudged by an able Physician to be incurable, he shall receive One Shilling and Sixpence so long as such illness or incapacity lasts. If any member of this Society shall feign sickness or lameness, or have the venereal disease, he shall not receive any benefit, and be for ever excluded.

These opening provisions reveal several essential features of the friendly society movement. The societies need young men whose income from uninterrupted work can serve to subsidize the older and ailing members of the community. Become old – that's to say, over thirty – and potentially ailing, and the society will not want you. (Indeed, in some societies, where young members were in a majority, resolutions were passed to expel the older and potentially costlier colleagues.) Yet some such young men, as those who make the rules are only too well aware, are by no means sure to behave themselves. That risk is all the greater where the society is linked, as

this one was and most of them were, to a pub – in this case, the
Crown (now demolished, and not the pub of that name that stands
close to the church today). Significantly, the snootier county society
met in the schoolhouse, which for young working-class men in a
village like Bishops Cannings was nothing like so alluring.

This link with drink suited the clubs because it offered the easy
conviviality that was just as important as the welfare benefits in
tempting new members in. It also suited the landlord: the rule book
specifically stated that money must be spent during the evening.
On the other hand, that also meant that rules would be needed to
cover situations that might all too often arise when several pints had
been sunk and the subsequent natural exuberance broke the bounds
of comradely membership. So there were rules for that too:

> 9. That if any member shall quarrel or fight at the six-weeks meet-
> ing, or in going home at night, or on our feast day; or if in going
> home he shall do an injury to his neighbour, and it can be proved
> against him, he shall, for every such offence, forfeit Five Shillings on
> the next meeting night following, or be excluded…
>
> 15. That if any member shall curse or swear, or offer to lay wagers,
> during the Club hours, he shall forfeit Threepence; and if any mem-
> ber come into the Club Room disguised in liquor, in the hours of
> meeting, he shall forfeit Sixpence for every such offence…

And even, though the proof must have been uncertain so long
before the breathalyser:

> 21. That when any member of this Society is on the box for sick-
> ness or lameness, he shall not be allowed to sit up in an ale-house
> and get intoxicated with liquor; and if it can be proved that such
> member has taken more than one pint, he shall not receive any more
> benefit from the Society for his sickness or lameness; and he shall
> not be allowed to do any kind of business whilst he receives full pay
> or half pay…

The rule books of these societies had enough in common to suggest that their framers started with a general model and amended

it according to local circumstance. At Kingston Deverill in the west of the county, one of these rules was perhaps devised to reflect past experience:

> If any person or persons belonging to the Society shall offer any challenge to any fellow Member or Members, or despitefully seize hold of any fellow Member or Members by the collar, or maliciously stamp on his or her feet… he or they so offending shall forfeit half a crown immediately…

And at Stapleton Royal's True Briton Friendly Society: 'That no person shall be admitted a Member of this Society but such whose character for Sobriety, Honesty and Industry will bear the strictest enquiry or who is not well affected to her present Majesty Queen Victoria and the British Constitution.' No such specific restriction was enforced on the tradesmen of Bishops Cannings, natural devotees perhaps of Her Majesty; but any such subversive talk could in any case be caught under a rule that said:

> 16. That if any member of this Society shall be unnecessarily talking of state or religious affairs, during the Club hours, he shall forfeit Threepence …

The publican at the Crown in 1820 is likely to have been a man in his middle thirties called John Bowden. He was certainly landlord there two years later. But soon after that he died, and his wife Sarah took over. In the following year, she married Silas Sloper, and he became licensee. Sarah herself died soon after, aged thirty-eight. When the tradesmen launched their society in the next decade, the landlord was Simon Sloper. Not much seems to have moved in Bishops Cannings then without some Sloper (or Slop, the alternative name in this family before the late eighteenth century) having a hand in it. The dynasty had in the past provided MPs and mayors of Devizes, as well as a succession of churchwardens at St Mary's. They must also have performed the irreplaceable rural role of feeding the village gossip machine. In 1598, on Whit Monday, one of them rode across the Plain to marry a woman from 'Wallope in Hampshire' – the equivalent in such a community then of espousing a Polynesian today. Some Slopers were classed as 'gentlemen'; some were farmers – others ran the pub.

The pub, too, was at the heart of the annual occasion that did most to enliven the life of a village: the society festivities, which here, as in most of Wiltshire, were organized for Whit Monday. The centrepiece of the day was the society's feast, which in the case of the tradesmen took place at the Crown on terms that the rule book defined:

> 24. That this Society shall keep a Feast on Whit-Monday, at the sign of the CROWN, unless the Society be removed to some other place. The landlord to provide the dinner, and each member to pay for it according to agreement made between the landlord and members before the feast day, and a half a gallon of beer for each member to drink; the beer to be paid for out of the stock. Any member not attending on the feast day, shall forfeit Two Shillings and Sixpence the next meeting night, or be excluded...

But these were serious times, and such organizations felt the need to have their activities sanctified. So before the feast they would need to thank God and be preached at. The same rule continued:

> ...and every member shall be required to go to Church on that day, (provided the Minister will attend,) or forfeit One Shilling, if he resides within ten miles of Bishops Cannings, or be excluded...

While rule 26 required:

> that there shall be allowed a half-guinea, out of the stock, to have a sermon preached to the members every Whit-Monday, at Church, (provided the Minister will preach one), and every member shall be obliged to attend at eleven o'clock in the morning, and answer to his name when called upon, and walk to Church in his place, and back again, or forfeit Threepence.

The minister pocketing half-guineas in those days – he was vicar from 1815 to 1862 – was the formidable Dr William Macdonald, Archdeacon of Salisbury, of whom Ida Gandy, daughter of his successor but one, records: 'In the year of Waterloo, a keen and lively young vicar… came to the village, married two wives, fathered ten children and stayed on for forty-seven years. This was Archdeacon Macdonald, who enriched Bishops Cannings with his scholarship and his deep interest in its history and its people. If they were simple he loved them the better for it.' Having listened to him attentively on a Whit Monday morning, they could all go off in good conscience to stuff themselves at the Crown.

This brings us to the reason why Bishops Cannings wanted a drum. The march to and from the church, and on to the Crown, was a ceremonial affair. At the head of it was the Society's flag, carried by someone whom members deemed worthy of such an honour. Sometimes the duty went to the oldest member – though in one Wiltshire village the right to carry the flag was put up to auction. The marchers decked themselves out in appropriate finery. In some villages they wore white cockades on their hats; in others, their hats had colours attached that were specified in their rule books. They carried carefully crafted emblems, some of which can be seen at Devizes museum. And year after year the whole village turned out to admire and applaud them – almost as if they were the Orange Order on the Twelfth of July, and this was the Crumlin Road or Enniskillen.

You can pick up some sense of the excitement of these occasions, and the part they played in binding such communities together, from the recollection of Wiltshire's 'hammerman poet' (so called because he laboured in the Swindon railway works) Alfred Williams, in his book *A Wiltshire Village*. Here is South Marston, in the north-east corner of Wiltshire, where Williams was born in 1877 and lived for much of his life:

'What a day the old club anniversary used to be in the village years ago, before the little society became enfeebled and crippled by other more powerful and national institutions! It was quite the event of the year; Christmas and Easter were nothing to it; it was, in truth, the red-letter day of all, young and old alike. There were about thirty members in the society altogether. These contributed a certain amount per month for sickness, and the club 'broke up' every five years; that is to say, the accumulated moneys were shared out to the members, only retaining a sum for present needs. The anniversary was held on the second Tuesday in May. This comprised a general assembly at the inn – the headquarters of the club – a general procession to church, headed by a brass band in the morning, and afterwards a parade of the village, with music and collections for the society's funds, at the manor, the farms and houses *en route*. At one o'clock, all sat down to a substantial hot dinner of roast beef, and other cooked meats and vegetables, provided in the club-room; the band played selections; the foaming ale was brought in in large two-gallon cans; the greatest good-nature prevailed. Farmers and all belonged to the gathering; it was no one-sided affair, and a great number of folk attended from the neighbouring villages; all the old people made it their business to come... The procession was headed by three men bearing blue silk flags with tassels and fringes, a large one first, and two smaller ones, one on each side. The members wore regalia, red and blue sashes and rosettes, and walked with blue staffs with gilt heads.

Jemmy Boulton always carried the big flag. He wore a stout leather belt, with socket in front; the flag-staff fitted into this; if there was a breeze he needed all his strength to maintain it. He was just in his element then; you may imagine how his eyes twinkled with pleasure, and what delight he felt. His old face was redder than ever; his smile was ineffable. How very proud he was of that fringed and tasselled silk! If the wind blew, he kept it upright and rigid; if it was calm he waved it about from side to side, and when the crowd was stationary before the farms, or near the club-room, he waved it so low as to touch the people's heads...

Yet, true to the village's reputation for daffiness, the big barrel drum in Devizes museum never quite played the role it was made for. The society commissioned the drum from a firm in the town called Bruton's, and since one of its employees lived in Bishops Cannings and was the village drummer, he was allotted the job. Since there wouldn't have been space enough in his home, he arranged with the landlord at the Crown to build the thing in one of its upper rooms.

But someone – indeed, several people – had blundered. When the moment came for the village drummer to take the drum out into the street ready for the parade, it was found that none of the pub's doors or windows was big enough to allow the great monster through. 'When, henceforth, the members of the Friendly Society "walked the village"', says Ida Gandy, 'resplendent in sashes of azure silk tied round their black coats, and carrying silken banners that depicted touching scenes of the succour of the old and sick, he would hurry to the Crown and, standing beside the open window of the upper room, hammer the drum with all his might... '

'Oh, the brave music of a distant drum!' wrote Omar Khayyám; though he did not, I imagine, have Bishops Cannings in mind.

4

TIDESWELL,
DERBYSHIRE

ROBERT BLINCOE SUFFERS WHILE PARSON
BROWN APPEARS TO HAVE LITTLE TO SAY.

᠁

*The only voice raised in defence of the apprentices seems
to have been that of an employee called William Palfrey,
who would knock on the floor and cry: 'For Shame! For
shame! Are you murdering the children?' But once he
had left for the night, the victims would be gleefully told:
'Old Palfrey is not here now.'*

THE FOURTEENTH-CENTURY parish church of
Tideswell, Derbyshire, dedicated to St John the Baptist, is
celebrated in the town as the 'Cathedral of the Peak'.
Visitors are invited to admire its memorials and wooden carving,
the occasions of justified local pride. Yet those who wander into the
churchyard should also look for the plaque on the wall of what
is now Tideswell library. The inscription is terse and chilling:
'The orphan children who died in Litton Mill are buried without
tombstones in this section of the churchyard – oral tradition in
the village.'

Drive south out of Tideswell towards Miller's Dale and just
where the road swings westward, opposite the little cramped church
of St Anne and before a great viaduct, you will see a signpost indicating a byroad to Litton Mill. A bubbling river runs to the right of
the road; fine woods and imposing crags loom to the left. And here,
past a pleasant scatter of houses, is Litton Mill. Little survives of the
original mill, but the adapted building, now converted into upmar-

ket apartments, retains the sense of solid, steady industry practised here in earlier days.

How exhilarating, one feels, it must have been for the orphan children brought as cheap and convenient labour from grim London workhouses to sense as they travelled this road the new dawn that awaited them here. All the more so when the workhouse masters had made life in these faraway mills sound like some foretaste of paradise. Here they were going to find vast uncluttered skies, high hills, woods and sweet, clean, rippling streams undreamed of in St Pancras or Bethnal Green. They were told, says poor blighted Robert Blincoe, who was one of them, that they would be 'transformed into ladies and gentlemen, that they would be fed on roast and plum pudding, be allowed to ride their masters' horses, and have silver watches, and plenty of cash in their pockets'. They believed it so readily that they jostled and clamoured to be selected.

The truth about these transactions was much less uplifting. Mill owners could not find enough local labour to keep their enterprises flourishing. Impoverished as the common people of places like Tideswell were, the long hours and ferocious disciplines of such workplaces kept them away. So employers and their agents looked for convenient substitutes, and the workhouses of the capital yielded a ready supply. Both sides would benefit. The mill owners got their cheap labour, while the workhouse masters were spared the cost of looking after the children. For those who, like me, intrigued by the little plaque in Tideswell churchyard, follow Blincoe's path to Litton, that enticing road and the handsome mill at the end of it may in this light seem suddenly ugly and sinister.

Years later, a journalist from Bolton called John Brown heard of Blincoe's experiences and set out to find him. 'If this young man had not been consigned to a cotton-factory,' he wrote, 'he would probably have been strong, healthy and well grown; instead of which, he is diminutive as to stature, and his knees are grievously distorted.' The results of their conversations appeared as a serial in a publication called *The Lion* in 1828 and subsequently as a book that became known as *A Memoir of Robert Blincoe* – or to give it its full comprehensive title, *A memoir of Robert Blincoe, an orphan boy: sent from the workhouse of St Pancras, London, at seven years of age, to endure the Horrors of a Cotton-Mill, through his infancy and youth, with a minute detail of his sufferings, being the first memoir of the kind published.* What Blincoe suffered at the end of this tranquil valley, the harsh conditions and hours of work, the privations and gratuitous cruelty to which boys and girls alike were subjected, produced a swelling outrage and a setting up of parliamentary inquiries. As John Waller argues in a book called *The Real Oliver Twist: Robert Blincoe: A Life that Illuminates a Violent Age,* published in 2005, Charles Dickens was greatly influenced by Blincoe's testimony and drew on it for his novel.

★

Blincoe was never sure who his father was. He believed him, perhaps quite wrongly, to have been a clergyman – a circumstance he may even have boasted about, since in his Derbyshire days the boy was known only as 'Parson'. When he was four or thereabouts, his mother had given him up, leaving a woman whose identity he never discovered to take him to the only available place of refuge – St Pancras workhouse. Like most workhouse children he dreamed of escape, and was even miserably disappointed when denied the chance to work as a chimney sweep.

Instead, he was taken by wagon in a party of thirty-two children to a mill at Lowdham, near Nottingham. What he found there made him long to be back at St Pancras. Even before he was eight, he told John Brown, he thought of throwing himself out of the window. He made one desperate bid to escape, but was caught at Burton-on-Trent by a tailor who had once worked at the mill and knew he would be rewarded if he brought an errant boy back. I have saved you from Hell, the tailor told him: 'I saw Satan behind thee, jobbing his prong into thy arse.'

Blincoe saw many children injured in accidents with machinery. Some, he told Brown, had the skin scraped off the knuckles, clean to the bone, by the fliers; others, a finger crushed, a joint or two nipped off in the cogs of the spinning-frame wheels. His own forefinger was cut off at the first joint, but a surgeon was called to sew it back on. He was there when a girl called Mary Richards was caught in a machine; and heard the bones of her arms, legs and thighs 'successively snap asunder, crushed seemingly to atoms'; nevertheless she survived.

Then came the news that Lowdham was closing. Those children who still had relatives back in London were told that they could return there. Those like Blincoe, who had no one to turn to, were marked out for transfer to Litton Mill. Its proprietor came to see them at Lowdham and made that prospect sound pleasing. 'To some,' wrote John Brown, reporting what Blincoe had told him, 'he gave money, to all, he promised most liberal and kind usage, he promised like a Titus, but he performed like a Caligula.'

The children were taken by cart to Cromford, where they stayed overnight, and were then marched to Matlock toll-bar, a distance of some three miles, before being restored to their carts for the rest of the journey. Their drive down the lane to the mill, according to Brown's account, had none of the enchantment one finds there today: 'The savage features of the adjacent scenery impressed a general gloom upon the convoy.' But what greeted them there was much worse. What they found at the prentice house, a quarter of a mile or so from the mill, was a wretchedly accurate portent of times to come. Hungry though they were after their journey, they could not manage the meal they were served with. But 'whilst Blincoe and many of his comrades went supperless to bed, their half-starved comrades, the Litton Mill apprentices, ravenously devoured what the more dainty Lowdham children turned from with loathing, and told them *their stomachs* would come to in a few days, and that they would be glad to pick up from a dunghill, the mouldiest pieces, then so disdainfully flung away'. That was not to improve. Later,

Blincoe narrates how he and his comrades would steal the pigs' food from their sties, preferring it to their own.

The working day was just as odious. They were roused at four from the dormitories where they slept fifty to a room. Anyone not immediately out of bed would be beaten. The factory where they had to work for as much as sixteen hours, sometimes without a break or a meal, smelled foully of oil and filth. The overseers treated their charges with brutal severity. Those already installed at Litton Mill when Blincoe arrived carried the marks of it: their bodies, he remembered, 'were literally covered with weals and contusions – their heads full of wounds, and in many cases, lamentably-infested with vermin.'

It is hard for a twenty-first century reader to read this account without a feeling of disbelief; but just as you start to think, can this really be true, Brown anticipates the question and replies to it. What he had been told, he says, had at first seemed almost incredible; yet Blincoe's testimony 'was afterwards confirmed by individuals, whose narratives *will be given,* and with whom no sort of acquaintance or intercourse had latterly subsisted'.

Both at work and in what passed for their leisure, the Litton Mill apprentices were subjected to vicious bullying. Some tried to kill themselves. A girl who attempted to drown herself was saved, but the mill's proprietor had her removed from the place for fear that her example might prove contagious. The worst of those who afflicted, and came near to breaking, young Blincoe, were two overseers called William and Robert Woodward. Robert Woodward had arrived, like Blincoe, from Lowdham; William was already installed. What the Woodwards and others did to him is described in painful detail. And yet, as he says, others were treated far worse. A boy called James Nottingham, who came like him from St Pancras, was subjected to such vindictive cruelty that his head became 'as soft as a boiled turnip'; his subsequent 'state of idiocy' simply increased the mirth of his tormentors.

Other apprentices tried to escape. The book describes how one fell to his death when the blanket down which he was climbing broke. Blincoe himself made more than one attempt to flee the place. Once he set off in search of a magistrate to whom he could make his protest. He found some gathered at the magistrates' court at Eyam, some eight miles distant, where he was heard with apparent sympathy, but told to go back to the mill. If he did, he said, he'd surely be beaten. They assured him that the master at Litton would not dare to act so defiantly. He returned, was duly beaten, and was made to promise never to make such a break for freedom again.

Those who complained of feeling unwell were kept working until they dropped. Inevitably, some of them died; primarily, the memoirs suggest, from years of too much labour and too little food, followed by sheer neglect. How many died from disease and how many from industrial injuries will never be established, though the fact that some of the victims were buried not where they died but in a neighbouring parish confirms the feeling one gets from the plaque at Tideswell churchyard that those in charge of the mill must have had much to hide.

The master at Litton Mill was man a called Ellis (sometimes spelled Ellice) Needham, a man, Brown's book suggests, who had risen from humble beginnings (though here he was wrong, in that Needham came from a well-established Derbyshire family). He had managed to set himself up as a man of some local consequence, and made enough money to move to a fine house near Buxton. He was also for some time a churchwarden at St John's. Needham, so Blincoe told Brown, never matched the outright viciousness of the Woodwards, but he practised his own indignities on the apprentices, and must certainly have been aware of their brutal inflictions – abetted by more junior overseers, of whom Blincoe poignantly says that the worst were most often those who had once been victims of similar treatment themselves.

Needham's son John was another oppressor, violent to boys and subjecting girls to indecencies which Brown abstains from describing. The only voice raised in defence of the apprentices seems to have been that of an employee called William Palfrey, who used to hear shouts and screams from below, whereupon he would knock on the floor and cry: 'For shame! For shame! Are you murdering the children?' But once he had left for the night, the victims of persecution would be gleefully told: 'Old Palfrey is not here now'. Yet others besides Mr Palfrey must over the years have learned of what was happening at Litton Mill. They must have known that Needham was ultimately responsible. His sins of commission may, compared with the Woodwards', have been minor. The evidence of his sins of omission, however, must have been overwhelming.

In that context, there's a second plaque at St John's, inside the church, which demands attention. It celebrates the Reverend Thomas Brown, who served this church for forty years until his death in 1836 in the eighty-second year of his age. So Brown – Parson Brown, as he was always known – must have been the incumbent here during the years when Ellis Needham and his assistants were running the fearsome regime that John Brown and Blincoe describe – and when those unnumbered, unrecorded children were dying a couple of miles down the road from his church, within his parish. If you credit what Robert Blincoe testified and John Brown recorded, it seems inconceivable that Parson Brown should not have heard some report of events in the valley – and certainly quite enough to incite a man of God to start asking pertinent questions.

What sort of a man was this Parson Brown? In the church where I saw his plaque, I found a leaflet entitled *Tideswell in the Days of Parson Brown* by one of his successors there, Canon Fletcher, who was vicar from 1900 to 1906. A drawing of Brown, taken from a contemporary woodcut, shows a sturdy, assertive man, showily dressed, with a broad-brimmed hat and a walking stick. There are many words one might use to describe his appearance, but pious is not among them. Canon Fletcher does the best for him that he can. He emphasizes the tough circumstances in which Brown arrived in the parish in 1780 as curate to a vicar called Richard Shuttleworth whose debts kept him out of the parish and possibly for a time in a debtors' prison. But his record at Tideswell was far from unblemished. When, after a spell in temporary charge of it, he applied for the permanent mastership of its school, the vicar objected, as did two newly appointed churchwardens, on the grounds that Brown's conduct during his temporary mastership had been weak and neglectful, and specifically, that Brown had been seen in the pub when he ought to have been at school. Charity commissioners who inspected the school in 1827 were also dissatisfied: they thought it wrong that the post of vicar and of headmaster should be vested in the same man.

For this and 'other reasons' (which he does not specify), Canon Fletcher relates, Brown gave up the headship in 1832. This must have made a hole in the family finances; but there were consolations. He had also by now become vicar of Seaton Ross, a village some eighty miles away on the road from Selby to Market Weighton in Yorkshire. All the work in that parish was done by a curate; even kindly Canon Fletcher feels bound to add at this point: 'I don't suppose that he ever set foot in the parish.' Nearer home, he supplemented his income by measuring hay, lettering signs for carts and houses and even by setting up as a moneylender. His standing in the town must have remained precarious. The support of big local figures was therefore worth seeking out and maintaining. And one of these was Ellis Needham.

Though accepting that all was not well at Litton Mill, Canon Fletcher makes a mild attempt to exonerate Thomas Brown. 'Wretched as the conditions of the apprentices at Litton Mill were in the days of Parson Brown,' he writes, 'I don't think that they were quite as bad as they were painted in the *Memoir of Robert Blincoe.*' The canon has not been alone in suspecting that Blincoe, or John Brown interpreting Blincoe, laid the suffering on too thickly; or that the uncounted numbers honoured by the plaque on the library wall might not have been as substantial as 'oral tradition' suggests. Yet certainly Blincoe, as Brown relates him, sounds like an honest witness. There are details here – the clerk of the magistrates' court at Eyam staggering back as the smell of poor importunate Blincoe hit him – which ring with a real conviction. John Brown emphasizes that he pressed his source hard on the most horrible points of the story, and traced witnesses, some of whom he cites, who were happy to endorse what Robert said.

Yet Brown himself was an unstable figure: driven, always suspicious, possibly paranoid, a troubled soul who in his distress would kill himself in his lodgings a year or so after he had finished writing the *Memoir*. In 1967, Stanley D. Chapman published a book which declared that Blincoe, as reported and amplified by Brown, was an unreliable witness. Life in those times of economic distress, he argued in *The Early Factory Masters*, was tough enough to drive employers like Needham into practices which might seem indefensible in our own more comfortable age. 'There can be little doubt,' he concluded, 'that *The Memoir of Robert Blincoe* was written by a gullible sensationalist, whose statements must be treated with the utmost caution... The proper historical context of the Blincoe Memoir is... a fast-declining industry. Ellis Needham, and his workers with him, were the unhappy casualties of rapid technical and economic change in a highly competitive industry.'

But not all that was said of Needham and his accomplices can be written off as the hyperbole of a gullible sensationalist. There's another piece of testimony to be pondered over in the church and churchyard at Tideswell. On the same shelf as Fletcher's account I found a further witness, named only as Orphan John (his name was in fact John Birley). Just as Blincoe told his story to John Brown of Bolton, John gave an account of his time at Litton Mill to the editor of the *Ashton Chronicle*, the celebrated radical Tory cleric Joseph Rayner Stephens. He looked, Stephens recorded, 'sunken, worn and haggard' and near to sixty, though in fact he was much the same age as Stephens himself – in his mid-forties. As with Brown and Blincoe, some of the language here seems to belong more to the interviewer than to the interviewee. But John, telling his story seventeen years after Blincoe, gives a portrait of life at the mill very much in line with Blincoe's, though attributing his persecution much more directly to Needham.

'Ellis Needham, the master', he says, 'had five sons: Frank, Charles, Samuel, Robert and John. These young men, particularly Frank and Charles, used us very cruelly, together with a man named Swann, an overlooker.' Even today, he told Stephens, he bore the marks of Swann's assaults on him, and still suffered the pain. Yet 'old Needham was as bad as any of the rest, or worse, if that was possible. He would sometimes come and begin to beat us as hard as he could, hitting us all over the body, until he seemed quite tired; he would then stop as if he had done, and move off as if he was going away; but he would come back again, and at it again, and move away and come again, time after time.' Like Blincoe, John insists that others suffered far worse than he did. Having run away from Litton, he was sent back to a second mill, at Taddington. Here, 'James Arnott had had the flesh and the muscles of the right arm torn off. Robert Gully, the overlooker, had struck him a heavy blow, which sent him spinning against the machinery… The driving strap caught him, and mangled his arm in a most shocking manner.'

Ellis Needham's last days, as John Brown discovered to his unconcealed pleasure, were bleak. In 1815 he and his sons went bankrupt. In 1817, this man who had once presented himself as the essence of Tideswell respectability was convicted, along with one of his sons, of assaulting a constable. 'Old Needham is now a pauper,' *The Lion* reported in March 1828. 'His wife now teaches a few little children their ABC at Hathersage, a few miles distant from Litton, and the sons are vagabonds.' The family had suffered, Brown says in the book, 'a visitation of calamities so awful, that it looked as if the avenging power of retributive justice had laid its iron hand on him and them.'

Needham died in 1830. For all the physical difficulties that beset him, the legacy of his days at Litton, Blincoe outlived his master by thirty years, though some were difficult. He became a mill-owner himself, saw a mill go up in flames on the day it opened, and ran up debts on a scale that landed him in Lancaster jail, but survived to continue in business. The boy who'd been jeeringly called 'the parson', and believed that a parson had fathered him, saw his son, also Robert, become a real parson, with a church in Old Street, London.

These matters of culpability – Needham's, certainly, for the treatment of the workhouse children at Litton Mill; John Brown's, possibly, for inflating what Blincoe had told him; Parson Brown's, very probably, for his apparent neglect and his acquiescence – can never be settled. The evidence of the ill-treatment that Blincoe and Orphan John complained of, and that Dickens wove into a story that left the country aghast, might not stand up in a court of law. But to me it seems largely persuasive.

We shall never know how many boys and girls apprenticed at Litton met with deaths they might have escaped had they stayed in the workhouse, or were left with physical legacies that blighted and foreshortened their lives. But Victorian England, with its passion for committees of inquiry and its restless eagerness to institute reform on the basis of what they discovered, brought in legislation that, though it could not eliminate, certainly curbed the freedom of ruthless employers to exploit the vulnerable in a way that even the most hardline preacher of laissez-faire would nowadays shudder at. Blincoe and Orphan John, for all the imperfections of their testimony, and John Brown and Stephens, for all that they were propagandists, helped convince enough open-minded people of the truth of the story they told to ensure that needful changes were made. As one leaves Tideswell church and looks back at the plaque on the library wall, one must surely wish to honour them – and to honour too the unnumbered children buried beneath this Derbyshire earth.

5

CRANE COURT, LONDON

*'The curtain drew up, and the action of the play began in
all serenity; but so soon as Hamlet made his appearance
an outcry, a burst of execration, rose suddenly. Hisses and
hootings, cries of "Off! off! – Blackguard! scoundrel!"
and the like were hurled at the actor; and the whole
performance was stopped...'*

O N   T H E   N O R T H   S I D E   O F Fleet Street in London, east
of Fetter Lane, there's a network of squares and alleys,
some of which still have a flavour of the days when this
was one of the liveliest and most talked about parts of the capital.
Tourists still come here in search of the house where Dr Johnson
held court, or to sample old wood-beamed pubs quite groaning
with ancientness, such as the Cheshire Cheese. But others have quite
lost their savour. Perhaps the dullest, the least beguiling, of all, its
surviving character effectively drained out of it by twentieth-century rebuilding, is the first you come to as you walk down the hill
towards St Paul's, which is known as Crane Court. And that is especially sad, since it was once the most talked about and turbulent
of them all.

Crane Court, according to the Victorian antiquary John Timbs
in his *Curiosities of London*, had long been a kind of nursery for

newspapers. It was here that in 1763 Dryden Leach was seized at night by the King's messengers, and his servants and journeymen with him, and arrested on a general warrant on suspicion of having printed John Wilkes's *North Briton no. 45*: a suspicion based merely on the fact that Wilkes had been seen entering Leach's house. 'Here', says Timbs, 'was the office of the *Commercial Chronicle*; the *Traveller* removed from Fleet-street, and remained here until its junction with the *Globe*. In the basement of another house were printed the early numbers of *Punch*... and in number 10... immediately opposite, was first printed the *Illustrated London News*...'

But here too, unmentioned by Timbs, perhaps because he recoiled from inflicting publications of such low reputation on his respectable readers, James Thompson, printer, unleashed on 10 April 1831 the first number of a concoction he called *The Satirist, or, The Censor of the Times*. No editor was named at this point, but it was very soon clear that the new paper's inspiration was a clamorous former schoolmaster, druggist, chapel-proprietor and itinerant preacher from Brighton called Barnard Gregory. Before long, Thompson's name had disappeared from the masthead and Gregory's had replaced it.

The front page of the *Satirist* declared itself to be '*pro rege, lege et grege*' (for King, law and people) below which appeared the motto: 'Satire's my weapon. – I was born a Critic and a Satirist; and my nurse remarked that I hissed as soon as I saw light.' It appeared every Sunday. In its early days, it carried straightforward reports from Parliament and the courts, together with patches of genuine news. The leader in the first issue championed the reform of Parliament, the hottest political issue of the day. But such purposes were clearly subordinate. Much of it was concerned to mock, defame and destroy people and institutions whom Gregory and his accomplices distrusted and despised. There were weekly columns directed at lawyers ('the black sheep of the law') and gaming houses. There were intermittent attacks on the church ('a mass of corruption'), judicial execution, and the stamp duty on newspapers, that 'tax on knowledge', as its opponents called it, which the *Satirist*, though deliberately unrespectable, obediently paid.

Scorn and derision were heaped week upon week on reactionary opponents of parliamentary reform, above all the Duke of Wellington, and on editors and newspapers aligned with that camp; though the *Satirist* was also full of contempt for such radical leaders as Orator Hunt – a political fraud, it maintained, and a secret friend of Sir Robert Peel – for the unstamped press, and for the Chartists. Queen Victoria was let off quite lightly, though rebuked from time to time for her lack of interest in English theatre, but Albert, her consort, was repeatedly dipped in obloquy, all the more so no doubt because he was a foreigner, and the *Satirist* did not like foreigners. Most of all it did not like Jews; to a reader today, its virulent anti-Semitism is one of the nastiest things about it.

One law for the rich, one for the poor, the *Satirist* always complained, was the watchword of our society. Rich and offensive aristocrats were constantly in its pillory, both for their public conduct and often even more for their private behaviour. The *Satirist*, above all, was a scandal sheet, trading in tales of hanky-panky and rumpy-pumpy in those classes, the aristocracy and the higher gentry, to which polite society accorded so much undeserved respect. The heart of the paper was a column that purported to give replies to letters from correspondents, though most of these correspondents were plainly fictitious. Gregory's method was to start a trail of malicious gossip in the expectation that assiduous readers might soon provide him with more of the same. Thus a correspondent using the pseudonym 'Veritas' was assured that 'particulars of the nefarious proceedings going on at the houses 10 and 11 King Street St James's... will be our attention next week'. 'We cannot really reply to "Looker-On",' the paper regretted, 'as to what the Countess of Beauchamp and William Burton are doing at Worthing. Perhaps our correspondent can inform us?' 'The correspondent who furnishes us with the facts in relation to the "duel years ago", "the death of one of the parties by 'a young military man'", "the 'smuggling of the survivor, dressed in women's clothes, to the house of a Good Samaritan in the neighbourhood" and "the recent act of ingratitude on the part of the delinquent", should furnish us with the name of the ingrate.' To which, with one of its regular claims to be acting in the name of good order and moral rectitude, the paper added: 'that he may be dished up, not as a feast for the gods, but to those who, like ourselves, despise ingratitude'. Sometimes, however, the paper dropped this device and went for the slur direct. 'Scandal in high life,' it said of another eminent target: 'A report is very current in the circles of high life referable to something more than a pla-tonic attachment between Prince George of Cambridge [a disrep-utable grandson of George III and for a time a lamentably inadequate commander in chief of the army] and a young lady nearly allied to a noble duke.'

In one of its many attacks on the libel laws, the *Satirist* claimed, with that bogus piety which was one of its hallmarks, that even very cautious writers and publishers sometimes inadvertently trans-gressed. That may have been true; but the *Satirist* itself was never cautious, and the offence that it gave was rarely inadvertent. Within weeks of its first appearance, lawyers were mustering against it – some of them plotting, the paper complained, to shut it down. There had been a cringeing apology in its seventh issue, expressing 'deep regret' for its 'want of caution' 'in giving admission to a statement in our columns, which, in justice to all parties, we are bound to ac-knowledge... is destitute of foundation'. That did not prevent it from recklessly inviting prosecution again when a Mr Neeld com-plained of what the Attorney-General called 'one of the most wicked and malignant libels' that had perhaps ever been brought to a court: an article that alleged that the birth of a child to Mr and Mrs Neeld had come as an utter surprise to the husband who had only recently married the lady, and suggesting that her 'close inti-macy with an officer in the Guards' might have had something to do with it.

Thereafter the threats to sue, and the actual successful suits, came thick and fast. In 1832, Gregory was convicted of libelling a lawyer called Deas; in 1833, of falsely accusing a Mr Digby of Brighton of cheating at cards. In 1839 he landed a three-month jail sentence for libelling the wife of a Tory MP called Hogg. More serious still was his defamation of a Mr Last, publisher of *The Town*, since the editor of that publication retorted with a denunciation of Gregory and his methods that spelled out what many had long assumed: that Gregory's intention in parading malicious gossip was to persuade his victims to pay him so that nothing further appeared.

Even more spectacular, since it involved a pillar (though, as the world would have known, a particularly wobbly pillar) of high society, was the case brought against him for impugning the integrity of the marriage of the deeply unappetizing Marquess of Blandford, son and heir of the hardly more reputable Duke of Marlborough, and challenging the legitimacy of the Marquess's children. Gregory's target here, a modern observer might feel, deserved the assault. The *Satirist* alleged that the Marquess had led a seventeen-year-old called Susan Lawson to believe they were married. They had gone through what she assumed was a legitimate marriage ceremony and had lived together in Scotland as Captain and Mrs Lawson. When the Marquess announced his intention of marrying a well-born woman called Lady Jane Stewart, Susan protested – only to be told by the Marquess, so the *Satirist* claimed, that their marriage had been a farce, and the clergyman who conducted it was no clergyman but an army officer dressed up for the occasion.

Mr Justice Denman, presiding, delivered a judgment patently torn between disgust for the Marquess and abhorrence of his would-be exposer. Had the Marquess alone been the victim of the *Satirist*'s accusations, the judge told the court, he would have found against him, for clearly he had badly misused a respectable young lady. But he also had to take account here of the Marquess's blameless wife and their blameless children. 'Considering the interests of the individuals I have mentioned,' he said, 'and the importance of warning those that are disposed to traffick in character in this way that they cannot be allowed to do so with impunity', he found the case proved against Gregory.

Even this joust with a very senior aristocrat was trivial compared with Gregory's long-running battle with the most cherished of all his targets: a very strange man indeed, certainly wildly eccentric and very possibly mad – Charles, Duke of Brunswick. More accurately, perhaps, Charles *ex*-Duke of Brunswick, for having succeeded to the dukedom at the age of ten and escaped from the care of a regent when nineteen, he proceeded to act in such a capricious and dictatorial fashion that his subjects in Brunswick resolved to get rid of him. Hurrying back in 1830 from Paris, where he spent much of his time, to deal with an insurrection, he found himself faced with a popular demonstration of fury before which he fled. Amidst general acclamation his younger brother was installed in his place.

Over the years, the duke made occasional efforts to recapture his dukedom, but appeals to the crowned heads of Europe to back him understandably found little response, leaving the duke to content himself with obsessional self-adornment, the acquisition of diamonds, amorous dalliance, and chess. There's a picture of the duke dressed, as he often was, as a lordly military man, which irresistibly suggests that the term popinjay, defined as a conceited figure and fop, might have been invented specially for him. That persisted, by furious effort, into old age. 'Discharged valets', a London paper called *Appletons' Journal* said of his last years in Paris when he died in 1873, 'used to gossip about the paint, and the wigs, and the enamel, and the pads, and the stuffings, the high-heeled boots, and elaborately-constructed braces, which converted the little pinched and haggard occupant of the ducal bed into the tall, stately and gloomy personage of forty, who with stalwart step stalked about the corridors of the Paris theatres, or was seen riding slowly alone in the Bois.'

In his London days, though, when he did battle with Gregory, he had seemed not pathetic but sinister: 'he was the subject of countless legends, and lived in a great, gloomy house at the North End, and inspired a sort of dread whenever he appeared… There was a prevailing notion that he had some time done something horrible; but no two gossipers agreed on what it was. Men, almost as dark and strange as himself, were said to be seen going in and out of his house after nightfall; but no result that a curious public could ever discover ever came of these secret conclaves.'

Being dead, he, for once, could not sue over that. Otherwise, this verdict might have added to the relentless string of occasions when he brought his detractors, or those who had somehow offended him, to court. Not all of these were cases for libel. He was said to have sued a washerwoman over a seven-franc bill, and to have filed a dozen lawsuits over a watch repair. It didn't take long for the duke to acquire an honoured place in the gallery of the *Satirist*'s cherished targets. In a characteristically snarly paragraph which it said it had picked up from Parisian chit-chat, it described the ex-Duke's habits as 'of a very unkindly and undignified nature'. He passed the greater part of the day smoking, it said, and thereafter part of his nights in gambling salons. His hosts were always happy to see the last of him, and had great difficulty in obtaining their payments.

The duke let these aspersions go, but as further pounding attacks were made on him over the years his patience dissolved, and by 1843 their confrontations had reached the point where he was bringing two very serious cases against Barnard Gregory, while Gregory was bringing an equally extraordinary case against the duke. Originally, the duke had charged Gregory with eleven offences of libel. But before the case could be heard, he was subjected to further assault. The paper, according to Brunswick, had now implied (though never specifically stating) that he was involved in the murder in the Waterloo Road of a prostitute called Eliza Grimwood. The charges arrived at a time when Gregory was engaged in a bid to launch his career as an actor. He had over the past four years been taking leading roles in the productions of a group he had founded called the Shaksperians.'Many distinguished individuals', one London journal commented, 'have declared that in these theatrical *re-unions* Shakspere was more efficiently represented than on any other stage, not excepting the two principal houses'; praise that might have sounded even more persuasive had the journal in question not been the *Satirist*.

In February 1843, Gregory accepted an invitation to appear at Covent Garden in the role of Hamlet. The performance was a disaster. As became apparent as soon as Horatio and Marcellus had left the stage after encountering the ghost, the house was packed with Gregory's enemies, who proceeded to set up a racket so intense and sustained that eventually the theatre's lessees had the curtain rung down.

Gregory had no doubts at all that this was the work of Brunswick. A club of ten, composed principally of 'foreign swindlers and blacklegs' who had come under the lash of the *Satirist* for their offences against society, had organized the disruption by assembling their own subordinate groups of ten, many of them hired from 'the filth of St Giles' (then a notoriously drunken, unruly and violent sector of London). These people, 'the most degraded of society', whom the plotter had hired and plied with liquor, had aided this foreign attack on an Englishman – 'a man whose great weight of offence, is, SPEAKING THE TRUTH, and EXPOSING THE VICES AND CRIMES OF SOCIETY'. The parties most implicated, said the paper, were Lord William Paget; 'the person calling himself Baron Andlau' (Andlau being a known associate of Brunswick); a long list of private gamesters, brothel-keepers and swindlers, and 'the St Giles regiment of ruffians'. Mr Bartley, who had rung down the curtain, was especially vilified; he had furthered the cause of these foreigners and their blackguard allies by this treacherous action. And yet Mr Gregory (the *Satirist* forecast) would rise above the malignity of hired ruffians, paid bravos and scoundrels, and above all, would resist 'the petty machinations of a "super-annuated" twaddler, who appeared to derive gratification from his own intemperance of folly, and the spleen of vindictive feeling.' The paper forbore to give the name of this twaddler; for regular readers, it didn't need to.

But had the disruption been orchestrated? Or was it rather, as some of the protagonists testified, a spontaneous outpouring of hatred against a man whom even a judge had condemned as a trafficker in character – in other words, as a scandal-monger? Mr Justice Maule was adamant when Gregory's case came to court that these demonstrations in the theatre should never have happened. Even so, as he warned the jury, to make his charges stick Gregory had to establish that the Duke of Brunswick had organized the proceedings: and that was another matter. Some witnesses had asserted, as if resentful that anyone should have thought otherwise, that they hadn't needed anybody's incitement to let Gregory know how they felt about him. Such people had sympathizers far removed from the squalid streets of St Giles. 'I begin to have hopes of the regeneration of mankind after the reception of Gregory last night,' Charles Dickens wrote to his friend John Forster. To the fury of the *Satirist*, hardly any London newspaper condemned what had happened. Even the *Theatrical Times*, while deploring the treatment of Gregory, felt bound to add that, like many others, his conduct as a member of the press had tended to lower the press in the public's estimation, and it held him blameworthy for his invasion of the sanctity of private life.

The radical journalist W. J. Linton fingered the duke for complicity, but made him seem an almost accidental contributor to the proceedings. In his memoirs, published in 1894, he recalled:

> The curtain drew up, and the action of the play began in all serenity; but so soon as Hamlet made his appearance an outcry, a burst of execration, rose so suddenly, and was so general, that one saw at once no opposition could make head against it. Hisses and hootings, cries of "Off! off!—Blackguard! scoundrel!" and the like were hurled at the actor; and the whole performance was stopped. Nothing was thrown except the storm of vociferation. Gregory faced it awhile,

undauntedly impudent, then tried to make his voice heard in protest, but it was drowned in the roar of indignation. I was but three seats from the orchestra, and I could not hear a syllable of his speech though I saw his lips move. At length he gave in, and as the curtain came down he seemed to cower and crouch beneath.

One of those most active in the storm was the Duke of Brunswick, who had been grossly assailed in the *Satirist*. He had taken a stage box, from which he acted as fugleman to a party he had organised throughout the house, so giving us most unexpected help. Gregory brought an action against him for conspiracy. Jem Mace, a pugilist and publican living in the neighbourhood of the theatre, was there, no doubt one of those hired by the duke, and prominently active. He was summoned as a witness, and did not deny the part he had taken, but denied having been hired for the conspiracy. He was asked: 'What made you active in such a matter? what interest had you in it?' His interest, he replied, was in public morality; he could not help protesting against such a man disgracing the stage – his words not these exactly, but to such purpose. The judge complimented him, and said he was glad to find so much public spirit in the parish in which he had his own residence.

Mr Justice Maule's jury, at any rate, found its decision easy. It took just half an hour to arrive at a verdict that cleared the duke. That left Gregory one down in the series, with two matches to go; and they would turn out even worse for him. The first case to come up, two days after the settlement of the Covent Garden proceedings, was that of the *Satirist*'s claims about the murder of Grimwood. That, in the end, was a walkover. Gregory had pleaded not guilty, but when the case opened his lawyers announced that he had withdrawn that plea, and now admitted the libel. He still denied imputing the crime to the duke, but accepted that what had been printed was designed to bring his highness into contempt and ridicule.

Gregory was sentenced to a year's imprisonment. He had planned, the *Satirist* disconsolately informed its readers, to explain to the court why he had printed this 'so-called libel', but because he had pleaded guilty, that right had been denied him. So his paper made his case for him. His statement might have been libellous, but that did not make it untrue. 'Legally libellous, as when measured by the late odious and detestable Law of Libel, such statements might be deemed; but it is one thing for a man to plead guilty to the publication of a libel, and another for him to be satisfied that he has not wilfully transgressed the boundaries of truth. If Mr Gregory is bound to admit the one, he ought not to be deprived of the opportunity of showing the other.'

Editorial condemnation and letters from outraged readers about both the Covent Garden event and subsequent judgment were now replaced in the *Satirist* by complaints of its former editor's treatment in Newgate jail. He had been exposed, his old paper protested, to restrictions, privations and torture, mental and physical. He was subject, it was claimed, to the pulmonary disease that had killed his father. His daughter had written a poignant plea to the Home Secretary, Sir James Graham, about her father's condition, but Sir James had replied that he could not intervene. Gregory's name was still for a time written across the masthead as printer and publisher, though the paper said he'd had nothing to do with subsequent publications, and printed what appeared to be a promise that under its new direction it would clean up its act: 'our shafts shall be fairly and impartially aimed, and our satire divested of a severity which much more certainly arouses bitterness and bad feeling than it reforms the offender, and, moreover, imparts to journalism its most objectionable feature.'

There remained the substantive matter of the eleven alleged libels originally brought to court before the case that had earned him his year in Newgate. But that for several years was deferred and deferred again. Because he had been in prison, he was too unwell to proceed with the case; physicians were willing to testify that to bring him to court in these circumstances might possibly kill him. Then, immured as he was, he had not been able to compile his defence. The

Satirist appealed to the duke and his supporters. 'Whom,' it asked 'do they hope to crush? A man once of great talent and indomitable energy, but now enfeebled, borne down, emaciated by prison fare, prison discipline, prison constraints, and prison cruelties!' The scenes in court had been so pitiable: 'the daughter of the sufferer – young, lovely and amiable – in filial and feminine tenderness attending to and solacing her father... brought up for a second indictment on the day immediately before the expiration of the first? O magnanimity! O justice!' And so on.

While the resolution of this case was awaited, a succession of further encounters ensued. The *Satirist* was sued for a report linking the duke with a murderer called Thomas Hocker. This time, the jury was unimpressed and awarded the duke damages of one farthing. Gregory, meanwhile, had been trying to resume his acting career, only to re-encounter the dregs of St Giles. Though this time the curtain stayed up, his appearance as Shylock at the Strand Theatre in December 1845 was so severely heckled that he stepped before the curtain when it was over to say he did not believe that it was in the British character to persecute the persecuted: a declaration rewarded, it was reported, by resumed noise and turmoil. (But even this had damaged the evening less, the *Satirist* judged, than the presence in the supporting cast of actors devoid of talent.)

Further stage appearances in the roles of Hamlet, Shylock and Othello, in the last of which, the *Satirist* claimed, Gregory, established himself as 'the true successor of Kean', were again howled down by 'the moral refuse of the metropolis', and a repeat of the *Merchant of Venice* occasioned such disgraceful scenes that the proprietor of the theatre wrote from the Isle of Wight, where he was taking a holiday, ordering that the house should be closed.

Gregory retaliated this time by publishing a pamphlet insisting that his journalist days had ended when he was jailed in March 1843. He went on to list those he held responsible for the latest attacks on him. They were, 'John Belasco, brother to the pugilist; The Count de Wuits, ex-equerry to the Duke of Brunswick; Goodered, of the Piccadilly Saloon; Wilmot, a Brighton coachman; Phillipson, better known as Jack Phillipson; Burton, "the advertising individual"; and Morris Barnet, a theatrical reporter and actor; Theophilus Echalaz, describing himself as "of the Stock Exchange"; and Lieut Philip Kemp, of the 9th Lancers.' This noxious ninesome were never given their chance again. On stage at least, the rest, for Kean's natural successor, was silence.

In other contexts, too, Gregory haunted the law courts. In one case he sued a Mrs Le Bas for denying him a legacy he believed he had been left by a man called John Thompson. But the case was never heard, since in the interim he married Mrs Le Bas. Together they then took on another disappointed claimant.

Gregory died in 1852 from lung disease, but the *Satirist* predeceased him. In spite of further declarations that it had now reformed and repented of some of its former excesses, there were more suits brought against it, culminating in its newly appointed publisher, Martin Hansill, being arraigned and convicted for aiding and abetting a woman who was trying to extort money from a rich manufacturer living in Twickenham. Hansill had threatened to treat his readers to an account of his victim's dalliance with two named women unless the man made it worth the editor's while not to do so – which, of course, was exactly what Gregory had been constantly accused of doing during his editorship. Despite the jailing of Hansill, the *Satirist* announced in its edition of 15 December 1849 its certainty that those who were trying to crush it would never succeed. Two weeks later, however, it failed to appear: suppressed by the government on the urging, it was asserted, of the Duke of Brunswick.

The duke, now based in Paris and grown grossly corpulent, not least because of his habit of visiting sweet shops and eating their wares until he could eat no more, survived until 1873, when, leaving the table during a game of chess with a warning to his opponent not to cheat in his absence, he went to his room and died. Despite his rackety life he had reached the age of sixty-nine. They don't, as they say, make people like Charles, Duke of Brunswick, or Barnard Gregory any more; which, despite the way their adventures cheered up a populace greedy for scandal, is probably just as well.

6

BIRMINGHAM

✒

'We saw him first in the street. We saw a man apparently about fifty years of age, walking slowly and with heavy steps along the pavement. He possessed a beard of astonishing proportions. It was jet black and completely covered the lower portion of his face. He is renowned for this beard. It is thick, and long, and bushy, and as he never has it combed or trimmed, it gives him the wildness of a demi-savage...'

O N   A   B E D R O O M   W A L L in the house of a friend I saw a group photograph of the new House of Commons elected in 1892. Rather to my surprise, most members were conspicuously, even extravagantly, hairy. A formidable contingent were sporting beards, and most of the rest, though falling short of genuine beardedness, compensated for that by other forms of display: sideburns (a curious term, which is said to derive from a US army wearer of sideburns called Burnside); clumps, even thickets, of heavy foliage sprouting all over their cheeks; little goatees; or the sort of false beard that starts not at the leading edge of the chin but somewhere in the region of the upper throat.

As to the beards, some were wispy and tentative, but others, particularly among the Scots and the Irish, were nothing less than majestic, suggesting in some cases that their owners must surely have needed beard-bearers to carry their growths before them. Strong though he looks in this picture, it is difficult to imagine a man so monstrously bearded as A. J. Mundella (Liberal, Brightside) walking without such assistance. Mr Gladstone, newly reinstalled as prime minister, has hefty side-whiskers, but his chin is naked. Sir H. Hussey Vivian (Liberal, Swansea) and S. D. Waddy (Liberal, Brigg) do the same kind of thing, only better. The most awesome figure in the collection is J. Rigby (Liberal, Forfarshire). His head is rectangular. His beard is immense. Laser-like eyes burn through vicious glasses. Second only to Rigby is Isaac Holden, MP for Keighley. This Holden installed in his grand house at Oakworth a galaxy of bathrooms and wash basins, a personal Turkish bath, a shower and a douche bath. He also constructed three reservoirs. When you contemplate the potential for infestation within this beard, you can see that he may have had need of them.

Was this some epidemic notion affecting only the newly elected? Not at all. For soon afterwards I saw, on the wall of a mocked-up Victorian bank at the Blists Hill industrial museum at Ironbridge, Shropshire, a group photograph of Lloyds Bank managers at a conference in 1898. They too were mostly extremely hairy, and many had lavish beards. These were people – like the MPs – the essence of whose employment was the need to generate trust. Their success would depend on suffusing their clients with an unwavering confidence in their diligence, honour and total reliability. Clearly their hair was not counted against them.

And yet through the subsequent century and into the twenty-first, such ostentatious hirsuteness was a matter for distrust and suspicion. Conservatives who stood by their beards in the heyday of Margaret Thatcher were taken aside by the party whips and warned that their beards might deny them preferment, which was why John Selwyn Gummer, for one, got rid of his. Likewise when Tony Blair was prime minister, the *Guardian* reported: 'Faced with the prospect of humiliating defeat at the hands of the clean-shaven Ken Livingstone in London's mayoral race, Labour's highly vaunted strategists have come up with a master plan: tell Frank Dobson [who much against his will was Labour's candidate for the mayoralty] to shave his beard off. Drawing on evidence from psychologists that men with beards are regarded as untrustworthy, Philip Gould, Labour's senior pollster and interpreter of focus groups, told grey-haired Dobson the beard should go, saying it would reveal the party's candidate as a reinvigorated figure ready and willing to beat Livingstone.' Dobson kept his beard; and he lost. Robin Cook too refused to give up his beard, which made him the first bearded cabinet minister since Sidney Webb; but even the prime minister's faithful henchman Peter Mandelson thought it wise to discard his moustache.

Much of sensible, stolid England now seemed to assume that men with beards were probably feasting on muesli, wearing sandals and reading the *Guardian*. The very fuzz that partly concealed their faces suggested they might have something to hide. So how was it that beards had conveyed exactly the opposite message a century earlier? One answer is Queen Victoria. Another is G. F. Muntz.

'At about this period,' wrote William Andrews in his *At the sign of the Barber's Pole: Studies in Hirsute History* (1904) – he was speaking of the 1840s – 'only one civilian of position in England had the hardihood to wear the moustache. He was Mr George Frederick Muntz, a Member of Parliament for Birmingham. He was a notable figure in the House of Commons, and is described as manly in appearance, with a handsome face, a huge black beard, and the moustache.' (Note that 'manly': it may be the key to this business.)

Muntz was first elected in 1840. His arrival at Westminster was one of the fruits of the Reform Act of 1832, for which he had been a prominent campaigner in Birmingham. A determined and turbulent figure, he was put on trial for his conduct in the campaign against church rates. Though the court threw out charges of riotous behaviour, it convicted him of causing an affray; but he won his case on appeal. That episode didn't deter respectable Birmingham from turning out to support him in the election. His pleasure at winning his seat would have been all the greater since the Tory whom he ousted was perhaps the most stuck in the mud of all opponents of electoral reform, Sir Charles Wetherell.

Muntz was not in any sense a conventional politician. His ancestors were Poles who had fled to France, where they became people of wealth and consequence. His father, Philip Frederick, had crossed to England where he set up in business in Birmingham. George Frederick, who inherited the business when only eighteen, introduced an ingenious adaptation to its methods of manufacturing, devising a compound metal, cheaper than the bronze that was used until then, which in time was adopted across the world and became known as Muntz metal.

Though popular enough in the city to retain his seat until his death, he was not a team player. In 1847, standing for re-election alongside a fellow Liberal called William Scholefield, he declined to campaign on behalf of his colleague. Appearing at an election meeting, he took a seat at the back of the hall and opened a bag of oranges, which he stoically munched and sucked while successions of speakers denounced him for failing to come to the aid of the party. Eventually as the onslaught continued, he climbed on his seat and addressed the meeting, insisting that it wasn't his business to tell his constituents who they should vote for. He then settled back in his seat and resumed his assault on the oranges.

Though he shook and stirred the great open air reform meetings in Birmingham, he was never a fluent or polished speaker. In the House he was loud, but rarely effective. He seems not to have been offered ministerial office and had offers been made he might well have rejected them. Outside Parliament he had sometimes had a decisive influence on events: it was he, says the Birmingham historian, Eliezer Edwards, who in 1830, when the Duke of Wellington was set to obstruct reform, told a vast meeting at Newhall Hill, Birmingham: 'To stop the duke, run for gold': that's to say, start a run on the banks – an invitation so readily taken up, says Edwards, miscounting slightly, that 'in half a dozen words he sounded the death knell of the new Tory ministry'. Yet his greatest achievement once he got into Parliament, Edwards sardonically noted, was inducing the government of the day to perforate stamps.

He was better known as a rough and mighty eater, about whom Barnard Gregory's *Satirist* paper published this rhyme:

> 'Dinner for six,' roared Muntz. The waiter stared.
> 'For six, sir?' quoth the man, awake to tricks;
> 'Where are they, Sir?' Poor devil, he was scared
> When Muntz exclaimed in anger, 'I'm the six'.

But most of all he was known for the wildly unorthodox picture he presented to public scrutiny. One observer, David Bartlett, author of *What I Saw in London; or, Men and Things in the Great Metropolis*, wrote of him:

> In personal appearance he is the most singular man whom we ever saw. We saw him first in the street. We saw a man apparently about fifty years of age, walking slowly and with heavy steps along the pavement. He was about the middle height, and possessed a beard of astonishing proportions. It was jet black and completely covered the lower portion of his face. He is renowned for this beard. It is thick and long, and bushy, and as he never has it combed or trimmed, it gives him the wildness of a demi-savage… He has a fine forehead and brilliant eyes, but his terrible beard completely spoils his personal appearance. It has been the laugh of England for years, but he is fonder of it than ever.

And that wasn't the only curious feature of the eye-catching public spectacle that was George Frederick Muntz. 'In his dress he is peculiar. His pantaloons', Bartlett reported, 'are generally constructed of coarse material, and are broad and flowing, and in England, where everybody wears pantaloons tight to the skin, they have a singular appearance.' He further noted that Muntz always walked with a stick. This, the bearded Midlander used to maintain, was because he might at any time be attacked by the scoundrelly Marquess of Waterford, who had threatened to publicly shave him.

He sounds an unlikely role model. Yet despite the reputed

awfulness of his beard, and its alleged risibility, it set a trend which others followed and which culminated in the beardorama of the House of Commons of 1892. In 1858, the year after Muntz's death, William White, a House of Commons doorkeeper who wrote vivid and evocative parliamentary sketches for the *Illustrated Times* newspaper on the side, reported that beards and other forms of hairy display were breaking out all over the place. The specimen that intrigued him most hung on the awesome countenance of the bestselling novelist Bulwer Lytton. 'We suspect that he has good features generally,' White wrote, 'but we cannot vouch for this, for they are for the most part entirely concealed by an extraordinary growth of hair… His hair proper is all dishevelled and unkempt, and his beard and moustache grow according to their own will. We have many extraordinary beards and moustaches in the House: we have flowing beards, and stubby beards, and curly beards; we have moustaches light and delicate like a lady's eyebrow, long and pendant like a Chinaman's, bushy and fierce like a brigand's. Some men wear beards, whiskers and moustaches; others shave the whiskers and beard and leave the moustache; whilst others preserve the moustache and part of the beard, but eschew whiskers; but in all these varieties, and a great many more, there are marks of design. But Sir Bulwer-Lytton despises all art, and lets Nature take her own way, and the result is probably the most astonishing human face in the world.'

White also spotted what would in time become perhaps the mightiest beard of them all: that of the subsequent Tory prime minister, Lord Salisbury. Lord Robert Cecil, as he was then – White noted in 1864 – looked older than thirty-four. 'His bearded face is not youthful; his head at the top is partially bald; his hair is getting somewhat thin and straggling; he might well pass for forty-four.' Yet see him today as he was in the days of his greatest eminence – on the cover, for instance, of Andrew Roberts's life of him – and here is a beard to be marvelled at: so vast and capacious that it might almost have been Lord Salisbury whom Edward Lear had in mind when he wrote:

There was an Old Man with a beard,
Who said, 'It is just as I feared!
Two Owls and a Hen,
Four Larks and a Wren,
Have all built their nests in my beard.

By now, though, nearly all men seemed to be at it. Lawyers were discouraged from joining the trend: in mid-century, a barrister named Brierley, who appeared in court with a flowing beard and a thick moustache, was told to get rid of them; when he declined, a vote of censure was passed on him and he disappeared from practice. Army officers were limited to moustaches; but beards flourished in Her Majesty's navy. Senior churchmen largely abstained – Rowan Williams, taking office in 2003, was said to be the first bearded man to become Archbishop of Canterbury since the beheading, beard and all, of Laud in 1645. But huge writerly beards – notably, Tennyson's – and science beards, such as Darwin's, were everywhere now, while radical beards were profuse: Shaw, William Morris, Sidney Webb, Keir Hardie, Karl Marx; as well as anarchist beards like Bakunin's, and more wondrous still, that of Kropotkin. And at the other end of the political scale, dispelling any notion that beards were somehow subversive, or out of keeping with the highest reaches of British society, Edward VII grew one, and George V grew another.

And here we come to the factor that may have licensed the spread of a practice which seemed so eccentric when Muntz brought his beard to Westminster. In a book called *Beards: Their Social Standing, Religious Involvements, Decorative Possibilities, and Value in Offence and Defence Through the Ages* (1949), Reginald Reynolds noted what a tour of the National Portrait Gallery tends to confirm: that beards were at their most fecund when a formidable female monarch was on the throne. So it was with Elizabeth I (who introduced a tax on beards, but soon dropped it); and so above all with Victoria. That manliness, which William Andrews diagnosed in Muntz, may have been the ingredient that caused his example to spread. Men had somehow to show that, despite their subordination to the reign of a woman, they remained the dominant force, because they were demonstrably manly. Here was one field where even the most formidable of women could not compete. Elizabeth and Victoria, political dominatrices though they aspired to be, could never grow beards, or even side-whiskers.

George Frederick Muntz was returned for the fifth and final time as a Member for Birmingham in March 1857. As in the previous election five years earlier he and William Scholefield were unopposed. But he was by now in every sense a diminished figure. Though *Aris's Birmingham Gazette* believed the news of his death only four months later would be greeted with 'unfeigned regret' throughout his constituency and indeed in a House of Commons that had come to respect his individuality, Eliezer Edwards thought he had been in steady decline from the time he was first elected. What Edwards calls 'his hereditary tendency' had pushed him steadily to the right. He was, Edwards adds, a very vain man, and had always told his friends, publicly and privately, that at least he was politically honest and consistent. So though he shifted his views, he tried to live up to that character: 'Hence all sorts of eccentricities, inconsistencies and absurdities. Hence his constant habit of speaking one way and voting another...' And hence too a sensitivity to criticism that led him (so Edwards claims) to come close to shaking to death a bookseller for selling a paper he thought had defamed him. His egotism ran out of control, so much so that it was said of a speech he had made in the town that no printer could have printed it, since none would have had a big enough stock of the letter 'I'. Moreover, the big black beard belonged, Edwards says, to a bully: 'he was always declaiming against despotism and tyranny in the abstract, yet he was domineering and arbitrary in his household, in his family, and in his business'.

Yet his final days made him an object of pity even to Edwards. The death of his youngest daughter in 1852 left him grief-stricken. 'His robust frame began to exhibit tokens of decay'; his hair turned grey and 'streaks of silver were seen in his magnificent beard'. By the time of his last re-election in March it was clear he was greatly changed, and soon after it was made known that 'tumours of an alarming nature' had formed. His once imposing and outsize frame was diminished 'to a mere skeleton'. He died on 30 July 1857.

Edwards complains that Muntz left nothing of his mighty fortune to the town that had long sustained him, and it cannot be said that Birmingham has done much to remember him. That would have shocked as well as saddened him since he patently regarded himself as a great man. There's an unremarkable street just south east of the city centre called Muntz Street, which runs up from the Malt Shovel pub on the Coventry road past a fast-food shop and a couple of schools until it appropriately transmogrifies into a street named for his fellow arch-promulgator of nineteenth-century British beard-edness: *Victoria* Street. It was once a more rousing place than it is today. In its earlier years as Small Heath Alliance, then Small Heath, and finally Birmingham, the football club that is now Birmingham City used to play there, but in 1906 they sold the ground and moved half a mile to their present home at St Andrew's.

The Cheshire cat in Alice slowly faded away until there was nothing left but its grin. It might equally be said that little of G. F. Muntz survives in his city today, apart perhaps from the occasional evocation of that mighty black beard; and even that is all but forgotten.

7

KILWINNING, AYRSHIRE

THE FLAGS, THE TRUMPETS, THE LISTS AND
ABOVE ALL THE RAIN BRING ABOUT THE LATE
EDUCATION OF ARCHIBALD, EARL OF EGLINTON.

🙡

*The young in the villages jeered them. 'It is said that not
a few of those who experienced this treatment, began with
laughing in good humour at the jests of their little
tormentors and ended with removing some of their once
attractive adornments, the young men especially tearing
their feathers from their bonnets and trampling
them in the mire...'*

TO THE UNTRAINED EYE it might have looked like business as usual. Here were the fluttering flags and the trumpets and the heralds ready with grandiloquent proclamations, and the armoured knights aboard fine caparisoned horses, and the Queen of Beauty, pavilioned in splendour and surrounded by gorgeous handmaidens – all part of a ritual stretching back to misty origins in eleventh-century France. Yet in several significant senses this occasion was not authentic. No one would die, as knights often did in genuine tournaments; indeed, apart from a minor injury to his wrist sustained by the Hon. Mr Jeringham, no one would even get hurt. And, perhaps for the very first time in the history of this art form, large numbers of those who assembled to watch the proceedings had come by train.

The event set up for this day – 25 August 1839 – was an exercise in romantic nostalgia, contrived by the twenty-six-year-old Scottish nobleman Archibald William Montgomerie, 13th Earl of Eglinton, in the grounds of his fine 1,200 acre estate, Eglinton Castle, on the edge of the Ayrshire town of Kilwinning. After an adolescence and early adulthood devoted – his more austere relatives had cause to complain – to drink and debauchery, Archibald had come back to Eglinton to reinvent himself as a serious person. An account of these proceedings by the Revd William Lee Ker, M. A., minister of Kilwinning, in his history of the town published in 1900, suggests two motives for the earl's determination to go ahead with this wildly ambitious enterprise. He wanted to recreate the glory days of the Montgomeries, who regularly sallied into rather more solemn battles, and did not always emerge from them; and he did it to give his friends and neighbours and indeed the whole locality a thumping good time. The 'geniality and kindness of his disposition, and his capacity to adorn, and his pleasure in participating in public festivals, which urged him... to do what he could, and that, too, often regardless of expense, for the promotion of the pleasure and the happiness of those around him...': these above all, Mr Lee Ker concluded, were what drove him to devise this lavish occasion and spend such startling sums in bringing it off. But other accounts of the Eglinton tournament suggest a sharper, more political motive, which Lee Ker either did not know about or forbore to mention. This was to spite the Whigs.

The Whig government had decreed that the coronation of Queen Victoria in June 1838 should be shorn of some of the pageantry of previous investitures. The reason they gave was the need for economy in difficult times. They may also, however, have had in mind the less than glorious record of similar recent occasions. According to the historian David Cannadine, at the funeral of Princess Charlotte in 1817 the undertakers were drunk. George IV's coronation four years later was 'so overblown that the grandeur merged into farce', with prizefighters stationed on doors to control the more troublesome guests, while the queen, Caroline, (whom the new king had shunned) clamoured vainly at the door of the Abbey to be admitted. George's funeral in July 1830 was hardly more decorous. 'We never saw so motley, so rude, so ill-managed a body of persons,' said *The Times* of the mourners. The young earl, however, was intent on putting the curmudgeonly Whigs in their place. He would show that the nation could still stage pageantry in the high tradition of earlier ages. And money, he seems to have told himself, would be no object.

There are several accounts of what happened at Eglinton, some by more accomplished and worldly-wise writers than Mr Lee Ker. In *The Knight and the Umbrella*, first published in 1963, Sir Ian Fife Campbell Anstruther, of that Ilk, 8th Baronet of Balcaskie and 13th Baronet of Anstruther, describes the event as 'the greatest folly of the century'. The value of Lee Ker's account, apart from its gentle and sometimes wry charm, is that he lets you see the occasion through the eyes of Kilwinning, where, when he wrote his book in 1900, he had been minister for thirty-four years. When he came to the parish it was not much more than twenty-five years since the tournament, and over those years he had talked at length to some of the local people who had been there to see it. His account is broadly approving. He admires the thirteenth earl – though they would never have met; the earl had already, as he says, 'passed to the great majority' five years before he arrived in Kilwinning. But the truth must be told, especially by ministers of the Church of Scotland, and despite his respect for the great local family, this writer cannot conceal the fact that the ambitious, rampagingly colourful and exceedingly costly celebration envisaged by the young earl did not always go according to plan. Indeed, there lurks not far beneath the surface of his account a word that was afterwards joyfully scattered about by the Earl of Eglinton's critics: the word 'fiasco'.

This was not for any lack of commitment. As the moment approached, there was high excitement in unexciting Kilwinning. 'In the parish of Kilwinning in which the Castle is situated,' says Lee Ker, 'in Irvine and other neighbouring towns there never had been, and probably never will be, so much stir and bustle. For months before... even the new railway which was being constructed between

Glasgow and Ayr received but small attention in comparison with the great outgoings at Eglinton Castle.' The expenditure alone was spectacular: perhaps as much as £40,000 (nearly £2 million today), the minister speculated, though he could not be sure and suspected that the earl had no clear idea either. To the disappointment of some local tradesmen, much of the money was spent in London, in line with the earl's conviction that only the best would do.

An invitation list was prepared, packed with the day's celebrities, of whom the most conspicuous was the thirty-year-old Louis-Napoleon, the subsequent emperor Napoleon III. The role of Queen of Beauty, to whom the contending knights traditionally dedicated their victories, was assigned to Jane Georgiana Seymour, a granddaughter of the playwright Sheridan, and wife for the past nine years of Lord Seymour, later 12th Duke of Somerset. The Reverend Mr Lee Ker did not fail to acquaint the ladies of early twentieth-century Kilwinning with the details of what she wore: 'Morning: Saya of violet velvet, having armorial bearings on front, emblazoned on silver in azure velvet; jacquet of miniver, spotted with ermine; partelet of sky-blue satin, worked with silver; mantle of rich crimson velvet, furred with miniver; gauntlets embroidered and fretted with gold; crown of silver set with rich jewels. Evening: a superb antique brocade silk kirtle, raised with silver, gold and various colours; vest of white velvet with demi sleeves of silver tissue and damask wire; stomacher of gold, set with precious stones; skayne or veil of silver canvass, and chaplet of flowers.'

The castle itself was garnished and beautified for this occasion 'as probably no other dwelling in Scotland was ever adorned'. 'With its ornaments of cunning work, its tapestry and needle-work, its ancient armour, its vessels of silver and gold, its lights from a thousand lamps, its beautiful and rare flowers, its still more beautiful women, and its noblemen dressed with the clothing which only wealth can provide and sparkling with jewels and diamonds, it must have presented the appearance of a fairy palace if anything ever did so'. But because the dining and drawing rooms of the castle were too small to accommodate the whole of his glittering guest list, Archibald had ordered the construction at the back of the castle of a grand saloon divided into three compartments, one for the banquet, another for the ball, and in the centre, a conservatory for some of the rarest and most beautiful plants and flowers. Mr Lee Ker can barely restrain his local pride as he conjures up the scene that, as he'd been told, was thus created: 'When one remembers that the various structures around the lists were erected after the most approved fashion and gaily adorned with flags of various colours, and that during the tournament they were occupied by the youth and beauty of the day, attired in all the splendour that taste and wealth could provide, it will at once be realised that the chroniclers of the event are not exaggerating when they say that the spectacle was one of great splendour and beauty when seen in all its grandeur.'

And the great day started so well. The townspeople of Kilwinning woke to a brilliant morning, and soon the world was on its way to their doorstep. Quite how many were there on 25 August will never be known. Lee Ker hazarded a figure of 60,000, but some – including Mary S. Millar in her account of the earl in the *Oxford Dictionary of National Biography* – put it nearer 100,000. Never in the history of Ayrshire, says the minister of Kilwinning, had such crowds assembled within any part of it, nor had such crowds come together since. 'Steamers filled with passengers from stem to stern came to Ardrossan from Glasgow and places on the way down the Clyde, and steamers from Liverpool and Stranraer came equally heavily laden. The Glasgow & South Western Railway, which had but recently opened a branch between Irvine and Ayr, did its utmost to bring crowds from the neighbourhood of these places. The horse railway between Kilwinning and Saltcoats, though it could only run one carriage at a time, lost not a moment in bringing up its load of eager sightseers from Saltcoats to Kilwinning, and returning empty for more. Vehicles of all kinds were pressed into service and filled all the surrounding public highways with carriages, 'busses, gigs, carts, vans of all sorts and sizes. It is said that nearly twenty miles of the road between Glasgow and Kilwinning was covered with a continuous line of coaches and other vehicles. And thousands who could not obtain any means of transit took lightly to the road on foot, and in hundreds from Kilmarnock, Ayr, Dalry and many other places further distant from the great centre of attraction, wended their way right cheerfully... A more gladsome, more eager crowd never probably assembled anywhere...'

They proved to be as patient as they were numerous. The proceedings were due to start at half past twelve, but one o'clock passed and one thirty, without any sight of the knights on their prancing horses whom they had come to see. This was because of a circumstance which, although he'd spent much of his life in the west of Scotland, the brash young earl had failed to allow for. It started to rain. What Lee Ker calls a 'perfect deluge' had begun to drench the place. And even when it abated, the principals did not appear. They were waiting, he suspected, for a glimpse of the sun. Still, eventually, at around three, a great buzz of excitement greeted the long-awaited procession; the thousand seats in the Queen of Beauty's pavilion were graciously occupied; and the first encounter was due to begin.

Yet the afternoon, in other respects besides the weather, did not live up to the public's expectations, or, for that matter, the earl's. Only thirteen knights, of the forty or so he had hoped to enlist, had made it to Eglinton. The proclamation of the start of the tournament, to be prefaced by summoning trumpets, had to be ditched because of the weather. And the way the participants fought when they at last appeared seemed to some eager spectators too gentlemanly by far. They fought, of course, with blunted swords and lances, as even contenders in ancient tournaments had been required to do, but were further regulated by an Eglinton set of rules – drawn up after a warning from the sheriff of Ayr that should a fatality occur there might be a charge of manslaughter – designed for their health and safety, to which even the notoriously madcap Marquis of Waterford had to subscribe.

This marquis, Lee Ker notes, had been one of the potent attractions:

'the Marquis… was one of the best known, if not one of the most distinguished of the illustrious men and women whom his Lordship had invited. Of course he was the observed of all observers, and drew from the crowds of girls and boys who gazed upon him as he rode along, expressions of wonder and delight, which he seemed greatly to relish.' Today he was, by his standards, restrained, though at least in the sixth of the contests he 'shoved his lance against his opponent with such force that part spun up 100 ft into air'. Even so, in the first four jousts of the day, not one lance was broken, 'much to the disappointment of our onlookers, some of whom could not refrain from ironical ejaculations'. And by now the rain, after its brief remission, had set in once more, further dampening and depressing the already uneasy proceedings.

Soon the day's entertainment was over. And then the earl encountered a further setback. 'Alas! his Lordship, standing in front of the Pavilion, had to announce that the cause of disaster outside had proved equally disastrous inside, for the rain had destroyed all the magnificent arrangements in the dining and ball rooms, and that consequently only his friends in the castle could be entertained… that evening'. The trouble was that although the London contractors had built a solid floor for the temporary accommodation, they had roofed it with canvas. 'Many', the Reverend Mr Lee Ker records, 'did not hesitate to say that if persons in the neighbourhood had been entrusted with the work no such mishap… would have happened.'

The nobility and gentry accommodated in the castle were safe from the disappointment thus visited on the second rank of celebrities. Even their deprivations, though, were hardly to be compared with the fate of less eminent visitors, most of whose journeys home were utterly wretched. They had trouble enough to fight their way through the mud to get out of the arena, but what faced them when they reached the railways compounded their misery: 'And then a scene was exhibited by the assembled multitude which really beggars description… Some… left the grounds in comparative leisure,

but these were the fortunate ones who knew of lodgings in neighbouring towns. As for the rest they rushed helter skelter for the
different gates... and amid mud and mire went along the roads to
the different destinations they had in view. Hundreds found their
way to the railway station at the Dirrans, near Kilwinning... to endeavour to reach Saltcoats and Ardrossan... But it was a railway with
a single line of rails, it had only one carriage running at a time, and
it was drawn by horses. [Perceiving] that to wait there till they could
obtain a chance of locomotion in this manner, might be to wait till
midnight... hundreds at once started off to walk... It was only a
distance of some four miles to Saltcoats, but the ladies' garments
were soaked with the rain, and the garments of the gentlemen were
in a similar plight, and the roads were ankle deep with mud...''One
who was there told the writer that the road to Kilmarnock was
crowded with wayfarers, and it was simply pitiable to see the "fair
dames" of Killie with their faded finery. They had eight miles to
walk from Irvine before they reached home, and though the men
and women of these days were in the habit of walking much longer
distances than now, there were scores of them very faint and weary,
almost, indeed, "dead beat" before they reached Kilmarnock.'

Nor did the neighbourhoods through which they passed regard
their plight with sympathy. The young in the villages jeered them.
'It is said that not a few of those who experienced this treatment,
began with laughing in good humour at the jests of their little tormentors and ended with removing some of their once attractive
adornments, the young men especially tearing their feathers from
their bonnets and trampling them in the mire.' Meanwhile there
was comparable suffering for those who made for the railway station
at Irvine: 'True, the train there was drawn by a locomotive, but the
train was a short one, and there was only one line of rails... thousands took to the roads rather than wait, which, however, some did
not do till 12 o'clock, when the last train for the night was run.'
Some supposed they'd be safe for the night in the inns and hotels
of Irvine, but there too they were foiled. Mr Lee Ker observes at

this point of this tatterdemalion army: 'Not a few never overcame
the effects of their exposure.' That, I fear, must indicate illness, and
possibly death. To catch a cold in the 1830s was often perilous, sometimes fatal. The old warning to children – 'you'll catch your death
of cold' – meant what it said in those days.

Such was the earl's wet Wednesday. Tempestuous Thursday was
hardly better. Storms raged all day. The advertised programme was
cancelled: the crowds who came were treated to the marching of
Highland regiments accompanied by their bands and the Queen of
Beauty parading herself and her acolytes. The knights were also in
action, attacking dummy figures and savaging them with the kind
of gleeful viciousness that many spectators would have hoped to
have seen directed at real opponents in the lists. One suspects that,
back in Kilwinning, some of the Reverend Mr Lee Ker's flock must
by now have concluded that these sad, damp days were a well-
deserved judgement of God on the vainglory and ostentation of
the earl and his not uniformly God-fearing friends.

Still, such forecasters as then existed thought Friday was going
to be better, and the earl announced that the tournament would be
resumed. He sent messengers around the district, and even drove
through the streets of Kilwinning himself to spread the good news.
And the day was bright enough to suggest that God had suspended
his wrath. Where on Thursday, play had been abandoned without a
lance being thrust, now the advertised contests resumed, while at
the end of the day banquet and ball went ahead as planned. The
crowd, Mr Lee Ker proudly reports, was orderly and perfectly sober:
Dr Campbell, his predecessor as minister of Kilwinning, stated that
not a single intoxicated individual had been seen within the gates:
'nor was this because there were no opportunities of obtaining re-
freshments'.

But again, it seems there was less than they had expected for the
groundlings to savour. The tilting duly began. 'It is said, however,
that there was at once exhibited a want of that enthusiasm which
characterized the crowd when the Herald sounded the onset on

Wednesday. There was, no doubt, much excitement, but it was not of that feverish kind that had been seen before. It seemed as if the assembly in general knew all about what was to happen, and that having seen it before they were not very deeply interested in seeing it again.' True, the headstrong Marquis of Waterford raised the spectators' spirits. 'The Hon. Mr Jeringham had his wrist slightly hurt, and the Marquis of Waterford and Lord Alford plied their swords as if in downright earnest – indeed they had to be requested to cease fighting, as they were violating the rules laid down for the conducting of the Tournament...'

For all his respect for the earl and the earl's commitment to spread pleasure and happiness, the minister feels bound to admit to the presence of dissatisfied customers, some of them not above heckling. 'Though, probably, none would have liked to see any of the knights permanently injured, many would have greatly enjoyed harder hitting and greater risks. This feeling, indeed, appeared again and again during this famous Tournament. Many people jeered at the mock contests which they saw enacted before them... Many... thought the tilting after the first course or two very tame work, not half so exciting as a horse race, and would have greatly enjoyed the unseating of a knight or such wrist wounds as the Hon. Mr Jeringham received at the end of this great occasion.'

Archibald had thought at one stage of stretching the public show into Saturday, but Friday's banquet and ball continued till five in the morning and at this point he called the show off. There was never another Eglinton tournament or indeed one remotely like it either in its ambitions or in its outcome. The earl made his name from now on as a buyer and owner of racehorses – he won the St Leger three times, in 1849 with a horse, The Flying Dutchman, that had earlier won the Derby – and as an increasingly serious politician – a popular Lord Lieutenant of Ireland in two spells under the premiership of Lord Derby in the 1850s. His statue, says a history of the Irish administration, stood for years on St Stephen's Green, 'with its eyes fixed on the card room of the University Club at, tradition asserts, Eglinton's own request'. He also developed an interest in golf, which in 1861 took him to a tournament in St Andrews where he suffered a fit of apoplexy, and died. He was forty-nine.

What he'd spent on the tournament left a dent in the already denuded family fortunes (his predecessors had already lost great sums of money on schemes like the development of Ardrossan Harbour) from which the house of Montgomerie never recovered. The estate fell into disuse. In 1925 the contents of the castle were sold by auction and the roof was removed. The army, which occupied the place during the Second World War, reduced it to an even more dire condition. It was finally razed in the 1970s, leaving only its tower. By then the estate had come into the hands of a food processing firm run by Clement Wilson, which specialized in Kennomeat and Kattomeat. The company tastefully landscaped the grounds and when it closed down in the 1990s the estate was given to the community. It is now within the Eglinton Country Park, which in turn is part of the new town of Irvine.

There's a model of the castle in its heyday, made out of matchsticks by the curator Jim Miller, in the museum close to the abbey church. What purports to be a re-creation of the tournament bridge has been built in the park, but local historians say the model used was a bridge that was only erected six years after the tournament, has only two spans where the tournament bridge had three, and is a hundred yards downstream from the original. In honour of the events of 1839 there's a tournament café, and a statue of a knight and a charger. A belvedere with a folly survives, as does a stable block, but incongruously alongside it in the midst of an otherwise placid and well-nurtured scene are the crumbling remains of the company's canning factory, which no one has yet got round to removing.

As for William Lee Ker, soon after completing his book he fell ill. In May 1902, his congregation met to choose an assistant and putative successor. A few days later, he died, much mourned across the whole town whose history and institutions – especially its role as the birthplace of Scottish freemasonry – he had lovingly chronicled. There's a window dedicated to him in the abbey church. It looks across the building to an opposite window given by Mr and Mrs Lee Ker in 1890, commemorating their daughters Nettie and Alice, who died young.

More sophisticated historians than Lee Ker take more complicated views of the tournament. Some see it as pure fiasco – an appropriate price for the earl to pay for his hubris: 'that grotesque revival of medieval mummery' as one nineteenth-century Liberal historian called it. Others see it as the precursor of political themes that produced the Young England movement in the Conservative Party and bred the cultural medievalism that, to the disgust of Hugh Miller (see chapter 11) inspired, or infected, the Oxford Movement. The verdict of Kilwinning on these proceedings, or at least that of its minister, is notably kind. 'There are few,' the Reverend William Lee Ker, writing the final page of his account in his manse in 1900, concludes, 'who remember the Tournament fetes. But though another generation has arisen who know only by hearsay of the marvellous scenes of August, 1839, nevertheless the people of the district have great pleasure in telling each other the story of what they know of the great doings which then took place, and in endeavouring to hand down to their children's children a record of that festival which rendered the name of their town and parish famous for the time, and attracted to the district greater crowds than ever previously assembled, or are ever likely to assemble, on the banks of the Garnock and of the Lugton… It is surely right and proper that for the sake of the general public the history of this magnificent undertaking should not be allowed to pass into oblivion.'

To which I shall say: Amen.

8

BROADWAY,
WORCESTERSHIRE

*At Middle Hill, rain had poured in through the ruined
roof; marauders had made off with whatever they fancied;
handrails, banisters, even in time the staircase, had been
taken. Not a pane of glass, it was said, was left in the
windows. 'In the drive,' Henrietta noted,
'every tree is cut down...'*

IT WAS ALL RATHER SUDDEN, and at first was probably
meant to be secret, but word must have got around, for at eight
o'clock in the morning a crowd had gathered at the gate of the
parish church of Broadway in Worcestershire to see the bride and
the bridegroom arrive. Few had ever set eyes on the groom before,
but the twenty-two-year-old Henrietta Phillipps was well known
in Broadway, principally because everyone knew of her father, the
irascible baronet and book-collecting obsessive who lived a mile or
so out of town in a house called Middle Hill. It would hardly have
surprised the people of Broadway that Sir Thomas was not present
at the ceremony. In his famously intolerant way, he was boycotting
the occasion; though at least he had not precisely forbidden it. That
must have made church gate gossip all the more juicy.

This was August 1846. Sir Thomas had long been established at
Middle Hill with his wife, also Henrietta, now dead, and three

daughters. But their presence was merely incidental, compared with the love of his life, which was books. Don Juan in pursuit of some ravishing beauty was a model of self-denial compared with Sir Thomas on the trail of some lusted-for book or manuscript. The word bibliophile fell hopelessly short of describing his condition. Some called him a bibliomaniac. Sir Thomas himself went further. He described his disease as 'vello-mania', since manuscripts and every kind of original document were a part of his addiction too. He could never resist a purchase. When he said at the end of his life that his ambition had been to possess a copy of every book in the world, that was taken to be a joke; but some who knew him best thought it came tellingly close to the truth.

There were signs of his addiction even before he left school. Already, when sixteen, and at Rugby, he owned over a hundred books. At Oxford he was even more out of control, and turned in vain to his father to rescue him from his debts. His father was a Lancashire textile manufacturer who at the age of fifty had begun an affair with a working girl, of which Thomas was the outcome. Yet even the combination of his father's coldness and the hot breath of creditors could not keep him out of booksellers' premises. He went on buying books in their hundreds with money he had not got – a practice that continued to the end of his life. He regularly neglected to pay his bills. At least one bookseller went out of business purely on account of Phillipps's refusal to pay for his purchases.

His father had bought the house and surrounding grounds at Middle Hill in 1794. He died two years later, leaving the place to Thomas, though under a will that would set up irresolvable troubles for the family later on. Immediately the new owner began to fill the place with his books. He also bought Broadway Tower, a folly built in 1799 on the heights above Middle Hill by the 6th Earl of Coventry as a gift for his wife. Here he installed a man called Brightley, the first of a number of printers who soon gave up the struggle to get their hands on their wages, especially when they discovered the hardships of living in Broadway Tower. The place, Brightley warned his master, was in a wretched condition and infested with people who came there in search of shelter. He and his sister had been forced to leave the place and stay in the pub. Getting no satisfaction, he went on his way, as did a string of successors.

Such events gave Broadway plenty to talk about – and the wider world too. Sir Thomas – he owed his baronetcy at the age of twenty-nine to manoeuvrings by his wife's father – was in some senses a respected figure; clearly a clever, accomplished man, a Fellow of the Royal Society, an acknowledged expert on books. On the other hand, he was stubborn, quarrelsome, extremely litigious and reliably unreliable in matters of money. Unlike his printers, his wife Henrietta Molyneux, and their three daughters – Henrietta (known at home as Harriet or Harry), Mary and Kate – had no hope of easy escape. They were slaves to the great obsession, pressed into service to sort, lug about and catalogue the books and manuscripts, which increasingly took over the house, and even to take on domestic chores as Sir Thomas sought to offset his debts by sacking the servants.

The place was full of evidence of things not done that ought to have been done. The walls of the once fine house were stained and peeling. Every room was full of piles of paper scattered negligently over the tables and floors. The drive to the door of the house was muddy and potholed and sometimes unnavigable. The household also had to cope with the press of importunate creditors. His father-in-law, concerned for his daughter's welfare, rebuked him, but Sir Thomas was unrepentant. True, he said, two attempts were being made to distrain on him, but the first man concerned was a rogue and the second a Quaker – 'each of them a race of beings which ought to be banished to some uninhabited island'.

Sir Thomas and Lady Phillipps became estranged. She took to drink and died at thirty-seven, in 1832, from what was described as a fit of oppression of the brain. The oldest daughter, Henrietta, was only thirteen. Increasingly it was she who accompanied her father to high social occasions – in the country, but more especially in town – a role she enjoyed. She charted her days in a series of diaries. Left by her widower to Edinburgh University, they were read by a latterday Shakespeare scholar, Marvin Spevack, who in 1999 published selections as *A Victorian Chronicle*. Odd that it should have taken a publisher based in Hildesheim, Germany, to present us with this endearing portrait of Henrietta, her husband, her lively daughters, her sisters, her cherished friends and her often indefensible father. One of the earliest entries (in December 1838; she was nineteen) records that she danced with Prince Louis Napoleon, a performer in the Eglinton tournament eight months later: 'an agreeable quiet person & spoke English well'. By now it was clear to all three daughters that marriage was their only hope of getting away from their father. Henrietta had already had suitors, one of whom offered marriage. On her twenty-first birthday in 1840, her sister Kate wrote in her pocket book: 'KP wishes HP many happy returns of the day and hopes that this time next year she will have a "nob" [husband]'. In fact it took two.

Sir Thomas, tyrannical and selfish though he so often was, was not devoid of humanity, even, in certain circumstances, of conspicuous kindliness. He delighted in the company of scholars, whom he welcomed to Middle Hill (unless they proved to be Catholics, in which case he sent them away) and treated with generosity. One of these was a young Cambridge man whose reputation had preceded him and whose arrival would drastically alter the lives of Henrietta and of her father. His name was James Orchard Halliwell.

Halliwell arrived in February 1842 at a delicate moment in the fortunes of Middle Hill. Ever since the death of his wife ten years earlier Sir Thomas had been looking around for a suitable and preferably well-heeled replacement. Now, at fifty-six, he had picked out a twenty-seven-year-old called Eliza Mansel. It is hard to see why she remained undaunted by what she was taking on. There were now well over 10,000 manuscripts and countless books in the Phillipps collection. The dining room was so full of books that it stayed locked up for most of the day and only opened for dinner; in time even that was not permitted. To get through the hall and the passageways you had to fight your way through thickets of books and boxes. The house was strewn with wooden boards smeared with plaster as a deterrent to woodworms. There was no ventilation. Windows were never opened. The wind howled through ill-fitting casements, never repaired. Yet Eliza was unrepelled. After last-minute wrangles over the marriage settlement, so severe that Henrietta thought the wedding might have to be cancelled, Sir Thomas and young Eliza were united at Leamington Spa on 2 June 1842 with Henrietta, Mary and Kate among the bridesmaids. 'The bride,' Henrietta wrote in her journal, 'is very fair with tight ringlets, short and rather stout… rather pretty and very amiable'.

Henrietta herself appeared by now to be well on her way to marriage. Halliwell had proposed soon after his first visit to Middle Hill. Sir Thomas, who greatly admired the young scholar, seemed at first to favour their union and gave it what Henrietta called his partial consent. But doubts began to set in. In the light of his debts, the baronet hankered for a rich son-in-law, and Halliwell had little money. Indeed, he too was no stranger to debt, and for reasons Sir Thomas must have well understood and perhaps had good reason to fear: James too was a besotted buyer of books.

Sir Thomas had also received a letter, signed 'Truth', warning that Halliwell was not a suitable husband for Henrietta. The potential bridegroom's father, it said, had been a draper at Chorley in Lancashire, while his mother was the daughter of a publican at Ewell in Surrey. He was also, the writer alleged, a debtor, a deceiver and a thief. Yet, remembering perhaps how long ago he had determined to wed his own Henrietta despite her father's objections, Sir Thomas relented a little. You can marry him if you must, he told her, but don't think that you have my approval, and don't expect me to come to the wedding. At which point he became 'very angry', locked up most of his daughter's clothes, and confiscated her journal.

Next day James went to Worcester for a marriage licence. In the evening, while her father was out to dinner, Henrietta collected and packed such clothes as she could find. And next morning – this from her journal, with her own never very reliable punctuation: 'I got up early & walked through the plantation with Mary & Kate & met James at the end & walked with him to the church at Broadway. Lucretia and E Marshall were my bridesmaids we were married at 8 o'clock by Revd Wm Battersby. I parted with my sister Mary in the plantation at Middle Hill. After our marriage, which took place in presence of a great many people from Broadway – who wished health & happiness and threw immense bouquets of flowers into the carriage, we started for Cheltenham & then posted to Cirencester whence we proceeded by rail to London. Called at Alfred Place & James introduced me to his father & mother... I grieved to part with my dear sisters but they like James & were very glad I was going to marry him... '

There then began – in a man with a particular talent for feuds and unquenchable hatreds – the greatest feud and hatred of his life. Until now, Sir Thomas's greatest animosity had been reserved for Catholics. He had banned them from Middle Hill. He had written to the Athenaeum, the London club to which he belonged, demanding that they should cease taking the Catholic publication, *The Tablet*; when they refused, he resigned. He came to believe that Jesuits from a nearby monastery were interfering with his mail at Middle Hill. 'He delighted,' wrote his biographer, A. N. L. Munby, 'to discover in his library and publish to the world evidence of unchaste practices in nunneries or the more curious details of Papal elections.' He wrote to Disraeli, begging him to warn the Queen against visiting Catholic institutions. Yet even that obsession paled beside that which he now developed against James Orchard Halliwell – also to some extent, though here the degree of passion varied from time to time, against Henrietta, for having married him.

His ostensible reason for this animosity was that he now believed that Halliwell was indeed, just as the anonymous letter had claimed, a deceiver and thief. There were allegations, which only came to public attention three years after the marriage, but with which Sir Thomas was already by then well acquainted, that Halliwell, when a student at Trinity College Cambridge, had stolen manuscripts from its library and sold them to pay for his habit – that habit being the buying of books. To Henrietta's horror, the case against him was advertised when in 1845 he was summoned to London to face allegations of theft and was banned from the British Museum. It will never be known whether these allegations were true. Henrietta could not for a moment believe it. The charges were later withdrawn, and his right to use the museum was reinstated.

The Halliwells were now established in Brixton Hill, London, where James worked on a sequence of books, varying from erudite explorations of Shakespeare to more crowd-pleasing works like his *Dictionary of Archaic and Provincial Words*. Henrietta was an eager and faithful assistant, copying and pasting and saving him from the editorial chores that might otherwise have distracted him. But she also maintained a life of her own, pursuing her interests in flowers and books and music and producing in time four daughters: another Henrietta, born in 1843; Charlotte in 1847, Ellen in 1854 and Kate in 1855 when she was thirty-five.

From time to time, as Henrietta's diary shows, reports would arrive from friends in Broadway or from her sister Kate about her father's latest excesses, and the sufferings of the new Lady Phillipps. Kate called on Henrietta on her way to France in September 1855 and reported that 'the water comes into several of the rooms & he has filled the drawing room with packing cases full of books leaving a narrow passage to walk between them & this is the only room they have to live in every other room being filled'. Sir Thomas himself admitted as much in a letter to Edward Edwardes: 'we have nowhere to dine,' he wrote, 'except in the housekeeper's parlour'.

A regular visitor over the years, Frederic Madden of the British Museum had noted in 1854: 'The house looks more miserable and dilapidated every time I visit it, and there is not a room now that is not crowded with large boxes full of MSs. The state of things is really inconceivable! Lady Phillipps is absent, and were I in her place I would never return to so wretched an abode... Every room is filled with heaps of paper, manuscripts, books, charters, & other things, lying under your feet; piled up on tables, beds, chairs, ladders &c, &c, and in every room, piles of huge boxes, up the ceiling, containing the most valuable volumes! It is quite sickening.' Sir Thomas must be mad, he reflected, to go on buying manuscripts at the prices he was willing to pay (prices Madden had been unable to match) but the ruling passion in him was too strong to resist: 'he certainly could have expended £600 in a better manner, for the sake of his wife and children'.

At least these, for the Halliwells, were distant troubles – as was the incident, a year after Sir Thomas remarried, when the baronet, who was a magistrate, was tried and convicted for hitting a tax collector. But what Henrietta could never escape was the fanatical feud between her father and her husband. The journals are full of the baronet's attempts to take his revenge on his son-in-law. The most persistent of these concerned the woods around Middle Hill, part of which under the terms of the will of Sir Thomas's father, were to become Henrietta's, and therefore her husband's, inheritance.

In May 1857, James received a letter from the Reverend Mr Franklin of Broadway, who said he thought it his duty as a clergyman to warn that Sir Thomas had contracted to sell all the timber on the Middle Hill entailed estates that were above six inches in girth, and that if this were done, it would take generations to restore what had been lost. Mrs Chandler, an old family servant, had written to Henrietta in similar terms. More warnings from Broadway followed, persuading James that his father-in-law would have to be sued. His solicitor went down to investigate. Henrietta recorded what he told them: 'The timber is the talk of the whole country round, even the poor people say what a shame it is... The house, farm buildings and stables are all in bad repair and some of them in a dilapidated state.'

Then came news that Sir Thomas was planning to cut down every tree in Childswickham, another part of the Halliwells' destined inheritance. James Halliwell duly took his father-in-law to court, but the influence of Sir Thomas was strong in these parts, and the Halliwells lost.

Now and then Sir Thomas would state his terms for a reconciliation. These always involved some transaction which the Halliwells felt, and their lawyers confirmed, would benefit Sir Thomas and be detrimental to them. One favourite notion was that Sir Thomas should be allowed to determine whom his grandchildren married. His hope was to leave his properties to the grandchildren, thus denying them to James – something that was in fact impossible because of the terms of the entail. His candidate as a fit spouse for one of his granddaughters was a man called Phillips, unrelated to Sir Thomas but increasingly close to him, who was steward of the estates at Broadway. Henrietta's diaries are measured and rarely betray strong feeling, but the thought of any such matrimony offended her: the man was a mere common farmer from Somersetshire. The singling out of May, her sister Mary's eldest daughter, particularly disgusted her, especially since May was not yet fifteen and this common man was much older.

Interspersed with such demarches there were cruelly wounding letters to upset the Brixton Hill breakfast table. In one, Sir Thomas said he understood that Halliwell was so much in debt that he was planning to sell his Shakespeare collection; he had also heard that the couple were intending to separate. He was anxious to help if he could. Henrietta's inquiries indicated that these rumours had emanated from Sir Thomas himself. Another letter suggested that the Halliwells' eldest daughter was half-witted. Not so, Henrietta told him; all of her daughters were clever. On a further occasion where she defied his will, he wrote back to say she was cursed. There were also chilling accidental encounters during his visits to London. Twice when he and his daughter came face to face with each other, he purported not to know who she was. On one ill-fated day Sir

Thomas and James Halliwell had to wait for an hour on the same station platform at Paddington. 'They passed and repassed each other without speaking,' Henrietta recorded.

The allegations over the Trinity documents had almost faded from view, but Sir Thomas kept doing his best to revive them. He tried to use his role as a trustee of the British Museum to reopen the case. He sought to get Halliwell expelled from the Royal Society of Literature, and when this was not accepted, he resigned himself. At one stage, the director of the British Museum, Anthony Panizzi, with whom Sir Thomas was also at odds, warned Halliwell that his father-in-law had challenged a payment to his son-in-law for a book he had recently sold them, on the grounds that the book had been stolen.

When Henrietta's sister Mary died in January 1858, the Halliwells could not attend the funeral for fear of offending Sir Thomas. Henrietta's other sister Kate was still in close touch with the baronet and kept her informed of events. At one point a letter from Kate, which had to do with the affair of the Trinity College papers, greatly offended Henrietta; but later Kate said that her father had locked her in a room, dictated it to her and forced her to send it. Lady Phillipps, Henrietta was warned, was in declining health, and Sir Thomas was often away, either in London or a nearby farm in Worcestershire, Kite's Nest, which he was also filling with books.

Then came news from Broadway that Sir Thomas was planning to leave Middle Hill. Unable to prevent the Halliwells inheriting it when he died, he had resolved to leave it to rot and to move himself, his long-suffering wife and his books somewhere else. The place he chose was Thirlestane House, Cheltenham, which he acquired in March 1863. He moved some of his books across as soon as he could, but the main contingent had to be shifted in 103 wagonloads between July of that year and March of the next. He rented it first, but planned to buy it, as Henrietta reported her brother-in-law John Walcot telling her: 'When he has it, he means to build a circular room like the British Museum Reading Room, to contain his books which are now in packing cases many of them have not been unpacked – he does not know where to find any book he wants & his memory being bad he is obliged to write everything down on paper.'

As Sir Thomas soon came to accept, his new address was not a hospitable place. Lady Phillipps, now nearly fifty, complained of being 'booked out of one wing and ratted out of the other'. When she could, she hid herself away at healthful Torquay, but Sir Thomas had by now forbidden her to write to the family and such letters as she received were copied out by a maid and submitted to him, even before Eliza was allowed to read them herself. In the drawing room he hung up his first wife's picture facing his own. Kate and her family, invited to stay at Thirlestane House, declined because they found it so cold and uncomfortable. Eventually, a quarter of a century after their marriage, Lady Phillipps nerved herself to complain of her predicament, lamenting to him in November 1868: 'Oh, if you would not set your heart so much on your *books,* making them an idol, how thankful I should be!' But Sir Thomas merely told her she must have been got at by Puseyites. One visitor discovered that he was sleeping with a couple of pistols under his pillow, on the grounds that he might have need of them to defend himself from the Pope.

In the end, though, he died without the Pope's assistance. On 6 February, 1872, Henrietta learned from a relative that her father was very ill and his doctors held out no hope of recovery. Next day she heard he was dead. Kate, who attended the funeral, wrote afterwards to say that Eliza, his widow, who had lived with him for thirty years, went into violent hysterics the moment he died. 'Papa never spoke of me,' Henrietta wrote in her journal after reading this letter, 'and carried his revenge beyond the grave – I was much shocked and distressed.' He was buried at Broadway (the church has a memorial to him) on Shrove Tuesday. He left his books and documents and other prized possessions to Kate and her third son Fitzroy. Such land as he could bequeath was left to his allies, the Phillipses; but the

Middle Hill estate, together with the villages of Buckland, Lavington and Childswickham, went, as he'd always feared, to the Halliwells – or the Halliwell-Phillippses, as the entail required them now to become, thus allying Sir Thomas's family name with that of his hated son-in-law.

The Halliwells set off to visit their new possessions, arriving to great acclaim and the ringing of bells in Broadway and the villages. But Sir Thomas's endeavour to leave them little in which they could take any pleasure had largely succeeded. James and his solicitor carried out a melancholy inspection. At Middle Hill, rain had poured in through the ruined roof; marauders had made off with whatever they fancied: handrails, banisters, even in time the staircase had been taken. Not a pane of glass, it was said, was left in the windows. 'In the library,' Henrietta noted, 'the water has swollen the boards of the floor so much that they cannot get it out. One of the pillars in the Dining Room is broken in two & altogether it is in a sad state In the Tower drive every tree is cut down it was a beautiful drive of a mile through an avenue of trees at the end of which a gate opened on a turf road which led to Broadway Tower…'

The Halliwells set to work to refurbish the place. But they were never to live there. Five months after her father's death, Henrietta came off her horse while riding in Tarring, near Worthing. Her journal made little of it, expressing her gratitude that her injuries had not been worse. But the entries thereafter become increasingly fitful and muddled, and the last of them make no sense. Once, her father had said she was cursed: perhaps in these final days she remembered that. She died on 25 March, 1879, aged fifty-nine. Halliwell lived a further ten years, becoming established as the most eminent Shakespeare scholar of his day, justifying the quiet pride that Henrietta took in him on almost every page of the journals.

The collection of books and manuscripts that had dominated Sir Thomas's life and imposed such cost on his family did not survive. It had been the greatest private collection ever assembled. He had promised to leave it to Oxford University – but, characteristically, only on terms that the university could not accept. Even so, in some eyes that achievement offsets his epic selfishness and the tyranny he exercised over those who were close to him. 'For thirty years', wrote A. N. L Munby (who devoted five volumes to him, which Nicolas Barker later summarized in one), 'he conducted single-handed the administration of a library which ranked as a national institution... the greatest library of unpublished historical material ever brought together by one man. He extended hospitality to hundreds of visiting scholars, who were charmed by the courtesy with which they were received and by the attentive solicitude with which he aided their studies...'

Middle Hill was sold and partly demolished. It is now quite hidden by trees. Broadway Tower still stands on the top of its hill, the highest vantage point, it is claimed, in the Cotswolds. Its advertisements make a great deal of the place's connections with William Morris, who used it very occasionally as a country retreat, but have far less to say about Sir Thomas. From the roof on the clearest days, it is said, you can see a dozen counties. Whichever direction you choose, the views are sublime.

9

CHELTENHAM, GLOUCESTERSHIRE

GEORGE JACOB HOLYOAKE PREACHES WHAT IS
SAID TO BE ATHEISM AND FALLS FOUL OF THE
SAVONAROLA OF GLOUCESTERSHIRE.

❧

*'With many blasphemous and awful remarks', said the
Chronicle, 'which we cannot sully our columns by repeating, the poor misguided wretch continued to address
the audience. To their lasting shame be it spoken, a considerable portion of the audience applauded the miscreant
opinion...'*

NO ONE EVER ELECTED THE Reverend Francis
Close. He never gave them the opportunity. But as rector for thirty years at St Mary's, the principal church of
Cheltenham, he was much the most formidable figure in the town.
Cheltenham, said Tennyson, who lived there for a time, was 'a polka,
parson-worshipping place of which Francis Close is Pope'. No one,
however mighty and eminent, was safe from the holy wrath of God's
Cheltonian agent – not even the local nobility and gentry. Delinquent aristocrats regularly felt the lash of his fluent tongue. He
vehemently deplored what he called 'the wide-spreading evils that
are poured upon the lower orders of society through the vain pleasures of their superiors'. His denunciations of the godless satisfactions
that its prosperous townspeople pursued, from the unsanctified entertainment of its genteel theatre (when the Theatre Royal was destroyed by fire in 1839, he fought a long effective campaign to
prevent its reopening) to the crowded, noisy and turbulent races

where the wickedness of bookmaking thrived, established him as the nearest thing the county had known to a Savonarola of Gloucestershire.

A book called *Occasional Sermons*, published in 1844, includes two that he preached against the town's annual race meeting. Not just because of the encouragement it gave to 'the foul spirit of gaming', which he called 'a vice more pre-eminently destructive both of body and soul than any other which Satan devised for the ruin of mankind', but because in his view these annual occasions promoted all the works of the flesh warned against by St Paul: 'adultery, fornication, uncleanness, lasciviousness – hatred, variance, emulation, wrath, strife – envy, drunkenness, revellings and such like... practised to a degree, and in an extent, at this season, that is truly frightful', and attracting 'numbers of the most worthless members of society from every part of the country to partake in this unholy revelry'. Bracketing these sin-fests with another institution he considered an engine of vice, Close warned his no doubt quivering congregation: 'I verily believe that in the day of judgment, thousands of that vast multitude who have served the world, the flesh and the devil, will trace up all the guilt and misery which has fallen upon them either to the race-courses or to the theatre.'

Yet few others affronted him – because he believed they so affronted his Maker – as much as those who challenged the established order of things: that's to say, radical Cheltenham, and especially that part of Cheltenham which did not say its prayers and in the most heinous cases did not even believe there was anyone there to pray to. Close was a churchman first, but only just short of that he was a Conservative. The two beliefs were essentially indivisible. 'In my humble opinion,' he told a meeting of the Church of England Working Men's Association, 'the Bible is Conservative, the Prayer Book Conservative, the Liturgy Conservative, and the Church Conservative, and it is impossible for a minister to open his mouth without being a Conservative.'

Although through much of the twentieth century Cheltenham

was cited as the epitome of a deep-dyed, red-faced-colonel-infested, reactionary Conservative community, at the time of Close's incumbency it elected Liberals to Parliament, members of the Berkeley family whose indulgences and support of the races earned them his mordant displeasure. As Owen Ashton, historian of Gloucestershire radicalism, has copiously established, there was also a radical element in the town strong and active enough to cause its rector the deepest disquiet. The town's popularity as a spa resort had swollen its population from 3,000 in 1801 to more than 24,000 thirty years later – and that was only the count of permanent residents in a town that thrived on visitors. The welfare of the prosperous required a sizeable presence of those of the lesser order who serviced them, from domestic servants and gardeners at the town's most handsome houses to the coachmen, saddlers and stable-keepers who looked after visitors' horses.

Such people, certainly, were subordinate; but they did not always accept their inferior status with the meek obedience preached every week at St Mary's. In August 1839, local Chartists invaded his church in protest against his preachings. Close told his regular congregation to pray for such people, even though they would not pray for themselves. They were plainly deluded. No country deserved such militant discontent less than England, for here was a land, more than any other, where the poor might grow rich and achieve the greatest honours bestowed by the state. And in no town in the country was there less cause for protest than here in Cheltenham, where examples of the benevolence of the well-to-do and the Church were everywhere evident.

In railing against inequality, Chartists were defying God's will. 'There is no such thing as equality. The book of Providence is one grand scheme of subordination. The book of Creation is one grand scheme of subordination and mutual help. The book which I have before me [the Bible] says that the poor "shall never cease out of the land"... there will be rich and poor, high and low; there will be men of different talents and different acquisitions as long as the world stands.' Socialism was a form of rebellion against moral codes for which husbands and fathers must be constantly on their guard: 'if any man among you has a wife, a daughter, a sister, let him look on her as a marked victim of sensuality, if the Bible be withdrawn, and Socialism substituted in its stead'. And addressing himself once more to the ranks of the ungodly (and unConservative) present, Close concluded with an extravagant flourish: 'Brethren! Do you want a charter? Here it is – the Bible is your charter – the universal charter of God to man!'

In a suitably subordinate thoroughfare called Albion Street, a few hundred yards from the church where these solemn warnings were issued, at about the point where today Marks & Spencer turns its unfriendly back on an abandoned cinema, there stood in those days a popular resort of the town's working class called the Mechanics' Institute, where meetings took place and the kind of books were available that in the view of its near neighbour, the rector, must have established the venue as a nest of vipers. This was the scene, on 24 May 1842, of a meeting that brought to a head the long hostility between Cheltenham's unrepentant radicals and their fundamentalist rector.

An unexpected late addition had been made to a list of speakers assembled, so the advertisements said, to discuss the apparently harmless topic, 'Home Colonization, Emigration, and the Poor Law Superseded'. The twenty-five-year-old radical writer, Chartist and apostle of the Owenite co-operative movement, George Jacob Holyoake, had come into the town on his way from his Birmingham home to visit a friend locked up, for having allegedly uttered a blasphemy, in Bristol jail. Holyoake, who had been standing in for his absent friend as editor of a publication called the *Oracle*, which was regularly condemned as hostile to Christianity, joined a group that went to the meeting.

According to a report in the *Cheltenham Chronicle*, towards the end, a questioner observed that while Holyoake had talked a lot about man's duty to man, he had said nothing of man's duty to God.

To this Holyoake had replied that he did not believe there was such a Being as God, and that if there was, He should be placed, as were subalterns, on half-pay. 'With many similar blasphemous and awful remarks,' said the *Chronicle*, 'which we cannot sully our columns by repeating, the poor misguided wretch continued to address the audience. To their lasting shame be it spoken, a considerable portion of the audience applauded the miscreant during the time he was giving utterance to these profane opinions.'

The sources of this report were two compositors employed by the *Chronicle*, a paper unwaveringly friendly to Close. 'Impressed by the responsibility attaching to the management of the Press,' it used to announce at the head of its leader column each week, 'we earnestly desire to exclude from our columns everything in the smallest detail calculated to counteract the influence of morality and religion.' Holyoake's theme for the night, it said, had been socialism, 'or as it has been more appropriately termed, devilism'. The paper appealed to those in authority not to let this matter rest, but to take immediate steps 'to prevent any further publicity to such diabolical statements'.

Holyoake by this time had pressed on to Bristol and then returned home, but when told of the report in the *Chronicle*, he resolved to go back to the town and repeat what he'd said. He and his wife knew very well the likely fate that awaited him. This time the audience in the Institute was joined by Superintendent Russell, who at the end of the meeting approached Holyoake and told him, very courteously, that he was under arrest, though he did not produce a warrant. Next morning he appeared before three magistrates, one of them a clergyman, charged with delivering atheistical and blasphemous sentiments. James Bartram, a *Chronicle* compositor, told the court he had heard the words complained of while attending the meeting of 24 May 'by accident' – a claim disbelieved by Holyoake's supporters, who were sure that he had been there as a Closeite spy.

Holyoake, representing himself, asked the magistrates whether anything he might say would make any difference to them, and was told it would not. As for the absence of any warrant for his arrest, one magistrate, Mr Capper, said that would not have been necessary when such blasphemous language had been used. The bench, he said, could not possibly continue in argument with a man who professed such abominable principles. Why, even the heathen acknowledged the existence of a deity, though for want of knowledge of the true god they made wooden ones to worship. Having been given the benefit of the bench's theology, Holyoake was handcuffed to be marched the nine miles to Gloucester prison, though when they passed a railway station his captors relented and he finished the journey by train.

The prisoner was subsequently bailed to appear at the assizes in August. As he left at that time for Gloucester, his daughter Madeline, who was not quite two, cried piteously after him, 'Dada, you won't come back again'. The outcome of the trial was inevitable. That he defended himself in a speech that lasted nine hours probably did him no good. He was jailed for six months. Even some who despised his opinions thought the case should not have been brought. The Home Secretary, Sir James Graham, tried to get the verdict reversed and the prisoner freed. He failed; but he told the prison governor that Holyoake must be treated 'favourably'.

That was certainly the view of the *Cheltenham Free Press*, a radical publication never slow to challenge the Closeite view of the world. Indeed, it seemed in this instance to be chiding the rector with Christ's remonstrance: 'Why are ye fearful, O ye of little faith'. 'We hold', it said, 'that in a Free Country, every man should have a perfect right to express his honest convictions, whether they differ a little or much from generally received notions, and all attempts to shackle the tongue or the pen are, we believe, unwarrantable and unwise. We cannot concur with those who in their practices declare that Christianity requires legislative enactments for its protection – that if not guarded by Policemen's truncheons and Soldiers' bayonets, it will be trampled under the hoofs of those Demons – Infidelity, and Atheism. We will not give any countenance to those who preach such blasphemy against the omnipotence of the God of Truth. We believe that Christianity has within itself resources sufficient to vanquish all the enemies that can be opposed to it – that the principles which were once promulgated by twelve poor working men, but which are now avowed by half the globe, have nothing to fear from the speculative reasonings of any man or body of men...'

The *Chronicle*, though, had no time for such liberal doubts. It was sure it had done the public a service, and that the principle of free speech, as correctly defined, had not been dishonoured. 'Christianity,' it riposted, 'is emphatically THE TRUTH, and therefore, every deduction of right reason must necessarily harmonize with its principles... Hence, though Christianity "has nothing to fear from the speculative reasonings of any man or body of men", it is quite certain that such reasonings often bewilder individual minds and confirm multitudes in a determined rejection of the only faith whereby they can be saved. Those that say the efforts of infidels are harmless, appear to overlook this consideration.'

It accepted that, as the *Free Press* had urged, it would not be wise to try to coerce unbelievers by means of legal penalties. Yet, 'the charge against Mr Holyoake was not disbelief in Christianity, nor an attempt to make infidels – 'but BLASPHEMY of the most revolting kind... The prevalence of the most revolting kind of a violent and insulting atheism... would absolve all bonds in which men are united in civilised life, and transform the world into a scene of boundless anarchy.' Likewise in August, after the blasphemer was jailed: 'Belief in God is absolutely necessary to society; for without it, society would soon lapse into a chaos of crime and misery... If the public demands that we punish the filcher of a pocket handkerchief, much more does it require that we punish the disseminator of a system which plucks terror from the heart of Guilt, and charters all the vices.' It might almost have been Dr Close who was speaking here. Perhaps it was.

George Jacob Holyoake was no tractable or subordinate prisoner. He refused to wear prison clothes or attend religious services. But the favourable treatment the Home Secretary had demanded was denied him by a visiting magistrate called Cooper, who, Holyoake says, shouted at him with great violence: 'I consider you worse than the greatest felon in the gaol – you have been guilty of the most atrocious crime a man could possibly commit – I have stated what you deserve to Sir J. Graham.' No doubt there were even those who thought he deserved the tragedy that followed in October. At the Bishopsgate Institute library in London, there's a letter preserved written to him in his cell by a Birmingham friend warning him that his daughter Madeline was gravely ill and not likely to live. During the previous night she had been saying her Dada was coming to see her. With it in the Bishopsgate file is a card announcing the death of Madeline, 'the interesting and beloved daughter of George Jacob and Helen Holyoake'; with this verse:

> Beauty and nature crowned thee!
> Death in thy youth hath found thee!
>   Thou art gone to thy grave
>   By the soft willow wave,
> And the flowerts [sic] are weeping around thee!
> The sun salutes thee early,
> The stars be-gem thee rarely,
>   Then why should we weep
>   When we see thee asleep,
> 'Mid thy friends who love thee dearly?

The governor and even Mr Cooper, the vituperative visiting magistrate, offered condolences: 'the general consolation offered', Holyoake recorded, 'is that she is taken from the evil to come. Mr Biley of Worcester remarked upon this – "and from the good, too."' When his wife came to see him in prison, she could not bring herself to speak of the child. This was not the only such tragedy in their lives. At the age of nine, their son Max was run over by a coachman in Tavistock Square. Holyoake says in his memoirs that he could not give evidence against the coachman because he refused to take the oath.

Holyoake was not overburdened with modesty. He liked to boast that he had introduced the terms 'jingo' and 'purchasing power' into the language and he seems to have coined the term 'secularism' for his beliefs, as opposed to the 'atheism' that others employed. In his frequently garrulous and not wholly reliable memoirs he claims at one point that a man in America had died of pleasure on reading words that Holyoake had written about him. He used to say proudly that his was the last trial by jury for atheism in Britain. Yet this celebrated skirmish in the battle between convinced religious belief and convinced denial had a curious postscript. The moral that those in the highest authority drew from the case (which amounted to: don't let us do this again) was not transmitted to others of lesser consequence, as Holyoake discovered more than a decade later when he heard of the prosecution at Bodmin, Cornwall, of a man from Liskeard called Thomas Pooley, for chalking blasphemous statements on gates and in other public places.

Pooley was sentenced to twenty-one months' imprisonment in a trial that was hardly reported anywhere. No one appeared to defend him. Bizarrely as it seems now, the judge, Mr Justice Coleridge, was the prosecuting counsel's father. Holyoake wrote an angry account of the case, which caught the eye of the historian Thomas Buckle, who denounced the proceedings in *Fraser's Magazine*. Pooley, Holyoake recorded, was a well-sinker, 'a tall, strongly-built man of honest aspect and good courage and fidelity', who had once descended into a deep well to rescue his master from death. Though not a philosopher, Pooley was 'a wild sort of Pantheist'. 'He thought this world to be an organism, and believed it to be alive; and such was the tenderness and reverence of his devotion that nothing could persuade him to dig a well beyond a certain depth, lest he should wound the heart of the world.'

Holyoake asserted that a barrister at the court was struck by signs of insanity in the defendant, and the same point was made in an article in the *Spectator*. Persuaded that this was the case, the judge ordered that Pooley should be released. He was taken home, after four months of incarceration, in the prison governor's private coach.

Had these events occurred in Cheltenham, would Francis Close, and the editor of the *Cheltenham Chronicle*, who championed free speech so long as it did not attack what he believed in, and the magistrates who assured the accused that nothing that he could say could possibly help him, have discerned the problem in the case of poor Thomas Pooley and responded with appropriate compassion? Let us exercise Christian charity here, and say: maybe.

10

AUSTREY, WARWICKSHIRE

MARY ELIZABETH SMITH BRINGS A SECOND EARL
FERRERS TO TRIAL IN WESTMINSTER HALL.

*And now the honour of the Ferrerses was once more at
stake in Westminster Hall; and though the occasion of the
dispute hardly matched that of 1760, the same flavour of
class against class, inferior against superior, permeated the
case and helped to make it, as a future Lord Chief Justice
later called it, 'one of the most remarkable trials which has
ever been brought into Westminster Hall
since the time that venerable building was
raised from its foundation...'*

ON AN EARLY SPRING MORNING in 1846 a nervous
congregation of people from an isolated village in the
northeastern corner of Warwickshire presented themselves at the doors of the mighty and intimidating Westminster Hall
in London. Their collective mood must have been pitched somewhere on the downward slope from apprehension to dread. Few
would have been far beyond their home village of Austrey before;
fewer still would have ever seen London. Theirs was a scattered
community of around 500 people: farmers and their agricultural
labourers, interspersed with shopkeepers and millers and tailors and
a smith and a wheelwright and servants for the grander local
houses. Two thirds of the population enumerated in the census
returns for Austrey five years later had been born in the village or
in neighbouring villages like Appleby just over the county border

in Leicestershire. Very few came from more than fifty miles away. One villager had been born in far distant Winchester; but he was the vicar.

And because, as in many such communities in those days, few ever ventured far from the place of their birth, Austrey families married into Austrey families, making this an inbred kind of settlement where most households were not just known to each other, but quite closely related. Nothing in life could have prepared such people for what was facing them now: a role in a trial before one of the highest courts of the land – one which that near-official chronicle of Britain's national life, the *Annual Register*, would call 'this remarkable case, as extraordinary as any that has ever come before a legal tribunal'; and that the Attorney-General, who took part in it, would record as the most extraordinary case in his long legal experience. The purpose of the occasion was the hearing of a suit brought by Mary Elizabeth Smith of Austrey against Washington Sewallis Shirley, 9th Earl Ferrers, for breach of promise of marriage.

The two most senior law officers of the day's Conservative government were pitted against each other here: for Mary Elizabeth Smith, the Solicitor-General, Sir Fitzroy Kelly; for the earl, Kelly's immediate superior, the Attorney-General, Sir Frederick Thesiger. The hall was packed for the occasion with a glittering assembly of high society, many of them come to support the earl but still more perhaps simply to enjoy this intriguing and glamorous spectacle. So full did the room become, the *Warwick and Warwickshire Advertiser* told its readers in Austrey and thereabouts, that several ladies, relatives of the noble defendant, were allowed to sit on the bench, close to the judge; a telling portent for the Austrey contingent, this, of the dominance of the proceedings by a class far above their own.

How awkward and intimidated they felt is clear from the answers some of them gave when they came to be questioned.

William Stanton, sworn, examined by Mr Robinson.

Are you a butcher at Appleby?

I believe I am.

Were you living at Appleby in the years 1840, 1841, 1842?

Yes, sir.

I do not know whether you are living there now. Are you living there now?

Certainly not. I am here now, but when I am at home there, I am there.

Or William Taylor:

William Taylor, sworn, examined by the Solicitor-General.

Do you live in Austrey?

Not when I am in London...

But after seven more answers, in one of which Taylor referred to having seen Mary Smith and Earl Ferrers together in 1814, before either of them was born, Mr Justice Wightman declared: 'This man seems exceedingly tipsy!' And though Taylor protested: 'No, I am not,' the judge ordered him out of the court.

Perhaps he had been drinking to nerve himself for the ordeal. For ordeal it certainly was. The peer against whom Taylor was trying to testify was not just some routine nobleman, but one of the Ferrers family; and the Ferrerses had a reputation for having their imperious way in dealings with their inferiors – even, in the most notorious example, talked about in awed tones for at least a century afterwards, of eliminating them: a circumstance that in the previous century, and in this very hall, had produced the last instance ever recorded of a nobleman being condemned to death for a felony. That offence had occurred at a place called Staunton Harold, just fourteen miles from Austrey.

★

Instability, of which their overbearing behaviour and their constant family feuding were only two of the obvious symptoms, stalked the

Ferrers family, though never quite as fatally as in the case of Laurence (often spelled Lawrence) Shirley, the 4th earl. He was consistently dangerous, most of all when drunk – but then he was frequently drunk, often from quite early on in the day.

One of those whom he most ill-used was his wife Mary, whom he had married in 1752 when he was thirty-one and she only sixteen. After six years of his relentless bullying, she took action against him in the London consistory court and succeeded in obtaining a divorce – a procedure that then required its own Act of Parliament. The term of the divorce stipulated that the countess should be entitled to specified revenues from the earl's estate. The task of ensuring that this arrangement was observed was entrusted to a steward called John Johnson who had been almost fifty years in the family's service. The choice was made by the earl, who clearly expected his steward to comply, as he always had, with his master's wishes. But here he had mistaken his man. Like some kind of north-east Warwickshire Thomas Becket, Johnson insisted on asserting his duty to an even higher authority.

The tension between them came to a head over a payment of £50 made to the countess against the earl's stated wish. On Sunday, 13 January 1760, Ferrers ordered Johnson to present himself at the house on the following Friday, at three o'clock. During the morning, the earl told his mistress, Mrs Clifford, who lived with him and their four illegitimate children, to leave the house at three and not to return until five. The menservants who lived in the house were given the same instruction, leaving only three maids present. When Johnson arrived, the earl took him into his room and locked the door. For perhaps an hour, he raged at his steward, demanding that he sign a statement admitting his offences. When the steward refused to obey, Ferrers shot him.

It took Johnson many hours to die, during which Ferrers taunted him, continuing to demand that he confess to his treachery. The steward was taken home, where, as the subsequent trial was told, 'he lay languishing till seven or eight in the morning, and then died'.

By now the news of the murder had spread through the surrounding village and a group of working men arrived at Staunton Harold and seized the earl. He was taken to Leicester jail, and thence, a coroner's inquest having reached a verdict of 'wilful murder', conveyed to the Tower of London.

On the morning of Wednesday, 16 April, the earl was brought from the Tower to Westminster Hall by the deputy governor, 'having', in the chilling words of the record, 'the axe carried by the gentleman-gaoler, who stood with it on the left hand of the prisoner, with the edge turned from him'. Ferrers pleaded not guilty, but given the weight of the evidence the only hope he could see of saving himself was to plead insanity. In his final statement before his sentence he virtually abandoned this doomed attempt at self-exculpation, saying he had been persuaded into this course by his family.

The earl was taken from court before, one by one, 116 peers of the realm delivered the identical verdict: 'Guilty, upon mine honour'. The Lord High Steward then delivered the inevitable sentence. Ferrers would be hanged by the neck until he was dead, and his body would be dissected and anatomized. The earl petitioned the king to be beheaded, as befitted a man of his station, rather than being hanged like a common felon, but George II rejected all such appeals, fearing that if the earl was in any way afforded special treatment it would reinforce the prevalent (and for the most part, entirely justified) view that the justice system in England had one law for the poor and another, much more lenient, for the rich.

On 5 May 1760 the whole town turned out for the big occasion. It took the grim ceremonial procession, in which Ferrers rode to his death in his private landau, nearly three hours to reach Tyburn. The earl was said to have comported himself with great dignity, even with elegance. But the hanging was somewhat botched, and he took several minutes to die; and an unseemly squabble broke out between the assistant hangman, to whom the earl had made a present of five guineas, and the hangman, who thought, with good reason, that the money had been intended for him.

★

And now, in the year 1846, thanks to Mary Elizabeth Smith, the honour of the Ferrerses was once more at stake in Westminster Hall; and though the occasion of the dispute hardly matched that of 1760, the same flavour of class against class, inferior against superior, permeated the case and helped to make it, as a future Lord Chief Justice, Alexander Cockburn, later called it, 'one of the most remarkable trials which has ever been brought into Westminster Hall since the time that venerable building was raised from its foundation – a case which deserves to go down to posterity as one of the causes célèbres of Europe, for a more remarkable case, in my view, has never been brought to trial'. And one which, as the Solicitor-General outlined the case of Mary Smith against the aristocratic lover whom she said had so cruelly abandoned her, must have seemed to spectators then, as it seemed to me when I discovered the transcript, to have only one conceivable outcome.

The essence of the story was this. Washington Sewallis Shirley was the son of Robert William Shirley, Viscount Tamworth, eldest son of the 8th Earl Ferrers. In 1836, his father died, leaving Washington as the heir to the earldom. In February 1839 he arrived in the village of Austrey to be tutored by a clergyman called Theodore Echalaz. At some point in the seventeen months he was there he made the acquaintance of Mary Elizabeth Smith, the fourteen-year-old-daughter (though the local newspaper reporting the case called her his step-daughter) of a farmer called Thomas Nicklin Smith.

The circumstances of the family are not easy to establish. There were references in the court to the Smiths' limited means, as, compared with those of the Ferrers family, they certainly were; yet the farmhouse where they lived, Elms Farm, which is still there today and is Grade II listed, is handsome and solid enough to suggest they were people of decent substance; they had several live-in servants, some employed in the house and some on the farm, which the 1851 census says covered 132 acres. Moreover, Mary's mother, whose name is variously given as Ann, Anne and Mary Ann, was related to the Curzon family and so, indirectly, to the Ferrers too. Certainly it was not every modest family who could have brought a case like the one before the Central Criminal Court meeting at Westminster Hall, with the plaintiff represented by so eminent a figure as the serving Solicitor-General.

The two young people, at any rate, became close friends, and exchanged protestations of love. They may even have talked of marriage – though that, as the young earl's defence made clear, was irrelevant to the outcome of these proceedings, for he at that time was too young for any such declaration to have a legal significance. The relationship was, however close enough to alarm the girl's parents, who may have sensed the unlikeliness of any eventual union between such a disparate couple. They sent the girl away, first to London and then to France. Ferrers, too, the Solicitor-General said, left Austrey to travel abroad, returning to live at what was now the family's principal residence, Chartley Castle in Staffordshire.

At this point, the court was told, Washington began to write regular letters, a sheaf of which the Solicitor-General produced. In these, the young nobleman – he was now the 9th Earl Ferrers after the death of his grandfather in September 1842, and free to do as he chose in the matter of marriage – declared his undying love for the girl from Austrey and time and again emphasized the impatience with which he awaited the day of their marriage. The letters were lively and colourful and packed with jaunty accounts of the young man's interests and activities, his political views as a Conservative whose Peelite tendencies had affronted some of his more conventional relatives, his nights out at the theatre and even (he regretted to say, and for which he hoped his beloved girl would forgive him) at the gaming tables.

The letters from which he was quoting, the Solicitor-General said, were somewhat chaotic – a point he proved by several times losing his place and confusing one with another. It was, he explained, this nobleman's curious habit to write his letters on odd scraps of paper. That was not, said Sir Fitzroy, a practice one might have expected at this level of society, but it was explicable here in terms of his somewhat skimpy education and unusual family history. This noble family, Sir Fitzroy informed the jury, had tended to marry persons far below themselves in status. 'I mention these circumstances to account for a lowness as well as caprice in the habits, thoughts and actions of this young nobleman.' Clearly, in the judgement of Sir Fitzroy Kelly, even if it was believed that bad blood ran in the Ferrers family, the world would need to accept that not all of that bad blood was blue.

In some of the letters read to the court, the earl told Mary how much he wanted to buy presents for her, regretted that he was at the moment unable to do so, and suggested she might buy them herself, and then he would reimburse her. Later, he said their marriage, planned for May, might have to be a little postponed, but that they would soon be united was not in doubt. Then came letters from the earl's brother Devereux, saying that Washington was ill; yet still the occasion seemed certain enough for the Smiths to buy the trousseau and the cake and for Mary to choose her bridesmaids. So the court, said Sir Fitzroy, might well judge the horror with which the Smiths then learned from a newspaper that the earl was betrothed to another: Augusta Annabella, daughter of Lord Edward Chichester. 'You will be able, I hope and I am sure', Sir Fitzroy told the jury, 'to sympathize with this young lady, whose peace of mind, whose happiness, whose prospects in this life are for ever sacrificed by the breach of faith, by the cruel perfidy of this young Nobleman.'

As maybe they did: but such sympathy may have ebbed as the procession of witnesses for Mary Elizabeth Smith took the stand to support the Solicitor-General's case – though he for the most part was not there to hear them, having been called away on other urgent business. Perhaps the most prized of his witnesses was the

Reverend Edward Francis Arden, until recently chaplain to the young earl and therefore, it must have been hoped, a particularly authoritative student of his behaviour. But why was Arden no longer in Washington Ferrers's service? He said he had left of his own volition. The Attorney-General, in a sharp cross-examination, said he had been dismissed and cited evidence of Arden behaving in ways not usually expected of parsons, involving a fondness for drink and a relationship with the daughter of a Staffordshire surgeon named Ingram, which led to her father banning them both from his house. Asked if he and the girl had been living together, Arden fortified the impression of truculence he had created throughout by saying he did not feel obliged to answer that question.

A succession of Austrey villagers followed, ready to swear they had seen the earl and Mary together after he returned from his spell abroad; but they seemed unsure of when they had done so and uncertain of quite what they had seen. The grand and glittering assembly in Westminster Hall cannot have been impressed by what it undoubtedly saw as a shambling parade of largely unlettered Midlands peasantry.

It was Washington Ferrers's case that once he'd returned from his time abroad he had never met Mary again. But her thirteen-year-old sister Ann gave confident evidence as the second day opened of having seen the young earl at Elms Farm. Though told by her parents to keep out of the way when he visited, she had seen the earl at the piano; her sister had entered the room and brought him a piece of cake. On another occasion, having been warned she'd be whipped if she did not make herself scarce, she had gone outside and peeked through the window and seen him leaning against the mantelpiece. Yet that did not square with the rest of her family's testimony. Mary's father had said he knew nothing of any visit by Ferrers – though that might have been because he suffered from a spinal condition and spent much of his time in bed. Mary's mother was a much more competent witness, as might have been expected of one who was kin to the Curzons, and she stoutly fought off the lawyers' attempts to bully her. Yet she too knew nothing of any visit by Ferrers.

It was clear from Sir Frederick Thesiger's questions that he took Mrs Smith very seriously. Some of the questions he wanted her to answer, the Attorney-General confessed to the jury, might seem a little odd. And they were. Was her daughter addicted to novels? Was she dark or fair? Was she short or tall? Did she ever, when she went to a ball at Tamworth, wear a white rose in her hair? In time, he promised, the jury would discover the relevance of these inquiries.

Still, at the end of the plaintiff's case, one consideration still seemed to work overwhelmingly in her favour: the letters. A succession of witnesses had testified that the writing looked like that of the young Earl Ferrers. On that count, it still seemed decidedly possible, as the Attorney-General rose, that Mary would win the case and perhaps collect the damages of £2,000 that she was seeking. Yet what followed was devastating. The Attorney spoke for almost three hours. 'I believe I may venture to say,' he said years afterwards, 'that I never did anything better than this while I was at the Bar.' Applause broke out as he sat down, which the judge had to repress.

Washington Ferrers, Thesiger declared at the outset, had no case to answer. There had been no further dalliance with Mary Elizabeth Smith, no kind of contact even, after their teenage acquaintance; there had never been any renewed talk of marriage (and Sir Frederick himself did not believe there had ever been such talk even during the seventeen-year-old Washington's time at Austrey). There had, he was about to prove (and the impact of this as the words were spoken in Westminster Hall must have justified that old reporter's favourite: 'sensation in court') not even been any letters. There had only been the fantasies of a lovesick girl, which had led her deeper and deeper into deception and falsehood.

The evidence submitted on the plaintiff's behalf had been largely worthless. 'The reverend – and I regret to use the title – Arden' had given a disgraceful performance, revealing to the court 'the history

and character of this degraded man', a man turned out by the surgeon Mr Ingram 'for seducing a child'. The evidence of the villagers
had been vague and contradictory. The decision to call the plaintiff's
thirteen-year-old sister – 'that child who was examined before you
yesterday' – had been the most distressing aspect of the case: 'that
this little girl has been brought forward to tell a story which is utterly without foundation in truth, I cannot but deeply reprehend'.

Unlike most of the other witnesses, young Ann had claimed she
was sure of the date of one of the earl's visits to Elms Farm. But the
family could establish that the earl had that day been lunching in
Welshpool; he could even produce the bill to prove it. Sir Frederick
was clearly enjoying himself. 'What will you say,' he said to the jury,
as if expecting a unanimous cry of 'we're deeply, deeply shocked!',
'to that mother who must have known it was false, who produces
her own child, of a tender age, to perjure herself in support of the
falsehood fabricated by her daughter and herself, without regard to
the consequences to her child, both here and [a fine Victorian flourish to end with] *hereafter?*'

But how to explain the letters from which such copious extracts
had been read to the court – and which the defence, he complained,
had never been permitted to see? Did they not reveal a depth of
knowledge about the earl's activities which Washington alone could
have drawn on? But these had been checked out as well, and many
were patent inventions. There were letters apparently written from
hotels that Ferrers had never stayed at; references to visits to relatives
who denied these had taken place; allusions to the private life of a
Mrs Hanbury Tracy in Brighton that could only have been based
on press reports featuring an entirely different Mrs Hanbury Tracy.
There were evocations of the prowess of the young earl's treasured
horse Zimro; yet the earl had never owned a horse of this name.
There were lamentations of the fate of a daughter of his kinsman
Evelyn Shirley, who had married a rascal called Walker, and who
nowadays looked like a corpse. 'A corpse? A phantom, I'd say', the
Attorney-General gloated. The child who was said to have wedded

the brute Walker, Sir Frederick revealed triumphantly, would at that time have been six months old.

On and on went the crushing catalogue of the letters' errors. And the explanation for all these errors, Sir Frederick thundered, was not the erratic memory or writing style of the earl, as the plaintiff's side had sought to establish, but a wicked resort to forgery in the expectation of financial gain by the plaintiff and her mother. The Solicitor-General, again absent on urgent business, was not present in court to witness the massacre of his case, but those of his team who were must have known by now they were beaten. Yet Sir Frederick's most potent moment was still to come. You'll remember, he told the jury, that I asked a number of questions which must have seemed bizarre, but promised that all would become clear in time? Now it will be. You may also recall that when cross-examining Mrs Smith I produced some letters and asked her to say if she recognized her daughter's handwriting, which she said she did. The court was asked to believe that these letters had to do with the forthcoming wedding. But I have these letters in front of me: and here are their contents...

They told a consistent story. Far from further establishing the earl's unsparing pursuit of the lady, they complained in pitiful terms of his neglect. The meaning of the mysterious questions Sir Frederick had asked about Mary's appearance – dark or fair, tall or short, the white rose she had worn in her hair for the ball in Tamworth – could now be revealed. Here was what had appeared in a letter purportedly sent to Washington by 'a well-wisher': 'There is a public ball at Tamworth every Christmas... Go, I advise you, go, there will to my knowledge be a young lady at the ball who I wish you to see and dance with; she is very beautiful, has dark hair and eyes, in short, she is haughty and graceful as a Spaniard, tall and majestic as a Circassian, beautiful as an Italian, I can say no more, you have only to see her to love her, that you must do, she is fit for the bride of a prince... She may wear one white rose in her dark hair... Farewell for ever...' 'I am afraid' Sir Frederick added ungallantly of this evocation of Mary Smith, 'not a faithful description.'

'The world, I am told, is wicked and deceitful' said a second letter. ('Who', Sir Frederick asked wonderingly, 'told her that?') 'Report says you are going to wed a lady of Wales... I am no Welsh lady...' ('I think,' said Sir Frederick, 'the people of Wales may be grateful for that.') 'They say that the blood of a Ferrers is not good, and that the generations of the Shirleys have mostly been men of ignoble minds, with one or two exceptions. Washington, add to the honour of your family; disgrace not further your name... Would we could meet!... Your friend, Marie.' And in a further letter: 'Days, even weeks, pass on, yet I hear not from you, or of you. Shall I ever again see your face?' (Yet according to Mary, Thesiger crisply observed, their wedding was set for May.)

All this, observed Thesiger, might seem deeply pitiful; but pity should not be taken too far. 'But from the various accidental circumstances which have intervened to shew where the truth is, and to protect justice and right, Lord Ferrers would have fallen victim to the snares with which he was encompassed, his honour blasted, his reputation gone, and what would have been of trifling importance, his wealth invaded by this infamous attempt to forge and to fasten an engagement on him.'

The case continued into its fourth day, but after this virtuoso performance, which still sizzles on the page as you read it, there seemed little left to establish. Soon after the morning resumption, the Solicitor-General reappeared. Because of his unavoidable absence from the court it had not been until the previous evening that he had become aware of the four additional letters and it was only on the morning that he'd had a chance to examine them. They had come as a complete surprise not only to him but to Mary's solicitor, Mr Hamel. Since he could not produce any explanation for what had now been uncovered, he would now withdraw from the case, leaving the plaintiff, in the terminology of such proceedings, 'unsuited'. Mr Justice Wightman, who knew a rout when he saw one, concurred. 'I think you have acted very wisely', he drily observed.

The Solicitor-General would by now have been wondering how he had let himself in for such a humiliation. Yet the state of the little party who had come from Austrey to London must have been still more grievous. The witnesses had heard their testimonies to having seen the couple together rejected with utter contempt as the work of simple countryside dolts or perjurers. And where did all this leave the Smiths – Mary and her mother, certainly, though Sir Frederick Thesiger had exonerated the father from any hand in the conspiracy?

Austrey was an insular village where gossip was one of the principal industries, and such gossip could often be cruel and poisonous. In the village churchyard there's a gravestone with this inscription:

Sacred to the memory of Harriot Langton, granddaughter of William and Ann Langton. Died September 22 1838 aged 19 years.

> My cruel foes against me rise,
> To witness things untrue,
> And to accuse me they devise,
> Of things I never knew.
> The good which I to them had done,
> With evil they repaid,
> And did by malice undeserved,
> My harmless life invade.

Harriot, people will tell you in Austrey today, was driven to her death by merciless local calumny – less than a decade before the public humiliation of Mary Smith. It is hardly surprising, then, to discover that within a year of the trial Mr Smith was reported to be away farming somewhere near Oswestry; though the 1851 census shows Mr and Mrs Smith, but not Mary, back in Austrey.

Mary, however, was unrepentant. She denied all the allegations made against her in Westminster Hall. Later that year she published a pamphlet defending herself – a melodramatic and florid affair, evoking her feelings when she heard of the earl's desertion, and the painful fate of a mother required to inform her daughter that 'her hopes were blighted for ever, her affection scorned and slighted, by the villainy, the treachery of one for whom had it been necessary, she would at the time have laid down her life.' 'My pen,' she interpolated at this point, 'even now trembles in my hand as I record that painful circumstance.'

An especially bitter complaint was that Sir Frederick Thesiger, in citing previous cases involving fantasies, had included that of a lowborn woman involved in a case he believed was comparable: 'Is a farmer's daughter, descended from ancestors as noble, if not as ancient, as my Lord Ferrers, and whose family is not devoid of wealth, and moreover, whose education has not been neglected, to be classed at once with an ignorant maid-servant of the last century?' There was also a risky allusion to Washington Ferrers as one 'whose parentage I shall not descend to characterize in the only terms which would describe the truth'.

A newspaper called the *Britannia* subjected this performance to a vicious review. Despite her previous public humbling, Mary determined to sue it and the case came to court in the following year. Mr Sergeant Talfourd, the eminent lawyer to whom Charles Dickens dedicated his *Pickwick Papers*, appearing for Mary, complained of a 'heartless, disgraceful and vicious calumny'. Mr Cockburn, the subsequent Lord Chief Justice, who appeared for the newspaper, asserted the right of the editor to speak as he found, emphasizing that this was a respectable Conservative and Protestant organ, which had never been sued for libel before. The paper, he conceded, had got one thing wrong: it had said the case had been thrown out of court, when in fact it had simply collapsed and no verdict had been recorded. In all other respects, he contended, the article had been justified. The writer had been doing his duty as a public journalist. Had Mary Smith wished to pursue her charges against the earl, she could have sought a fresh trial; significantly, she had not done so. She complained that because her suit was withdrawn she had been denied her right to contest what Sir Frederick Thesiger had said of her; yet in the light of what the trial had revealed about her falsehoods and forgeries, Sir Frederick's case was surely unanswerable.

The pamphlet that she had published was less a vindication of her own conduct than an attack on everyone else's. As for her reference to the troubled history of the Ferrerses, Mr Cockburn told the jury: 'The allusion, painful as it is, is one you will at once comprehend. We all know that in the family of Earl Ferrers there is one stain which all the pride of heraldry or ancestry cannot wash out. Is it to be tolerated that she, in vindicating herself, is to attempt to throw abuse and calumny not only upon Lord Ferrers but on his family?'

Mr Justice Cresswell, however, found another instance of error in the paper's assault on Miss Smith. In its closing lines it had portrayed her as a dangerous person, and possibly even insane, by implying that anyone who went to the lengths that she had might be capable of resorting to murder. The judge was in no doubt that in this context the paper had gone too far. It had crossed the line between attacking what Mary had written, that was a legitimate target, and personal criticism of Mary herself, which was not. No plea of justification had been entered by the *Britannia*; so in this case, he told the jury, it must be guilty. On the other hand, jurors should take account of Mary's behaviour. Had she invited notoriety? If so, that must be a factor in settling the case. The judge appeared particularly shocked by evidence that Mary's solicitor, Mr Hamel, had begged her on the eve of the case at Westminster Hall not to proceed if there was any flaw in her story that might come to light. He also read to the court the editor of the *Britannia*'s concluding sentiments: 'This is a lesson to be impressed on the minds of the young, that there is no crime, however monstrous, however repugnant to natural feeling, to which a course of falsehood may not lead. It is at the bottom of all depravity, as truth is the foundation of all virtue.' 'No fault,' said the judge, 'can be found with that.' The jury took its cue from the judge. It found the *Britannia* guilty of libel and it awarded Mary Smith damages of one farthing.

Thereafter Mary disappears into oblivion, which was probably the best address for her. Except that, reading the letters she was found to have fabricated, there's a terrible sense of waste. For a teenage girl in a remote Midlands village to imagine and, however fictitiously, to document the life of a man at the top of society argues a talent that might have been put to much better use. Her 9th Earl Ferrers - charming, capricious, headstrong, well-intentioned but deeply unreliable − may in sum have been a lot more intriguing, and even perhaps more alluring, a character than the real one. Her writing is often touching and sometimes beautiful. It would take things too far to pretend that Mary Elizabeth Smith of Austrey might in other circumstances have come to rival her near contemporary Mary Ann Evans (George Eliot), who came from Nuneaton, no more than a dozen miles away from Austrey. Yet she might have held her own with many quite successful Victorian lady novelists, writers of the kind of dewy romance that she herself used to devour. There was talent there in abundance. What a pity that, so far as we know, it blossomed only while being ill-used.

II

CROMARTY

❧

*'A stranger', wrote one admirer, 'would pause to look
after him and wonder what manner of man this could
be. If such a visitor ventured to question one of the
passing townsmen, he would be told promptly and
with no little pride, "That is Hugh Miller". No
further description or explanation would be
deemed necessary…'*

IN THE EARLY HOURS OF Christmas Eve in the year 1856,
in his house at Portobello on the east side of Edinburgh, Hugh
Miller, geologist, devout Presbyterian, author of many books,
editor of one of Scotland's bestselling newspapers, put a gun to his
chest and shot himself. In the morning a maid found his body, and
summoned a priest and a doctor to break the news to his wife and
their children. No one had foreseen this event. His wife and his
closest friends were aware that he had been haunted through recent
weeks by night-time horrors – less dreams than visions – peopled
by witches and demons. He felt on waking, he said, as if he had
been ridden fifty miles by a witch. He believed he had walked in
his sleep, and feared what he might have done on such excursions;
though when he examined his clothes he could find no trace of
having been out of doors. A few days before, he had seen a doctor,
to whom he said that he thought he was losing his brain. The doctor
felt he had simply been overworking. He prescribed him medicine

and advised him to rest, to trim back his shaggy hair, and to take warm baths at bedtime.

That evening before dinner a maid entered the room to find Hugh Miller's face convulsed with pain. Later he sat with his daughter Harriet, reading poetry. One work he read was the last that his favourite poet, William Cowper, wrote, 'The Castaway': lines steeped in the poet's diseased conviction that – justifiably, in the light of his sins – God had abandoned him, cast him away. Miller took the warm bath, but not the medicine. At some point in the night he got up, partly dressed himself, and wrote this note to his wife:

Dearest Lydia,

My brain burns. I *must* have *walked*; and a fearful dream rises upon me. I cannot bear the horrible thought. God and Father of the Lord Jesus Christ, have mercy on me. Dearest Lydia, dear children, farewell. My brain burns as the recollection grows. My dear, dear, wife, farewell.

Hugh Miller.

There was deep consternation in Edinburgh, where Miller had become a familiar figure, immediately identifiable by his shock of red hair and the Lowland dress – rough tweed suit, shepherd's plaid, stout walking stick – that he continued to wear as he had when he lived in the rugged north. 'A stranger', wrote one admirer, 'would pause to look after him and wonder what manner of man this could be. If such a visitor ventured to question one of the passing towns-men, he would be told promptly and with no little pride, "That is Hugh Miller". No further description or explanation would be deemed necessary…'

'Rarely', said the *Scotsman*, the only Edinburgh newspaper that outsold his own, the *Witness*, of which he had been the founding editor, 'are we called upon to perform a duty so painful, alike in itself and in the sudden circumstances of its occurrence, as to report the death of Hugh Miller.' 'It is this day our painful duty', said the *Caledonian Mercury*, 'to record the death of a fellow citizen, who, in some respects has left no equal behind him.' As a geologist, the tributes said, he had, though entirely self-taught, dealt on equal terms with the science's greatest figures, national and international. Some called him the nation's greatest figure since Walter Scott; the *Edinburgh Express* said he had been 'the greatest living Scotchman'. His funeral, the *Scotsman* reported, was 'both as to the attendance of mourners and the concourse of spectators... one of the most remarkable that has ever been witnessed in Edinburgh'. There were thirteen mourning carriages and nineteen additional carriages behind the hearse in an hour-long procession from Portobello to Waterloo Place, where Miller had been a Free Church deacon. The shops along the route were nearly all closed.

Edinburgh, though, had known, and still knew, other great men. The news of his death was most grievous for the little town of Cromarty, twenty miles north-east of Inverness at the point where the Cromarty Firth meets the sea. 'The news of this eminent individual's death', wrote the Cromarty correspondent of the *Dundee Courier*, 'is received in his birthplace with a universal expression of the deepest sorrow. Since the occurrence of the sad event nothing else has been talked about.' This was where he was born, where he grew up, and where, despite his departure for an eminent life in Edinburgh, he always belonged. Twenty years earlier he had written its history in a book called *Scenes and Legends of the North of Scotland; or, The Traditional History of Cromarty*, commemorating its heroes, the odd and endearing people whom Cromarty still liked to talk about, and the traditional tales, which, had he not written them down, might have been lost for ever. Here, now immortalized, was the woman dressed in green and bearing a goblin child in her arms who wandered at night from cottage to cottage, stealing their children and killing them to wash her own child in their blood; and the mermaid whom so many had seen by moonlight, sitting on a stone in the sea to the east of the town. Miller did not assert these tales were true, but the reader may sense his reluctance entirely to disbelieve them. His later book, *My Schools and Schoolmasters*, the nearest he came to writing an autobiography, was another warm celebration of the town. That his story ceased at the moment he left for Edinburgh further underlined the debt he owed to the place.

Cromarty had no newspaper of its own, but the *Inverness Courier*, for which he had often written, and whose editor, Robert Carruthers, had picked him out as a man of exceptional talent and become his mentor and friend, produced in its Christmas Day edition a long account marked by such anguish that Carruthers himself must surely have written it. 'God of our fathers, what is man!' it began. 'Through every parish and hamlet in our northern counties this event will be received and felt as a private calamity, no less than a public and national loss.' Having celebrated the chaste simplicity, terseness and elegance of Miller's prose and saluted his mastery of sarcasm and invective, the editor could write little more: 'The recollection of nearly thirty years rise up before us, clothed in the pall of a past friendship, and forbid further utterance. His death will be mourned and lamented, not only in the country which he loved so well, but in foreign lands and distant regions, wherever science, literature and virtue have a friend and admirer.'

Much more than in disparate Edinburgh, religion permeated the life of this region. That a man who so reverenced God, whom he used to call the adorable Creator, should have extinguished the life that God gave him seemed deeply shocking and sinful. Those about him in Edinburgh had been shaken by that thought and were anxious to banish it. His friend the Reverend Dr Guthrie, one of the first to reach Portobello, later recorded: 'In justice both to him and to religion, it was considered necessary that a post-mortem examination of the body should be made – that if, as was probably, the brain should be found to be diseased, that might be made known, and thus, along with other circumstances, remove the last lingering suspicion against Miller which the event might have raised, or his enemies been ready to take advantage of.'

The little town on the firth had by general agreement lost the greatest man it had ever produced. He is still so regarded today. This place has survived many vicissitudes. The original Cromarty, east of where the town stands now, was lost to the sea. In medieval times it flourished, then failed. At the end of the eighteenth century, an entrepreneur called George Ross returned with substantial money he'd made in London and set about redeeming it, knocking down its crumbling castle and erecting a home for himself on the site, building a courthouse where he presided as magistrate, and a harbour; establishing a brewery, a hemp factory, a log yard and a nail works and reclaiming land from the sea to extend its farming. In the early years of the nineteenth century, when Hugh Miller was growing up there, Cromarty prospered as never before. But then once again it fell into decline. The building of a new pier at Invergordon on the northern coast of the firth eroded its trade; the coming of the railway to the same town compounded the damage. One by one, Ross's industries failed. As early as 1843, three years after Miller left for a new life in Edinburgh, a visitor found its fishing town full of dilapidated houses, pigs, dead mussels and rotten fish. In 1875, another found 'streets deserted and silent, houses roofless and windowless'.

What saved it was the outbreak of war, making its fine natural harbour, with the two hills known locally as the Sutors standing sentinel on either side of the entrance, a precious place of refuge. In 1919 one prominent townsman asserted that the previous five years had been the most prosperous in its history. With peace came decline and distress, until, from the 1960s onwards, an ambitious programme of restoration saw it starting to flourish again as North Sea oil – an industry that owed much to Miller's cherished science of geology – brought money back to the town.

I arrived there on a sublime summer day, with brilliant but temperate sun. As I wandered through the main streets, with their handsome Georgian family homes interspersed with unpretentious houses in a townscape of unpremeditated harmony, as I sat in the evening outside the Royal Hotel on the waterfront, with the blue bay and the hills beyond lavishly laid out before me, this could almost have been Italy. ('If this is global warming,' said a deeply contented woman enjoying the sun outside the hotel, 'bring it on.') The effortless charm of the place and the friendliness of the people made London, momentarily, feel like some kind of disease.

And because, since the railways never reached it, its tourist potential has never been realized, you can still get a sense of what it must have been like when the young Hugh Miller was here. Wherever you go, he seems to be waiting for you: down on the shore where he wandered and made his geological discoveries, in the street named after him, in the house where he was born and the more substantial house next door built by his father, both now owned by the National Trust for Scotland and preserved as shrines to Miller. Yet it's never overwhelming or cloying like some of the places that live off the Dickens industry. This is Cromarty saying with justifiable pride, yet doucely, and with proper Presbyterian restraint: however great Hugh Miller became, this was the place that made him.

★

Miller was born in a dark thatched cottage on Church Street on 10 October 1802. It was a difficult birth: at one stage, he stopped breathing. The midwife who delivered him looked at his head and said he would be an idiot. Though he liked through his life to portray himself as a simple working man, that was not authentic. His father, also Hugh, was a coastal shipmaster rather than, as often depicted, a sailor, and as you can see from the house he later built next door to the cottage, a man of some substance. But he died at sea when young Hugh was five.

Thereafter, his mother's life was a struggle. Two of his sisters died; he overheard his mother saying she wished it was he who had died instead. He did badly at school. He was, on his own estimation, a

wild insubordinate boy. At fifteen he was expelled for wrestling with
a teacher. He had ready access to books, often borrowed from
friendly neighbours, graduating from an early taste for patriotic Scots
legend to English-based essayists, notably Goldsmith and Addison,
unexpected tastes in a Cromarty boy. His schools and schoolmasters
were two affectionate uncles, James and Sandy, the beaches and hills
and woods of Cromarty, and his own all-encompassing curiosity.

His uncles thought he should go to university; Hugh thought
otherwise. He would become a quarryman. That way he could
labour by day and read or explore through the evenings. His
mother's brother-in-law engaged him as an apprentice. The boy was
not as strong as he looked; the work took a physical toll that marred
the rest of his life. His assignments introduced him to the Highlands,
so instructively and provocatively different from lowland Cromarty,
but also to equally alien Edinburgh, where he shared his evening
accommodation with working men whose conduct shocked and
distressed him. They had no religion; their money as soon as collected was spent on drink and debauchery. The drink he could
understand; drink was a kind of defence against lung-clogging
stone dust. On one contemporary estimate, only one out of fifty
stone-cutters in Edinburgh survived past the age of forty-five. But
he could not condone it.

These Edinburgh days engendered in him a sense of despair
about proletarian life in the urban centres that conditioned much
of his later writings. Many of these lost souls, he noted, had come
from small towns where everyone knew them, where in consequence they had lived 'under the wholesome influence of public
opinion', to large towns where nobody knew them at all. Thus unless they were under the guidance of higher principle – which, he
believed, was impossible when they had no religion – they found
themselves at liberty to do whatever they pleased.

Back in Cromarty, Miller gave up the quarries and became a
stonemason, a less strenuous occupation but one that still meant
enduring choking dust every working day. In his new occupation

as much as his old one there was always a threat of silicosis, to which he duly succumbed. But where the quarrying had meant having company – and often, company one might otherwise never have chosen – both at work and at night in the barracks where quarry-men rested, his new avocation left him for much of the time on his own. 'Your solitude and seclusion are your best teachers', the shrewd and supportive Inverness editor Carruthers told him.

'I am much alone in this remote corner,' this self-taught prentice geologist wrote to a trained and established one, 'a kind of Robinson Crusoe in geology.' Though sometimes he ventured further afield in search of new discoveries, Cromarty and the coast to the south were his natural territory: a *terra incognita*, he called them, for few truly expert geologists ever came here. So much evidence lay before him, and before him almost alone. How, in such circumstances, Hugh Miller mused, could anyone *not* be a geologist? It was on one of these patient, diligent, obsessively repeated explorations of Cro-marty's old red sandstone that he made, in 1830, the finds that began to establish his reputation: the fossil fishes that would one day be given his name – *Coccosteus milleri* and *Pterichthys milleri*, names bestowed by a famed international geologist, Louis Agassiz.

Miller was also, from his childhood, a writer; and especially, at first, a poet – though not, as he came to accept, a good one. In 1829, a book of his poetry, *Poems written in the Leisure Hours of a Journeyman Mason*, was published, anonymously, in Inverness. Though one re-viewer scented genius, others were powerfully unimpressed. 'It is our duty to tell this writer that he will make more in a week by his trowel than in half a century by his pen,' one Edinburgh reviewer sniffed, while another gave him 'no chance whatever of being known beyond the limits of (his) native place'. Carruthers of the *Courier* had rejected his verse but divined his talent as a writer of prose; and indeed for a modern reader, there is far more poetry in his prose than there is in his poetry.

'Let it be my business', he said, 'to know what is not generally known.' There could not be a better resolve for any aspiring journalist. In the year he made his debut as a poet, he sent Carruthers a series of features on herring fishing and fishermen. Only a cloth-eyed editor could have failed to spot the wonderful windswept freshness and immediacy of his descriptive writing, and though contemporaries felt that his style matured as he grew older, these pieces, which the newspaper later issued as a booklet, seem to me to catch the best of Hugh Miller. He examines in learned and quite technical detail what he calls 'the peculiar arts of the fisherman', evokes the sea creatures, especially the whales, both real and legendary, of the firth (which he calls the frith), and charts a sharp encounter between the boat on which he was stationed and one of its rivals. But above all, as ever, he hymns the wonders of God's creation:

> The breeze had died into a perfect calm. The heavens were glowing with stars, and the sea, from the smoothness of the surface, appeared a second sky, as bright and starry as the other, but with this difference, that all its stars appeared comets. There seemed no line of division at the horizon, which rendered the illusion more striking. The distant hills appeared a chain of dark thundery clouds sleeping in the heavens. In short, the scene was one of the strangest I ever witnessed... I gazed on the sky of stars above, and the sky of comets below, and imagined myself in the centre of space, far removed from the earth, and every other world, – the solitary inhabitant of a planetary fragment...

Had he published such work today he'd have been snapped up within days by some television company and might have spent the rest of his life striding powerfully through picturesque glens and presenting his rugged profile to camera on convenient wind-blown cliff tops.

Wherever he went, he observed and made notes. His curiosity was unquenchable. Uplifting or degrading, sublime or squalid, every successive experience was part of his education, to be written about later on. The range of the subjects he covered is breathtaking: geology, and religion, but also psychology, the study of accents and patterns of speech, phrenology and what really amounts to social anthropology: 'even as late the year 1823,' he writes in *My Schools and Schoolmasters*, 'some three days' journey into the Highlands might be regarded as analogous in some respects to a journey into the past of some three or four centuries.'

Now and then chances occurred to leave his labouring life in the north and move to the south and to literature. Why not, invited the Revd George Husband Baird, Principal of Edinburgh University, continue to work in the north through the summer but take his winters in Edinburgh? Characteristically he replied with one of the fruits of his often exotic reading: 'Ortogrul of Bara,' he said, 'after he had surveyed the palace of the vizir, despised the simple neatness of his own little habitation.'

Miller feared, at this stage, the embrace of the intellectuals. He was happy with the rhythm of life of his own habitation. Cromarty too had brought him in time to religion. Once he had classed himself as a doubter – 'in the camp of the unconverted'. He found religious values appealing, yet suspected then that it might all be nothing more than a 'cunningly devised fable'. Peter Bayne, in his *Life and Letters of Hugh Miller*, prints a letter written by Miller on New Year's Day 1823 to his friend William Ross, in the course of writing which he effectively converts himself to Christianity – so much so that, reading it back, he thinks it is almost as if its thoughts and modes of expression had emanated from somebody else. From now on he starts to distinguish between a past and a present self.

That night was one of three decisive turning points in Hugh Miller's life. The next would come eight years later. As he worked at his inscriptions, visitors would sometimes appear, anxious to catch a sight of the stonemason-poet of Cromarty. One day a young woman called Lydia Fraser was brought by her mother to a school-yard where he was working – a decision the mother would later come to regret. Miller's lifestyle at this time clearly marked him down as belonging to the higher strata of working-class Cromarty. His young visitor, though, was a lady: the daughter of an Inverness merchant, though not a very successful one, she had been schooled at Inverness Academy, in Edinburgh, and more recently in Surrey. Lydia, he later recorded, was nineteen at this time (to his twenty-nine) but looked even younger. After some conversation, she and her mother left, but soon Lydia was back again, and this time unaccompanied. Her mother did not like the look of this association. Lydia was told not to see him again. On her solitary walks, however, she began to stray on to forbidden territory.

Hugh had until now seen himself as a perpetual bachelor: he imagined a suitable wife, but did not expect that one would ever present herself. Lydia was persistent. The ban on their meetings was modified, but not altogether rescinded: Hugh was still a mere mason and Lydia in her mother's opinion deserved better. They must wait, she ordained, for three years before they considered marriage. Miller made no objection to this requirement: indeed, he endorsed it. He too believed that Lydia ought to expect a better match than he could provide. He must find some way, he told himself, of attaining the social status that would make him worthy of her.

At this point, out of the blue, he was offered work in a bank. A man called Robert Ross was opening a bank in Cromarty and was looking for an assistant. Already, as stonemason-poet and much-discussed geologist, Miller was a well established and respected townsman, regularly invited into its finer houses, where he used to venture with some unease, feeling out of place. But this would be exactly the kind of move on to a middle-class territory that marriage to a lady required. So, not without some feelings of trepidation, he took up the offer, and after a period of training in Edinburgh and Linlithgow, took up his post in what is now Old Bank House in Cromarty's Bank Street. There was, however, an aspect of this employment whose implications could not have been predicted, but in the light of what would happen two decades on, might be seen as fatal. Because he carried the bank's money to other branches, he began to go about equipped with a gun.

With his new status established, he and Lydia were married in Cromarty on 7 January 1837. The following year saw the third great existential change of his life. The Scottish Church had long resented the rights given to patrons under Queen Anne, which debarred parishioners from rejecting a minister chosen for them by the laird. Both as a Scottish patriot and as a Presbyterian church-goer, Miller found this objectionable. The legislation, he argued, contravened the agreements on which the Act of Union was based, since it failed to respect the settled rights of the Scottish Church. In any case, the appointment of clergy ought to depend not on the will of rich and powerful landowners but on the will of God. In 1834, the General Assembly of the Church of Scotland passed what was called a Veto Act. No landlord, it said, had the right to 'intrude' a minister who did not command the support of a majority of male communicants.

Soon after, the issue came to a head when the laird of Auchter-arder, Lord Kinnoul, tried to impose a minister unacceptable to the congregation, which voted by nearly 300 to 3 to reject him. The matter went to the House of Lords, where the brilliant, headstrong, boisterous Lord Chancellor, Brougham, made a speech that dispar-aged and mocked the rebellious Scots. This provoked from Miller a characteristic retort – proud, aggressive, and seasoned with sarcasm and intermittent contempt.

'I am a plain untaught man,' he undeferentially declared, 'but the opinions which I hold regarding the law of patronage are those en-tertained by the great bulk of my countrymen, and entitled on that account to some little respect.' No knees, he made clear, would be bowed by good Scots in such circumstances. 'The Earl of Kinnoul is not the Church, nor are any of the other patrons of Scotland. Why, then, are these men suffered to exercise, and that so exclusively, one of the church's most sacred privileges?... My grandfather was a grown man at a period when the neighbouring proprietor could have dragged him from his cottage, and hung him on the gallows-hill of the barony. It is not yet a century since the colliers of our southern districts were serfs bound to the soil. The mischievous and intolerant law of patronage still presses its dead weight on our consciences...'

The writing of this letter led directly to an event that had never before seemed likely: Miller's departure from Cromarty. The church in Scotland was at this point sharply divided between two competing factions: those known as the Evangelicals, who wished to promote religious revival and were ready to take on all forces that stood in their way, and the Moderates, who regarded themselves as the children of the enlightenment but whom Evangelicals saw as sodden with compromise. The Evangelicals had been planning a newspaper to carry their cause to the public, and when some of their most prominent figures read Miller's letter to Brougham they believed they had found their man.

For a while he remained uncertain. The offer came at a difficult time. He and Lydia had recently buried their daughter Eliza, who, not yet eighteen months old, was taken ill and died in less than a week. He carved her gravestone – the last that he ever worked on. You can see it today in the churchyard of St Regulus. 'All the time she lay dying,' Lydia wrote, 'which was three days and three nights, her father was prostrate in the dust before God in an agony of tears... Yet, when she was taken away, a calm and implicit submission to the Divine Will succeeded.' This eagerness to submit to God's will must have been one of the motives for his decision to edit the *Witness*; though the chance to make his social and material fortune on such a stage must have registered in the equation too. So, leaving Lydia and their four children behind to join him later, he said a fond goodbye to his native town and in the final days of 1839 set out for Edinburgh.

★

And yet he took Cromarty with him. The way he dressed, in the tradition of working men of the Lowlands, in Bayne's words as 'a rugged plebeian' – and the unelocuted way he continued to speak even in genteel Edinburgh were evidence of a continuing allegiance to the town that had shaped him. At one point a visitor called

Robertson had taken temporary charge of his church in Cromarty. Robertson saw a further significance here: 'He affected (as I thought) indifference to gentlemanly appearance and fashionable manners, and adhered to a certain rusticity of aspect and style – possibly because he dreaded failure in any effort to become perfectly polished… his character, which seemed to me at one time harsh and even fierce and dangerous, dissolved into romantic heroism and almost feminine tenderness.' There was something of that in his life as an editor too – a fierce, unwavering onslaught on what he found wicked and wrong, a gentle reluctance in private life to wound those with whom he engaged in combat.

His progress was watched with the greatest attention a hundred and eighty miles to the north, in Cromarty, above all in 1843 when as editor of the *Witness* he became a prominent player in the drama known as the Disruption – a term some believe he invented. This again was fuelled by a boiling dissatisfaction with attempts by outside forces to dictate to the Scottish church. It culminated at a meeting of the General Assembly when many of the church's most prominent figures led their followers out of St Andrew's kirk and down the road to Canonmills Hall where they proceeded to stage the first assembly of the Free Church of Scotland. Four hundred and fifty-one ministers – about a third of the total serving the Church – seceded. Those who walked out stood to lose their churches, their incomes, and often (since these were owned by the laird) their homes.

At the height of these confrontations, the circulation of Miller's *Witness* overtook that of the *Scotsman*. The *Witness* was never devoted exclusively to religion. It carried, just as the *Scotsman* did, political, parliamentary and foreign news. It reflected, too, its editor's enthusiasm for science. The material that became his book *The Old Red Sandstone* appeared in his newspaper first, nicely timed to catch the attention of those about to assemble for a British Association meeting in Glasgow, where his findings were much discussed.

The hours at the *Witness* were long and the work demanding. Miller wrote much of the paper himself, which taxed his less than robust health. Now and then he took breaks from the treadmill. In one, he sailed with his friend John Swanson, one of the ministers who had lost his church, home and income in the Disruption, on a boat called the *Betsey*, which served as a kind of floating chapel for the isles where Swanson was minister. That led to yet another Hugh Miller book: *The Cruise of the Betsey or, A Summer Ramble among the Fossiliferous Deposits of the Highlands; with Rambles of a Geologist, or Ten Thousand Miles over the Fossiliferous Deposits of Scotland.* (No journey he ever made failed to include some geology.) A second took him to England, where apart from his habitual geologizing he visited principal cities, small towns, and places associated with his great English heroes, notably William Shenstone, as much perhaps for his gardens as for his poetry; also – the writer he cherished above all others – William Cowper, for whom he made a pilgrimage to Olney in Buckinghamshire. It's a book of great charm and perceptiveness, marked by a generosity towards England greater than might have been expected from Miller, though the English have from time to time to be castigated, especially for dishonouring the Sabbath.

Inevitably in such times Hugh Miller, geologist and deeply committed Christian, had to confront the apparent discrepancy between the implications of geology and the strict teachings of Genesis. When he died, some suggested – more recent writers have frequently done so too – that it must have been this unresolvable conflict that drove him to make an end of himself. In fact it seems to have troubled him hardly at all. He honoured science, but above all he honoured the God without whom there would have been no science. Why was the world that he found so wondrous? Because it was God's creation.

The rejection of science that he found in the work of some leading churchmen made him ferociously angry. He had no patience with those who, sticking close to the calculations of Archbishop Ussher, still tried to insist that the world was a mere 4,000 years old.

He railed against what he called the medievalism of the Oxford school, of false prophets like Pusey. Science would continue to grow, whatever the efforts of Oxford to stand in its way. 'The medieval miasma originated in the bogs and fens of Oxford, has been blown aslant over the face of the country,' he noted after attending a Puseyite service. Unlike St Paul's, Westminster Abbey failed to gain his approval. Its offence? It was medieval.

Yet the writings of pre-Darwin evolutionists also disturbed him. Animals had no souls. How could souls have developed from soul-less creatures? That was not, he believed, how God had devised things. There had been, he contended, not one continuous process of creation but something that more resembled a play comprising a long succession of separate acts, each with its own separate cast. Each act had ended in a catastrophe, to which a new act succeeded. As he wrote in *First Impressions of England and its People* (1846):

> Let it be admitted, for the argument's sake, that the earth existed in the dark and void state described here [in Genesis] only six days, *of twenty-four hours each*, before the creation of man; and that the going forth of the Spirit and the breaking out of light, on this occasion, were events immediately introductory to the creation to which we ourselves belong. And what then? It is evident, from the continuity of the narrative in the passage, say the anti-geologists, that there could have been no creations on this earth prior to the present one. Nay, not so: for aught that appears in the narrative, there might have been many. Between the creation of the matter of which the earth is composed, as enunciated in the first verse, and the earth's void and chaotic state, as described in the second, a *thousand* creations might have intervened.

As Miller's latest biographer, Michael A. Taylor, himself a geologist, sums up this theory, 'this series of catastrophes and creations suc-cessively modified the Earth's climate and life to give a habitat suit-able for humanity which was duly specially created after the most recent catastrophe, and would itself face the next and last geological catastrophe in the Last Judgment'.

No one would subscribe to such theories now. Miller died three years before *The Origin of the Species* blew such speculations out of the water.

★

In 1856, which would be the final year of his life, Hugh Miller entered the seventeenth year of his editorship. By now he was great with honours, though one that he hoped for – the chair of Natural History at Edinburgh University – eluded him. He lost out to a younger, more academically eminent, man. The book that Bayne compiled with the help and guidance of the widow Lydia portrays this as a truly grievous blow to him, though Michael Taylor thinks he must have well understood that the man appointed was a full-time professional in a trade where Miller, for all his virtues, was at base an unsystematic amateur. He had never set out his findings in learned journals. Indeed, through most of his explorations he had been dependent on more professional men to assess his findings, set them in context, and relate them to others' work.

He was now fifty-three, and even before he began to sink into a nightmare world his health was failing. The clouds were gathering well before the night of 23 December. Miller seemed pathologically anxious, fearing attack by enemies. He had been going about Portobello, where they now lived, asking people if they had seen suspicious figures lurking, possibly bent on doing him harm. Lydia, herself severely troubled by arthritis, watched his deterioration with mounting concern.

His reputation, too, was not as secure as it seemed when he died. His books are still read, but few nowadays have heard of his times at the *Witness*, while his standing as a geologist fell into decline from the time that Darwin published and would leave him almost forgotten by the end of the century. But latterly he has begun to be valued again, not for the teachings to which he attached such confidence, but for his strength as a writer: especially as a kind of geological evangelist, who engaged the attention of thousands, who without him, might never have developed a taste for it. 'His importance for nineteenth-century science,' says M. J. S. Rudwick in the *Dictionary of Scientific Biography*, 'lies... in his use of outstanding literary abilities to broaden the taste for science in general and geology in particular, and to encourage a humane concern for the fundamental significance of such studies...' 'What set him apart from other geologists,' says Michael Taylor, 'was not so much the quality of his science – or even his fine fossil collection, important as it was and remains – but the same literary activity that, ironically enough, limited his geology.'

On the hill of Cromarty – once the edge of a cliff high above the sea – looking down towards the shores where he walked, solitary and reflective, alive with curiosity and devotedly eager to explore the handiwork of his adored God, there's a statute of Miller on the top of a memorial pillar, cut from red sandstone by Alexander Handyside Ritchie in 1859. A plaque below says: 'In memory of Hugh Miller, and in commemoration of his genius, and literary and scientific eminence, this monument is erected by his countrymen.' Miller was as a rule sceptical about such commemorations. 'It is a bad matter,' he wrote, 'when a country is employed in building monuments to the memory of men chiefly remarkable for knocking other men on the head; it is a bad matter too, when it builds monuments to the memory of mere courtiers, of whom not much more can be said than that when they lived they had places and pensions to bestow, and that they bestowed them on their friends.' He had, however, just then been contemplating the Scott Monument close to Princes Street, which caused him to add: 'We cannot think so ill, however, of the homage paid to genius.' Miller thought of himself, by the end, as a great man; indeed even a man of genius – and I came away from beautiful Cromarty convinced that he was. One can take it, I think, that this memorial too, on its hill overlooking the sea, would be one that honoured Hugh Miller's own stern requirements.

12

HARTLEPOOL

RALPH WARD JACKSON CREATES A TOWN WHERE
NONE STOOD BEFORE AND SEVERELY UPSETS
HIS NEIGHBOURS.

'One and all', the Mercury *reported, 'resolved that they
would not leave the church, even though they should be
walled up within it… The strongest fellows who were
there now took a ladder, and, using it as a battering-ram,
sallied down the aisle, urged on by the throng behind,
and, with a force that was irresistible, swept down the
newly-built wall at the western end of the church,
resounding with cheers…'*

SATURDAY LUNCHTIME, a sunny day in early July and a
good deal of Hartlepool is gathered around its multi-million-
pound marina, built where the busy docks of West Hartlepool used to be. Few of the bobbing boats, people will tell you,
belong to pure Hartlepudlians, and the same is probably true of the
pleasant aspirational blocks of apartments close to the waterfront.
This isn't that rich a town. Yet on a day such as this, that hardly matters. Pure Hartlepudlians at ease in the sunshine outside the bars
and cafés for food, drink and conversation show every sign of enjoying the scene. Where once decline and dereliction reigned, all
about them today is lively, smart and colourful; and it's theirs.

There is a further ingredient, though, unpremeditated by architects and designers, that makes the picture complete. Across the
water towards the north-east, there's a promontory dominated by
the short sturdy tower of the church of St Hilda: arrayed before it

is a line of brightly coloured Georgian houses shimmering in the sun. This is old Hartlepool – or, as it's locally known, the Headland. It was there for a good 700 years before anyone thought of marinas. It was there a good 600 before there was any hint of West Hartlepool rising up on the other side of the bay. And though it is now forty years since the two boroughs were merged into one, there is still, when you take the bus round to the headland, the sense of a decidedly separate and disparate place, with some echo still of that smouldering resentment with which original Hartlepool used to look on this interloper as the place that had stolen its birthright.

That affront was the work of one man: Ralph Ward Jackson, product of Normanby Hall, North Yorkshire. He began his working life in a solicitor's office in Stockton-on-Tees, but it wasn't long before he wanted a life more adventurous, more pregnant with opportunity. Hartlepool, twelve miles away on the coast, seemed to him to throb with potential. There were those in the headland town who had seen that too. Christopher Tennant had planned a future for Hartlepool serving the south-west Durham collieries, with a railway to bring the coal to the water. But Jackson had a driving impatience that could not wait for the older entrepreneurs of old Hartlepool. He scuppered early attempts, from 1838 on, at cooperation. He wanted to build a great harbour and a sequence of docks to serve a far greater trade. He believed he could beat the powerful Peases, creators of burgeoning Middlesbrough, and capture the traffic of places as far to the south as Hull and Grimsby. He wanted, as he declared, to make the place the Liverpool of the north-east. And if that was going to be done, he would have to do it himself.

West of the water was the little village of Stranton, with a population of perhaps 350, against Hartlepool's 6,000. This was where he would start. He regretted having waited so long. When the first sod of his coal dock, in a scene of bleak grassy emptiness, was dug in 1845, he was only eighteen months short of his fortieth birthday. Thereafter the pace was frenetic. The first dock was completed in 1847. A second was ready five years later; a third in 1856. To ensure a heavier traffic for his creations he bought collieries and a small fleet of ships. But constructing these works and servicing them thereafter also meant bringing a whole new workforce into the area. So he built the town of West Hartlepool.

It must have seemed in those early days as aspirational an enterprise as the marina concept in the early twenty-first century. The centrepiece of the town would be Church Street, broad and elegant, with a church at the western end and fashionable shops and a building called the Atheneum, which would serve as its principal hall and a place for the town's commissioners to meet until the municipal buildings were opened, nine years after his death, in 1889. To build a church he intended to be as much a prideful landmark as a place of worship, he chose an architect, E. B. Lamb, whom Nikolaus Pevsner described as 'the naughtiest of mid-Victorian architects'. Its agreeable oddness suggests that he cannot have been disappointed.

Very soon West Hartlepool was considered as striking as Middlesbrough to the south or Barrow on the western side of the Pennines as a town that had grown in no time at all out of virtually nothing. According to the local historian Robert Wood, where Hartlepool had once had a mere vassal status as an outpost port for Newcastle, by 1857 the value of goods shipped through Jackson's creation was £1,767,160, which was £379,098 more than trade out of Newcastle. By 1861, the new town's population was not far short of the old town's 12,245. But that, in Jackson's vision, was only a start. His projected Cleveland railway would open up new swathes of territory whose output could be brought to and shipped from his town. The building of this north-eastern Liverpool required sharp ideas pursued with a degree of ruthlessness and a readiness to sweep past such obstacles as might stand in the way.

The progress of Ralph Ward Jackson had two distinguishing characteristics: a determination to do his best for the town through enterprise but also through benevolence; and an intransigent insistence that all should be done precisely as he wished. You can see them both at work in the story of Christ Church as recounted

in a book called *Jackson's Town* by the former town clerk of Hartlepool, Eric Waggott, who devoted his retirement to researching and
writing it. His publisher was Hartlepool Council. Though doomed
to go largely unread outside the place it commemorates, it's an essential and exemplary source for anyone hoping to understand how
such places came into being. In his town-clerkly way, Waggott says
in his preface: 'Some may feel that it would have been better not to
have resurrected some of the details which surrounded the early
days of Christ Church... and to have left in obscurity the strange
and sad record of Ralph Ward Jackson's downfall...' Thankfully, he
did not succumb to such wheedlings.

No one could doubt that Christ Church was Jackson's creation.
He raised much, though not all, the money needed to build it, and
provided both the site, and the stone – which like much else in new
West Hartlepool had been excavated to make space for the docks.
To superintend it, he established a board of trustees, one of whose
duties would be to act as patron and choose the incumbent. Alongside himself he named his aged father-in-law, who lived safely far
away in Lancashire; his clerical brother-in-law, who because of
indifferent health spent much of his time in Italy; the vicar of nearby
Seaton Carew; and a Durham clergyman. The cut and thrust of debate
was clearly not what he had in mind for their meetings. Nor did he
expect any trouble from the incumbent whom they, in theory,
and he in, practice, selected: a twenty-eight-year-old curate,
eager, energetic but usefully inexperienced, from Norton near
Stockton, called John Hart Burges.

Burges, however, proved to be less unquestioningly tractable than
Jackson had expected. They fell out over a plan to build new schools
for the town. As with the church, Jackson would provide the site
and the building materials, but Burges must raise the money. Burges
worked on the basis that the schools would primarily serve Anglican
children from his new parish; Jackson had always meant them to be
inclusive, to take in children from across his new town. Burges dared
to resist him, not least because much of the money he'd raised had

come from people who wanted Anglican children put first. A war of words, and in time rather more than words, broke out between them. In his unbending way, Jackson complained of his minister's 'unbending disposition'. 'I am bound to confess', he wrote, 'that you glaringly betray, in my opinion, a degree of obstinacy and perversion, which I am satisfied will be extremely obstructive to the well-being of this rising town.' What that sentence in turn betrayed was that the dispute had gone beyond a mere matter of scholastic intake. The issue now was what should be done with a man who had risen up in the midst of West Hartlepool and sought to thwart the will of the founder.

Burges began to backtrack. Just before Christmas 1855 he wrote to say he was now willing to accept Jackson's wishes. But too late: on New Year's Eve, Jackson wrote back to suggest the time was now right for Burges to go ahead with the plans he had several times hinted at, to leave Christ Church for good. Burges promptly denied having ever suggested that he might do so. Nor would he do so now. At a public meeting called to discuss the dispute he declared that Jackson knew that no power in the land could remove him from his incumbency. But in this, as it transpired, he was not as safe as he thought. For Jackson had discovered a defect in the documentation for Burges's appointment, which meant it had never been valid. And if it had never been valid, then it inescapably followed that much that had been done in the parish, including all the marriages that Burges had solemnized, was invalid as well, and many couples who thought themselves respectably wedded were living in sin; a matter that when conveyed to the Bishop of Durham made what until then had been an embarrassing local dispute look very substantially nastier.

Precisely what happened next is impossible to establish. Since, as Waggott points out, the sources are local newspapers, some partial to Jackson and another a keen supporter of Burges, the whole truth, one might say, can be known only to God. But in March, Ralph Ward Jackson and the vicar of Stranton – the parish that had been there before Christ Church was built, and so if Christ Church had no validity, was continuing parish now – posted a notice saying that marriages, churchings (ceremonies for the blessing of women after childbirth) and baptisms would not take place at Christ Church until further notice. Those who wanted them must arrange for them to be held at Stranton instead. Immediately Burges stuck up a counter-notice. Marriages, churchings and baptisms would continue as usual unless the bishop revoked his licence.

Very well: if that was the case, Jackson concluded, the licence must be revoked. The bishop, however, thought otherwise. And with no sign by midsummer of a peaceful resolution, the confrontation turned violent. Jackson now closed the church. As the *Stockton and Hartlepool Mercury* reported on 2 August, Burges's supporters broke the doors open and began what is nowadays called a sit-in. Jackson and his son arrived at the church and a confrontation with Burges ensued, in the course of which Jackson gave Burges what the Jackson-supporting *Mercury* called a light push, but a letter from a prominent Burgesite to the *Durham Chronicle* portrayed as a sharp assault.

Jackson now announced that if the forces of Burges would not accept that its doors should be closed, he would summon a force of workmen and brick the place up. A body of masons duly arrived, equipped with the tools of their trade. A cartload of bricks had already been delivered. They found waiting for them what Burges's side called the congregation, but Jackson's adherents described as a mob thirsting for battle. 'One and all', the *Mercury* reported, 'resolved that they would not leave the church, even though they should be walled up within it… The strongest fellows who were there now took a ladder which had been conveyed into the church, and, using it as a battering-ram, sallied down the aisle, urged on by the throng behind, and, with a force that was irresistible, swept down the newly-built wall at the western end of the church, resounding with cheers. The women then turned up the sleeves of their dresses, and, with broiling faces, pitched out the bricks, relieving each other by turns.' There followed what the *Mercury* called 'a scene such as is, happily, rarely enacted under the roof of a religious temple'. 'The mob were rushing to and fro over the tops of the sittings; fictitious marriages were celebrated at the altar; mock sermons addressed from the pulpit, the mimic priests indulging in the luxury of a cutty pipe; while mimic baptisms took place at the font.' Mr Burges had been absent, conducting a funeral elsewhere, but even when he returned the performance continued, with beer being sent for. 'Nothing was more striking', the *Mercury*'s reporter noted, 'than the excited and sometimes violent demeanour of the women – with few exceptions, all of the lower orders – who evidently would not have hesitated to pull down the church with their own hands if the signal had been given.'

The scenes in the evening were even worse. 'The mob with which the church was filled consisted of the lowest and most ruffi-anly men – drunken sailors, Irishmen and "navvies". They wandered up and down the church, in and out of the pulpit and pews and within the altar railing – shouting, whistling and smoking. A mock marriage was celebrated by a drunken sailor, he declaring it to be "the only legal marriage that had been celebrated in that church"... Meanwhile a brother navvy, self-delegated to the office of priest, was baptising an infant at the font. Hassocks were pitched about in every direction; the building rang with cheers and laughter, and the drunken oaths and fiendish threats that mingled in the uproar gave a crowning effect to the Pandemonium-like scene. The awful and disgusting threats uttered against Mr Jackson by many of the women offer the truest index to the character of the matronly enthusiasts in the cause of the rev. gentleman. They were, in fact – at least those which we heard ourselves – too revolting for repetition.' At around nine o'clock, Mr Burges, having, the *Mercury* alleged (Burges himself strenuously denied it), been in the church for these proceedings, thanked the mob for their support and suggested it was time they went home.

The *Mercury* chose to ignore the appearance at Christ Church of a body of men headed by a shipbroker called Newbiggin who tried to retake the church from its occupants and in doing so struck the sexton. The *Durham Chronicle*, however, printed a long letter, signed *Fiat Justitia*, which declared that the disgraceful scenes in the church had been enacted 'in Mr Jackson's presence and at his command'. This came in response to a letter which Jackson published in the *Mercury* and the *Durham Advertiser* addressed to the inhabitants of West Hartlepool. It spoke of 'scenes and pollutions of the vilest character – known only in the brothel and the lowest pot-house', and added to the catalogue of mock ceremonies and pipe smoking described by the *Mercury* the claim that 'fornication and other beastliness' had taken place even within the altar rails. He had, even so, Jackson went on to say, told Mr Burges that he was ready to pay him £150 a year until such time as he could find an alternative living or curacy. Burges refused the offer; he said he was staying put.

The next encounter in the series took place in West Hartlepool cemetery, where the West Hartlepool commissioners (the nearest thing the town had at this stage to a local government) with Jackson and his son William among them, arrived in a bid to prevent Burges officiating at the burial of a child. The vicar of Stranton attempted to read the service, but according to the *Mercury*, which as ever has to be treated with scepticism, 'the father of the child that was to be buried, and who was unmistakeably drunk, snatched up the coffin, and declared that he would take it home again'. He claimed to be armed with a pistol and said he would use it unless the vicar of Stranton desisted; which he did, and Burges was allowed to resume.

Burges, however, was beaten. Jackson had resorted to what even the usually neutral Waggott describes as 'dreadful measures', designed to deprive poor Burges not only of his income and of legitimate expenses, but of his rent-free house. At this point the Bishop of Durham retired on the grounds of ill-health and gave way to a successor less likely to protect the beleaguered priest from his persecutor. Burges preached his farewell service on 22 March 1857 and left for a post in Birmingham. Jackson now took swift and resolute action to put the affairs of the church in order and save numbers of Hartlepudlian children from the imputation of bastardy. A private bill was introduced at Westminster which remedied the defect in the first appointment and validated all marriages conducted in Christ Church from the beginning, while the right to appoint incumbents was transferred from Jackson and his complaisant nominees to the bishops of Durham.

And so, in 1857, the year he was fifty-one, Jackson could hope he had put such matters behind him. But here he was wrong. Though much of the local establishment had sided with him throughout, these shenanigans had fed some local unease about the founder and his imperious ways. And, even more dire for Ralph Ward Jackson, the history of these events helped to colour a truly more savage dispute that now overwhelmed him, and would finally bring him down.

It began almost accidentally. Ralph's younger brother Edwin had become involved in a dispute with a solicitor called Benjamin Coleman, who seems to have been by temperament a difficult and troublesome man. 'By no means a clean potato,' Alderman Major Robert Martin, VD, JP, says of him in his book, *Historical Notes and Personal Recollections of West Hartlepool and its Founder* – though Edwin, it seems, was not an entirely clean potato either. The details are complex – they are charted by Eric Waggott with his customary diligence – but essentially, Coleman accused Edwin Ward Jackson of failing to pay a debt. The dispute rumbled on for some time. On several occasions, Edwin thought he'd disposed of it, but Coleman kept coming back at him, and in time his brother Ralph (who after all had qualified as a solicitor) got sucked into the quarrel. Immediately, Coleman found a fresh target.

Edwin had written anonymous letters vilifying his assailant. One of these in which he was described as a 'deep-dyed scoundrel' and 'a designing plausible Jew', came into Coleman's hands. Ralph was one of those who came forward to say that the letters were not in Edwin's handwriting. In one of many pamphlets in which he prosecuted his case, Coleman said he had been to the north of England, where he 'heard such a character of Mr Ralph Ward Jackson, as satisfied me that the extraordinary and dishonest course of conduct pursued by him in his brother's case was precisely what might have been expected from his known antecedents' . He particularly cited the battle of Christ Church, 'where under the cloak of religion he did acts which stamp his name with infamy'.

Coleman now began to broaden his attack into a comprehensive indictment of the business methods and practices on which Jackson and his West Hartlepool Dock and Railway Company had built their success. By enlisting as a shareholder in Jackson's company he was able to turn up at an annual general meeting to make his case.

Though in theory what he said applied to the company, it was Jackson who needed to answer, since in essence, he *was* the company. What the company did was what he ordained. His board of directors was hardly better equipped for argument and resistance than the original trustees of Christ Church had been. Coleman listed them: Jackson; his son William, 'an inexperienced youth'; his father-in-law, now well past eighty, and still usefully out of the way in Lancashire; a woollen draper from Stockton, 'who, very wisely, never opens his lips, and never takes publicly a part in the Company's affairs'; and one Mr Cuthbert Wigham, 'also upwards of 80 years of age, very infirm, and who is, moreover, blind'.

There were two main charges in Coleman's case. One was that Jackson had set in hand illegal deals to purchase shipping and collieries in a manner detrimental to the interests of shareholders. This had been done to create such a sense of prosperity that other colliery owners and other shipowners would be anxious to trade with West Hartlepool. The other was that Jackson had been cooking the books, publishing what Coleman called 'delusional accounts'. In pursuance of his campaigns to tempt the timber trade away from Grimsby and Hull he had made reckless offers and had falsified figures. In modern terminology, he'd indulged in the practice of flattering the company's profits. He was also able to throw in the information that Jackson had been convicted (in 1861, the year he turned fifty-six) of an assault on the vicar of Greatham, where he lived, in a dispute over a right of way.

Jackson fought back with letters and posters, one of which offered a £100 reward for anyone who could produce the body of Benjamin Coleman, an adventurer and a libeller intent on causing panic throughout West Hartlepool, dead or alive. Coleman duly appeared at the company's annual meeting where he found no support, while Jackson was lavishly lauded for the job he had done for the company and the town and what he now planned to do for their further enrichment. Jackson, Coleman complained, had the gift of being able to mesmerize an audience. Certainly since his arrival he had always had an eye for the main chance and a habit of keeping everything else out of focus. He took risks, cut corners, brushed aside tedious regulations, because that was how things got done. Victorian England was full of such single-minded entrepreneurs, quite a few of whom were detected and sometimes jailed, while others, equally culpable, got through their lives unscathed and quite often wreathed in honours.

Coleman's complaints clearly had substance, and a couple of City houses endorsed them, to the point where the company had to concede that its practices must be regularized. Bills were drafted and put before Parliament. Coleman and his supporters objected; more tellingly, the Board of Trade, which monitored such matters, protested as well. The bills were dropped; a second attempt at remedial legislation was so amended that it left the company no less vulnerable than before. Jackson was now dangerously exposed, and the company with him. Analysis in the City showed it to be unsafe. Creditors mustered. On 10 April 1862, Jackson resigned from the board of his West Hartlepool Harbour and Railway Company and of the Cleveland Railway Company, which he chaired.

A new board was constituted, which in the company's precarious state began to sell off assets. In an echo of his treatment of Burges, it locked Jackson's office against him. When he offered his services as an adviser, arguing a depth of experience that the new regime lacked, he was snubbed and shunned, and although he argued that the bleak assessments published by City houses were based on error, it censured him for his past mismanagement. A Commons select committee set up to consider the bills put forward to try to regularize the operation in Hartlepool explicitly exonerated him from any taint of criminality or pursuit of personal benefit. But a Lords committee whose findings were published in 1863 was not so forgiving. 'Lord Donoughmore and the other members of the Select Commitee of the Lords on the West Hartlepool Bill' said *The Times* in a leading article, 'have performed a public service by investigating the frauds which have been practised on the shareholders and creditors of the company.' That provoked a 5,000-word letter from Jackson – which *The Times* published in full – denying any malpractice; and certainly Eric Waggott argues that Lord Donoughmore's report went further in its condemnation than the facts it presented could justify.

The following year the powerful North Eastern Railway took control of Jackson's company and all that went with it. That had always been a logical possibility. The Hartlepool enterprise was never really big enough to achieve what it sought to create. The NER was always happy to drive competitors out of business. Indeed, Eric Waggott suggests there may have been collusion between the company and Benjamin Coleman to break Ralph Ward Jackson – though the Peases of Middlesbrough may have had a hand in it too. Certainly West Hartlepool needed a rescuer, and if the NER was one, another appeared in the shape of William Gray, a son – and former mayor – of old Hartlepool, who established a shipyard that became the new town's greatest industry. In the year of its charter he also became its first mayor. The town continued to grow and by 1901 had 63,000 people – nearly thirty times as many as had lived in vestigial Stranton when the thrustful Jackson arrived there.

Yet whatever the town owed Gray, it owed Jackson more. It might not have become the new Liverpool he had dreamed of –

but that was never likely to happen. He had, even so, created a town of achievement and opportunity in a place that had started with nothing. He was flawed, but without those flaws, without that determination to press on regardless of considerations in the face of which others might have sensibly hesitated, the beanstalk growth of West Hartlepool could never have taken place. Now his reputation was sullied; but the town he had built did not reject him. That was clear when in 1868 he stood as Conservative candidate for the newly created parliamentary seat of The Hartlepools (the plural was still very necessary then) and won. The margin over his Liberal opponent, Thomas Richardson, was only three votes. The probability is that the many voters of West Hartlepool (whose population at the 1871 census three years later was 22,200) backed him strongly, while the voters of ancient but grievously overtaken Old Hartlepool (13,166 people in 1871) were solid for his opponent. The local historian Major Robert Martin certainly thought so. Richardson is on record as having declared: 'There ought to have been no West Hartlepool. Mr Jackson, in creating West Hartlepool, created it not precisely in opposition to Hartlepool but in opposition to the docks in Hartlepool. A feeling of animosity between the two towns grew up when those new docks were established, and the feeling has grown ever since.'

Yet Jackson was now almost done with the town he had founded. His mother had died in 1863 and his wife, at fifty-nine, two years later. His son had married. His parliamentary duties kept him in London. In 1874 he stood again against Richardson and this time lost by more than 900 votes. He gave up his house at Greatham and from now on appeared in the north only rarely. He dabbled in further entrepreneurial ventures – the provision, for instance, of a water supply at Cheltenham – but much of his time was taken up with disputes with his successors at Hartlepool, and in litigation.

He fought a long and burdensome battle with the North Eastern Railway. A man called George Leeman, once one of his closest associates, but now with the NER, accused him of deluding the shareholders of the West Hartlepool company to the tune of around £2 million. Jackson sued him for libel and won, though the damages awarded him were a mere 40 shillings and the finding was anyway reversed on appeal. His circumstances in these final years were sadly reduced. Robert Wood, in his book *West Hartlepool: the rise and development of a Victorian new town*, quotes the editor of the *Durham Advertiser*, musing on Jackson's fate in 1874: 'How little one suspects the strange romantic histories of the men who toil past us every day. As the elderly, bending figure with the white hair, bright eyes and ruddy cheeks (streaked with red like winter apples) trudges westwards and goes in to its unostentatious dinner at the Carlton every day, who would suspect it of founding a town? Yet one day the North of England will erect a statue to Ralph Ward Jackson's memory, and his name is everlastingly bound up in the history of English pluck and enterprise.'

Jackson died in August 1880, at seventy-four, and was buried at Kensal Green cemetery, 250 miles south of his town, though shops shut and flags flew at half mast there on the day of the funeral. And he did get the statue. It stands in Church Street, on the eastern side of his church, with William Gray installed on the western side. He looks out today on a sadly diminished street. Christ Church, at the top, has been deconsecrated and is now a tourist information centre and gallery. Church Square in which it stands, is little more than a traffic roundabout. The principal shopping centre has migrated to the area west of Church Square, which Gray surveys, up past Victoria Square with its imposing Methodist chapel.

Jackson on his perch looks stern and austere, a bit like Charles Dance as the cold lawyer Tulkinghorn in the television version of *Bleak House*. The plaque beneath the statue calls him the founder of the town, which was true enough when it was put there in 1897, since the town in those days meant West Hartlepool. It's no longer so true today, since West Hartlepool was merged with Hartlepool by parliamentary fiat on 1 April 1967. Some had campaigned for this marriage as far back as 1880, but old Hartlepool had always resisted. Independent out on its headland around ancient St Hilda's, still nursing the grievance that Thomas Richardson had identified, it did not wish to see its identity submerged in that of Ward Jackson's upstart community. In the 1950s, Hartlepool borough council agreed to a merger, but a plebiscite in the old borough rejected it by a margin of eight to one.

Eventually, however, distant commissioners declared that the two must be one. On the night of 31 March 1967, a 'small but vociferous' crowd sang 'Auld Lang Syne' outside the municipal offices of West Hartlepool; a rather larger one turned out for municipal fireworks. So on one assessment, Ward Jackson won: the old town is subsumed in the one he created. On another, though, the older community triumphed. It's the old town out on the headland whose name is used for the town that is there today: 'West Hartlepool' no longer appears on the map.

Shortly before Ralph Ward Jackson's death a fund was opened to sustain him through what would have otherwise been an impoverished old age. But he died before the proceeds could be passed to him. A debate arose on what should be done with the money. In the end they decided to spend it on a good traditional north country park, with a lake, a bowling green, a bandstand, a Boer war memorial, and a wonderfully ornate fountain, with cherubic blowers of conch horns performing under the presidency of a goddess on its summit. For years West Hartlepool used to ride out there by tram on high days and holidays. Less so now. The trams ceased running there long ago. Ward Jackson Park is no longer the draw it was – especially now when on sunny Saturday afternoons in July, Hartlepudlians have the marina.

13

NINE ELMS, LONDON

GIUSEPPE GARIBALDI RAVISHES LONDON AND
INSPIRES ADULATION EVEN IN BASINGSTOKE.

🐌

*'Never, in the memory of living man, has such a scene
been witnessed as that which was produced by the
reception of Garibaldi. It was a greeting that any
sovereign might envy and one which perhaps no
sovereign ever received...'*

THE JUBILATION BEGAN AT Southampton. It was
unexpectedly muted, for this was a Sunday, and the cele-
brations of even the greatest earthly heroes had to be
tempered out of respect for the Sabbath. The General should have
arrived the previous day. As the *Southampton Times* reported,
throughout Saturday everyone in the town had seemed to be 'on
the tiptoe of expectation'. But the weather had been against them,
and the good ship *Ripon* had failed to arrive. 'The people', wrote
the *Southampton Times* reporter, 'were so earnest and hearty in their
desire to welcome this great and good man... that they persisted in
hoping against hope until long after the dark mantle of night had
o'ershadowed the glittering splendour of the day.'

But on Sunday morning, 3 April 1864, word arrived that the
Ripon was now off Hurst Castle and was due to dock in about two
hours' time, and immediately the flags of England and Italy were
being hung out on buildings and the townsfolk began to assemble,
clambering over the boats in the harbour and crowding around the
berth where the *Ripon* was due to dock. And this time they were
rewarded. Dressed in his trademark red shirt and grey coat, and

leaning upon his stick – for the wounds he had suffered two years before at the battle of Aspromonte still troubled him – General Giuseppe Garibaldi, Italian patriot, revolutionary leader and for much of the western world the very spirit of liberty, was deluged in Southampton's welcome.

Because it was Sunday, formal addresses prepared for this moment went undelivered, but soon he was on his way to meet the first of the contingents of local dignitaries he was doomed to encounter in the course of his visit. There followed a recuperative visit to the Isle of Wight as a guest of the Liberal MP Charles Seely. The harbour at Cowes was decked out for his arrival. In his few days on the island he would be introduced to most of the island's most celebrated figures, especially Alfred Lord Tennyson, with whom he swapped quotations from favourite poets, and on whose estate at Farringford he planted a tree. On Saturday he visited Portsmouth, which had failed to prepare for his visit, the corporation having voted against an official welcome. Inevitably, though, news of his arrival spread through the town, and what the *Hampshire Advertiser* called 'a large accession of workmen' rushed to acclaim him; to which he responded by frequently doffing his hat and bowing. Before long, a more general crowd had gathered, cheering and waving flags, and climbing aboard the boat on which he was due to tour the docks.

On Monday, 11 April, he was back in Southampton to start his journey to London. The London and South Western Railway had furnished a special train of twelve carriages, its engine adorned with Italian flags, for the seventy-seven-mile journey. Adoring crowds packed the station, desperate to shake the hand of their hero, some even climbing on the top of his carriage. At Bishopstoke (now Eastleigh) the train slowed to a crawl to let people see him; at Winchester, where the platform was full to overflowing, it came to a halt, as it did again even at the lonely wayside station of Micheldever. Wild scenes of adulation followed at Basingstoke, and again at Woking. 'Not only', wrote the *Southampton Times* reporter, 'was there at every station a gathering as demonstrative as numbers and cheering could make it, but all along the country there were really surprising signs of the universality of the Garibaldi sentiment. Far away at cottage doors women waved their handkerchiefs, and from lonely plantations there burst out unexpectedly the shouts of a group collected for no other purpose.'

The culmination came when, at about half past two, the train pulled in to Nine Elms, the original London and South Western terminus in the district of Vauxhall. Already by then superseded as a principal destination by Waterloo, the station had been named after a group of trees on the side of the road which served it. No trace of the trees or the station remains today; the site is now part of the fruit and vegetable market relocated in 1974 from Covent Garden. The drab streets here had never seen such excitement before. 'For some minutes before the platform was reached', wrote the man from the *Southampton Times*, 'there were heard shouts that seemed to come from all quarters, above and below, and on every side; and the eye took in a confused and bewildering vision of men and women, chiefly railway workmen and their wives; on lines of trucks, on piles of timber, on idle locomotives, on roofs of dizzy height, on walls and parapets, on mountains of luggage – everywhere huge mounds and thick long lines of human beings, instinct with one emotion, expressed by feature, hand and voice; an emotion of overwhelming gladness at the arrival of a long-expected, much-honoured, and beloved guest.'

Outside the station, marching in from every quarter of London, representatives of working-class organizations – benefit societies, friendly societies, temperance societies, trade associations – had gathered with flags and banners. The London *Times*, though conceding that they were 'as docile and as easily managed as so many regiments', was unimpressed with their efforts, finding them shabby and poorly organized. Such a shame, it lamented, that the planning of this occasion had been left in the hands of working-class men; that offers of cooperation from the upper classes, who organized such events so much more effectively, had been rejected.

Yet, imperfect as they were, they now waited with cheerful patience outside the station while the rigmarole of the day proceeded within. A little child came forward to present the general with a bouquet: 'with the most perfectly natural and fatherly manner he took the child in his arms, kissed it, patted its curls, and tried as well as he was able to speak to it in English'. Then came a succession of formal addresses, the first from the City of London, which greeted Garibaldi as 'Sir', and the second from the working men, which began 'Illustrious Chief'. To their joy, he replied: 'I like to see working-men particularly. I am very grateful, and will forget not all my life this welcome of the class I have the honour to belong to. They like to call me the brother of the working men of every part of the world.' And then, unprogrammed, an Italian woman came forward to offer her thanks to the English, the most powerful of the world's nations, for the honour they had done to the general for his defence of Italian liberty against despotism. On most occasions, said *The Times*, such an interruption might have been coldly received; but not on this one.

And now, at last, the formalities over, Garibaldi appeared before the fervent crowds on the streets. Here and throughout his slow and stately progress beyond, there were scenes the like of which, it was agreed, had never been witnessed before in the capital. The general was now on the home ground of the *South London Chronicle*, one of the very few suburban newspapers publishing at that time, and eager to pronounce on behalf of the people it served. 'The enthusiasm of South London', it declared, 'has been wound up to the highest pitch. Never, in the memory of living man, has such a scene been witnessed as that which was produced by the reception of Garibaldi. It was a greeting that any sovereign might envy, and one which perhaps no sovereign ever received. Its glory consisted in its spontaneity. Every man, except here and there an entrammelled spiritual slave, held in bondage as well as kept in ignorance by an elaborate and crafty superstition, went forth eagerly to add his voice to the long loud chorus of welcome. And such cheering! It was the language of the heart, unrestrained, unimpeded by prudential considerations.'

That sentiment went well beyond London patriotism. The *Manchester Guardian*, a newspaper not easily impressed by London excitements and London excesses, called it 'an event almost unparalleled in the history of the metropolis... The crowd exceeded anything ever before witnessed.' *The Times* declared: 'Yesterday witnessed one of those extraordinary spectacles which show that under the thick crust with which natural seriousness and the habits of a material age have overlaid the character of Englishmen there burn the fires of an enthusiasm as strong as animates any nation on earth.' Even when he rode triumphant into Naples, the paper suggested, he had not received such a welcome. London, John Morley, Liberal politician and Gladstone's biographer, would later write, had seldom beheld a spectacle more extraordinary or more moving: 'such scenes of passionate curiosity, delight and enthusiasm; and this not for some much loved prince or triumphant captain of our own, but for a foreigner, and the deliverer of a foreign people.'

Slowed to less than walking pace by the huge enthusiasms of the crowds in the April sunshine, crushing together and striving to touch their hero, the procession made its difficult way through the streets of London south of the Thames, by way of Kennington, where radical and perhaps even revolutionary aspirations had been crushed by the failure of the Chartist demonstration sixteen years before, to Westminster bridge and the fashionable side of the river. South of the river, wrote the man from the London *Times*, the gathering, except among some who waved from the windows, had been unmistakably plebeian, but now as it closed on Pall Mall 'there was an infusion of higher elements...'

Yet this clamorous fervour north and south seems wholly to have transcended class divisions. People, rich or poor, leaned out of every window, perched on roofs, clung to railings, lampposts and signboards, and risked being crushed by passing trains as they massed on railway bridges. The better off, who had paid good money for privileged vantage points, cheered the revolutionary hero as eagerly as any working man. From Westminster up Whitehall and in to the great arena at Charing Cross, the general's procession fought its way through the clamorous throng. There were, some reporters believed, at least 100,000 people assembled at Charing Cross, packing the square and spilling into the streets as far back as the Strand, as the bells of St Martin's rang out in salutation.

For those in distant parts of England who could not be there, there were pictures in the *Illustrated London News* in the following weeks to show them what they had missed. A journey of perhaps three miles from Nine Elms to the general's destination – Stafford House (now Lancaster House), behind Pall Mall, home of his host in London, the Liberal Duke of Sutherland – had taken on different estimates between four and six hours. The number of those who from Southampton to Charing Cross had come on this day to salute their hero was beyond computation: perhaps, it has been suggested, a million. The one disappointment was that, once he had arrived at Stafford House this cynosure of all eyes would not come out to address the crowds that still clamoured for him. Garibaldi, it could be explained, was not a well man: one of the reasons for his visit to London was to consult its distinguished medical men. But more likely he did not come out because he was not allowed to. As subsequent events would show, some senior London politicians thought that this adulation of a revolutionary leader had already gone far enough. Too far, in fact.

What did it really signify, this spontaneous unrestrained outburst of admiration, rising to outright love, for a foreign visitor? Some of it must have come from the kind of greedy delight in gazing on and getting near a celebrity that infects our own times. This was a man, matched in recent history only perhaps by Nelson Mandela and possibly for a while by Barack Obama, of overwhelming charisma; also, as the reports of the day make clear, of exceptional sexual appeal. Several newspapers noted how fervent, even verging on shameless, normally modest and respectable women became in his presence. From the Duchess of Sutherland, who could not disguise how smitten she was, to the railwaymen's wives at Nine Elms, women doted on Garibaldi – despite (or in some cases perhaps, because of) his notorious adventures with women. At one point he had proposed in the space of two months to three different women, while a fourth was having his child.

Everyone, as we now say, wanted a part of him. Garibaldi effigies, Garibaldi mugs, flooded out of the potteries. Garibaldi biscuits appeared on middle-class tea tables. A manufacturer in Leeds marketed Garibaldi overcoats. Garibaldi red shirts sold lavishly. The players of Nottingham Forest FC refused to perform unless the club clad them in shirts of Garibaldian red – as they still are today.

Yet the Garibaldi sentiment, as the man from the *Southampton Times* had called it, went far beyond fashion. For it also reflected the easy unpretentious humanity that London had witnessed in his response to the address of the workers, or his kindly treatment of the child who presented him with flowers, when he arrived at Nine Elms. It had to do, too, with the conspicuous heroism and the commitment to liberty that the English public had been reading or hearing about ever since, four years before, the general and his 'thousand' had landed at Marsala and taken the town in the name of Italy without a shot being fired. Garibaldi's character and his record had made him a hero – especially, a working-class hero, which was why much of the pressure to bring him to England had come from working-class radicals – but a hero also at this moment to even such unradical figures as the editor of *The Times*. 'Some were drawn by his daring as a fighter,' John Morley wrote, 'and by the picturesque figure as of a hero of antique mould… but what fired the hearts of most was the thought of him as the soldier who bore the sword of human freedom.' In the North and the Midlands, people counted the days until Garibaldi would come among them.

There was, though, a darker side to this astonishing outburst of mass adulation. Garibaldi was revered and loved not just because of what he was seen to stand for, but because of what he was seen to be standing against. As the *South London Chronicle* explained to its readers, Garibaldi had been the target of 'French influence and French hatred' designed to discredit his cause. Here was a chance for the populace to demonstrate what it thought of the French. And even more, to show what it thought of another of Garibaldi's antagonists, the church of Rome. Rome regarded him as a dangerous atheist, with designs to erase the Vatican's independence, a view to which many Catholics in England subscribed. That was what the *South London Chronicle* meant when it bemoaned the failure of entrammelled spiritual slaves to join the popular welcome. More crudely, thousands sang in the streets: 'We'll get a rope and hang the Pope, so up with Garibaldi.'

There were others, more influential, who also forbore to join the general welcome. Chief among them was Queen Victoria. She was said to have observed that she felt ashamed to be the head of a nation capable of such folly as its worship of Garibaldi. She feared – and not without reason; this had been one of the reasons why radicals had been so keen to invite him – that his presence must encourage political dissent to flourish. But she must also have observed, as again the *South London Chronicle* had noted, how much more warmly the people responded to Garibaldi than they did to their queen. In fact, the epic events at London came at one of the lowest points of Victoria's reign, in the midst of her apparently interminable mourning for Prince Albert, who had died in the closing weeks of 1861. It was in this year of Garibaldi's visit, 1864, that a notice was found pinned to the railings at Buckingham Palace: 'These commanding premises to be let or sold, in consequence of the late occupant's declining business.'

The monarch's prime minister, Lord Palmerston, a Liberal of deep conservative instincts, was hardly happier. *The Times* had said of the visit: 'It is in England only that associations of workmen could conduct a revolutionary hero through a capital thronged with their own class, and yet not excite a fear in the mind of any politician that danger might spring from the gathering.' But in fact there were politicians on both sides of the party divide who feared the prospect that the visit seemed to induce of middle- and working-class radicals allying to force through change. Palmerston hoped that by ensuring that this inflammatory Italian spent much of his time in London in the care of a Liberal, but far from radical, aristocrat, the Duke of Sutherland, the general's appeal could be muffled. The radicals knew exactly what he was up to, complaining of an 'aristocratic capture' of Garibaldi.

The crucial figure here was Palmerston's chancellor, William Gladstone. Gladstone had been slow to respond to the cause of Italian liberty, but having been converted, he now characteristically reproached himself for his earlier sloth. Even now, however, his feelings about the distinguished visitor remained ambivalent, for much as he admired him, he deplored, and was even repelled by, his irreligion – Garibaldi's 'attenuated belief', as he called it. He greeted the general warmly and staged a party in his honour. His intention, none the less, was to ensure that the Garibaldi sentiment was defused.

The general had continued to command vast acclaim, at two great public meetings at the Crystal Palace, and at Covent Garden, where he was treated to a night of opera: Bellini's *Norma* and *Masaniello* or *La Muette de Portici* by Daniel Auber, a work so suffused in revolutionary sentiment that some believed it had sparked the uprising in 1830 that led to the establishment of the Belgian state. (That towards the end of this opera the revolutionary leader goes mad was presumably overlooked.) The expensive audience for the evening, which included Gladstone, were so eager to lay hands on the visitor that it seemed at one point quite possible that the opera would never begin. When he left at the end, the crowd that had waited four hours for this moment obstructed him, clung to his carriage, and refused to disperse. Still ahead lay a tour of provincial towns and cities – Birmingham, Leicester, Manchester,

Liverpool, York, Newcastle, Ralph Ward Jackson's West Hartlepool, Edinburgh, Glasgow, Dundee and Greenock – where the demonstrations were expected to be just as vivid and turbulent.

But then came the sudden announcement that Garibaldi was going home. His health, it was stated, was proving too frail to sustain the rest of his programme, and rather than fulfil some engagements while cancelling others, he thought it more just to abandon the lot. This decision was announced in the Commons by Gladstone. The *Manchester Guardian*, speaking for one of the towns now denied his inspiring presence, unreservedly accepted the reason that Gladstone had given. Garibaldi had after all come to England partly to take advice from medical experts, and the eminent Dr Ferguson had counselled against any further exertions. Some, the *Guardian* warned, would seek to attribute this outcome to political calculation; yet no shred of evidence could be found to support that conclusion. Others were not so sure. Was it really no more than coincidence that the eminent Dr Ferguson was Palmerston's personal doctor? The radical journalist and Member of Parliament Joseph Cowen denounced the official story as fraudulent, while Gladstone's parliamentary statement was greeted with protests and a certain amount of 'rude laughter'. A protest meeting called by the radicals who had done so much to bring the visit about was broken up by the police.

So a visit that had opened with unprecedented scenes of enthusiasm tapered away, though the crowds persisted to the last. One of the towns that had long been preparing for his arrival was Plymouth, where the Duke of Sutherland's yacht, the *Undine*, was waiting for him in the harbour. But the crowds that mustered for him on the appointed date, 22 October, and the dignitaries assembled to present their addresses, waited in vain. The general, it transpired, had gone to Cliveden instead. Still, apparently all was not lost: he would be passing through the town in a railway train, Plymouth was told, in three days' time. Again, he did not materialize. 'Never on any day in April', the *Western Morning News* complained next morning, 'have the inhabitants of Devonshire and Cornwall been so thoroughly deceived as they were yesterday.' The line had been thronged across the two counties by people hoping to catch a glimpse of him. At Exeter, 'the indignation of the multitude rose to a dangerous pitch'. At Plymouth, 'a hundred thousand persons, many of whom had sacrificed a day's work' were finally informed that their hero had gone to Weymouth.

Garibaldi did indeed pass through Plymouth, but in the early hours of the following morning, when few were around to see him, on his way to Par, where on the 27th a delegation from Plymouth presented him with the town's address. From here he went on to Fowey, where he joined the Duke's yacht: the inhabitants here, said the *News*, were 'fully alive to the honour done to their quaint and interesting little town'. Even that was not quite the end: the yacht docked at Falmouth, from where the general despatched a message of thanks to the people of England, before finally sailing away in the early hours of the following day.

And in time it transpired that in the matter of his departure, the sceptics and rude laughers were right and the *Manchester Guardian* wrong. A private conversation with Gladstone had persuaded Garibaldi not to proceed with his schedule. That was why great towns like Birmingham and Manchester had been denied the high excitements that London had enjoyed. Such dispossessed places had to make do with the second-hand testimony of Garibaldi's home-bred enthusiasts – though some of those must have been very effective too. It was one such meeting in his native Dundee that persuaded William McGonagall to become a poet. As he later recalled of that occasion:

> Rev. George Gilfillan of Dundee
> There is none can you excel;
> You have boldly rejected the Confession of Faith,
> And defended your cause right well.

The first time I heard him speak
'Twas in the Kinnaird Hall
Lecturing on the Garibaldi movement,
As loud as he could bawl.

14

BLOOMSBURY, LONDON

§.

*'Tricks of a most unwomanly nature were resorted to,
their frames and stools were covered with ink, to destroy
their dresses unawares, the letters were mixed up in their
boxes. Men who were induced to come into the office to
work the presses and teach the girls had to assume false
names to avoid detection, as the printers' union forbade
aiding their obnoxious scheme...'*

A SELF-RESPECTING THOROUGHFARE called Great
Coram Street – long ago cut short by developers, and now
merely Coram Street – used in the mid nineteenth century to run through the London district of Bloomsbury as far as
Brunswick Square. Here, at the eastern end, there would gather
every weekday morning for some years in the 1860s a diligent
platoon of young women who in the view of many in the neighbourhood should not have been there.

They were training to be compositors in the printing trade.
Some who noted their morning musterings with distaste would
have believed, with the then fashionable poet and social philosopher Coventry Patmore, that the role of a woman should be, in the
term he used as a title for his most famous book, that of an 'Angel
in the House' – inspiration, consolation and helpmeet to her husband. Others, from rather less privileged sectors of society, objected
that these girls were stealing work that rightly belonged to men.
Here they were, even so; all eager, and all as the rules of the house

required, not yet sixteen, summoned to work by Emily Faithfull, founder and proprietor of the Victoria Press and engaged on the superfine production of the book that was destined to make the company's name: an anthology of prose and poetry called *The Victoria Regia*, devised, designed and edited by Emily's close friend of those days, Adelaide Anne Procter.

The Victoria Press had emerged from a network of feminist organizations that began with a publication called the *English Women's Journal* and developed into a sorority called the Langham Place Circle, named after the place where they met. Their aim was to see that work until now almost universally regarded as the preserve of men should be opened up to women. That was the impetus for the establishment in 1859 by Adelaide Procter and Jessie Boucherett of the Society for Promoting the Employment of Women, with Emily Faithfull, the boisterous daughter of the rector of Headley in Surrey, who turned twenty-five that year, as its secretary. Despite the group's belief that women were as capable of running such organizations as men, the circumstances of the time required the recruitment of men as allies, and the women enlisted the help of the National Association for the Promotion of Social Science, chaired by Lord Shaftesbury. Six men and six women made up its founding committee; but when a joint meeting of the two groups was held at Langham Place in June 1860, papers written by women were all read to the audience by men.

Starting out as printers of various publications, among them the *Journal*, the Victoria Press soon became a publisher too. Adelaide Procter's book *The Victoria Regia* was chiefly designed to demonstrate the expertise of the Press's compositors, but by seeking the Queen's permission to have it dedicated to her, it hoped to allay any taint of subversion. And the list of writers recruited by the thirty-six-year-old Adelaide further emphasized the organization's status. The most eminent was Alfred Tennyson, who furnished her with a poem called 'The Sailor Boy', but here too were Thackeray, Anthony Trollope, along with his brother Thomas Adolphus and sister-in-law Theodosia, Matthew Arnold, Harriet Martineau and even that decidedly unfeminist figure Coventry Patmore. Leigh Hunt contributed a poem on death, but died before it appeared.

Adelaide included a piece of her own, a maudlin affair about the death of a child, called 'Links with Heaven'. She was already well established as a popular poet and would soon become perhaps the most cherished of all in Victorian England with the exception of Tennyson, the only poet who outsold her. She was always said to be the Queen's particular favourite. The poem that cemented her reputation – though by then she was already thirteen years dead – was called 'A Lost Chord':

> Seated one day at the Organ,
> I was weary and ill at ease,
> And my fingers wandered idly
> Over the noisy keys.
>
> I know not what I was playing,
> Or what I was dreaming then;
> But I struck one chord of music,
> Like the sound of a great Amen...

Try as she might she could never discover the chord again...

> I have sought, but I seek it vainly,
> That one lost chord divine,
> Which came from the soul of the Organ,
> And entered into mine.
>
> It may be that Death's bright angel
> Will speak in that chord again,
> It may be that only in Heav'n
> I shall hear that grand Amen.

In 1877, the composer Arthur Sullivan, whose collaboration with W. S. Gilbert had already given Victoria's England *Trial by Jury* and would soon delight it still further with *HMS Pinafore*, *The Pirates of Penzance*, *Patience* and *The Mikado*, went to say goodbye to his dying brother Fred in Chelsea. He already knew Procter's poem and he now resolved to set it to music. 'The Lost Chord', as he renamed it, became the most pervasive work in the repertoire, sung and even recorded by Caruso and Dame Clara Butt, and a staple of every musical evening when families and friends gathered around a piano. 'Such songs as "The Lost Chord" ', wrote the affectionate chronicler of the age E. F. Benson, who was Adelaide's cousin, in his memoir *As We Were*, 'were accepted as test-pieces for tears...'; though in Arnold Bennett's novel *Clayhanger*, a family begs for mercy when Papa proposes to sing 'The Lost Chord' yet again; and in the twentieth-century revulsion against Victorian England, the poems of Adelaide Procter fell not just out of favour but into virtual oblivion.

'She was the author', wrote Margaret Drabble and Jenny Stringer, sparing her a paltry nine lines in the 1987 edition of the *Concise Oxford Companion to English Literature*, 'of much popular sentimental (and often morbid) verse.' And indeed, for most modern tastes she is unashamedly sentimental and often mawkish. One flinches, turning the pages, in the expectation of yet another contingent of angels, yet another evocation of suffering, yet another suffusion of cloying piety, yet another encounter with death. Death, though, is not an occasion of fear for Procter; often it is to be welcomed. Mothers long for the deaths of their children, as they do in the poem she includes in *The Victoria Regia*, and understandably so when the circumstances of life for a great many children were so utterly and irredeemably wretched. Death will be not just escape but the moment of transposition into a higher and happier existence. Often Procter, like Keats, seems 'half in love with easeful death'.

Yet to relegate Adelaide Procter to the ranks of the merely morbid and mawkish is a bit like writing off William Wordsworth as clumsy and lumpish on the grounds that he sometimes perpetrated such lines as 'Spade! with which Wilkinson hath tilled his lands!' There is far more to Adelaide than a penchant for wallowing in suffering and misery. The best of her writing is honest, direct, full of irony spilling over at times into a mordant bitter sarcasm. Take the poem 'A Parting', one of several suggesting rejection in love, which begins:

> Without one bitter feeling let us part—
>   And for the years in which your love has shed
>   A radiance like a glory round my head,
> I thank you, yes, I thank you from my heart.
>
> I thank you for the cherished hope of years,
>   A starry future, dim and yet divine,
>   Winging its way from Heaven to be mine,
> Laden with joy, and ignorant of tears…

But continues:

> Yet how much more I thank you that you tore
>   At length the veil your hand had woven away,
>   Which hid my idol was a thing of clay,
> And false the altar I had knelt before.
>
> I thank you that you taught me the stern truth,
>   (None other could have told and I believed,)
>   That vain had been my life, and I deceived,
> And wasted all the purpose of my youth.
>
> I thank you that your hand dashed down the shrine,
>   Wherein my idol worship I had paid;
>   Else had I never known a soul was made
> To serve and worship only the Divine.
>
> I thank you that the heart I cast away
>   On such as you, though broken, bruised, and crushed,
>   Now that its fiery throbbing is all hushed,
> Upon a worthier altar I can lay.

No soppiness there. There's a mixture in Adelaide Procter of the soft and the genuinely tough, reflecting perhaps the very differing characters of her parents – 'a lemon and honey partnership' as it was said. Her father, the B. W. Procter and Barry Cornwall (his pseudonym) of *The Victoria Regia*, to whom she was devoted, was a friend of several great writers but was himself a poet of limited talent or consequence, who turned to the law and specialized in cases of lunacy. His was the honey side of her inheritance. The lemon came from her mother, Anne, a tough and spirited woman, the friend in her youth of Shelley, Byron and Keats and later of Hardy, but possessed of a sometimes acerbic and quite often wounding tongue. 'Our lady of bitterness', somebody called her, and that caught on.

The wealth of talented and sought-after writers whom Adelaide was able to muster for *The Victoria Regia* was to some extent a mark of the broadness and eminence of her parents' circle, but it clearly also reflected respect for Adelaide too; she had from the start rejected the temptation to trade on her parents' connections. Some of her earliest work was published in *Household Words* by Charles Dickens. To be certain that it was judged on its merits, and not favoured because her father and Dickens were friends, she submitted it under a pseudonym, Mary Berwick. It was only when Dickens, on a visit to the Procter household, began to enthuse over Mary's qualities that her true identity was revealed.

In a tribute to her after her death, printed in a book of her work called *Legends and Lyrics*, Dickens mused with regret on the impression that some of her poems gave of a gloomy, despondent person. Not at all, he said, this was a woman of great humour, generosity and vivacity – and one who rejected mere contemplation in favour of practical action: 'always impelled by an intense conviction that her life must not be dreamed away, and that her indulgence in her favourite pursuits must be balanced by action in the real world about her, she was indefatigable in her endeavours to do some good' – visiting the sick, sheltering the homeless, teaching the densely ignorant, raising up those trodden under foot, and pursuing new job opportunities for women.

This last was a side of Adelaide Procter largely unknown to many who reverenced her memory as the author of 'A Lost Chord'. One aspect of that was her part in helping to run a Catholic refuge for the homeless in a street behind Finsbury Square, Providence Row. The proceeds of her last book of poems, *A Chaplet of Verses*, went to this cause. The other was her intense and controversial involvement with the feminist activists of Langham Place and the printing press in Great Coram Street.

Any woman who worked in an organization like the Victoria Press had to be ready for battle. The London printing trade seemed determined to stop the exercise. As Gladstone, one of their dedicated supporters, wrote: 'The printer's monopoly is a powerful combination, which has for its first principle that no woman shall be employed – for reasons obvious enough – viz., that women are admirably suited to that trade, having a niceness of touch which would enable them, to handle type better than men.' Bloomsbury's girl compositors, Emily Faithfull would later record, were subject to all kinds of persecution. 'Tricks of a most unwomanly nature were resorted to, their frames and stools were covered with ink, to destroy their dresses unawares, the letters were mixed up in their boxes, and their cases were emptied of "sorts". Men who were induced to come into the office to work the presses and teach the girls had to assume false names to avoid detection, as the printers' union forbade aiding their obnoxious scheme.'

The unions were especially keen to deny any woman a place in their ranks for fear that this might open the way to more general female employment. 'If it were not for the union in London,' one of its organizers boasted, 'I venture to think that women would be all over the London trade. Fortunately, the London union has been strong enough to keep them out.' The Victoria Press was awarded a royal warrant; Emily was appointed Printer and Publisher in Ordinary to the Queen; and the jurors of the International Industrial Exhibition in London in 1862 – a far less successful repeat of the Great Exhibition of 1851 – awarded it a medal for good printing. Yet even Adelaide seems sometimes to have had her moments of doubt about their employees' competence: 'the women', she once noted, 'are enough to make anyone swear. I would not have believed how careless they are – such disgraceful carelessness.'

Adelaide herself, one may take it, would not have sworn, even under such trying circumstances. Though few of her poems preach – only one ever made the hymnbooks – they are often suffused in religion. Adelaide was a Catholic convert, a move which two of her sisters followed, one becoming a nun. It is fair to call her devout. Yet her personal life took her into a world where religious teachings were sometimes ignored or defied, among people whom God-fearing folk must surely have regarded as indefensibly louche. Though Queen Victoria was held to be totally unaware of such matters, there was avid speculation about the sexuality of some of this sisterhood.

In 1864, Emily Faithfull found herself at the heart of a first-class scandal when Admiral Sir Henry Codrington sued his wife for divorce. He accused her of misbehaviour with a number of men, and particularly with an officer in the guards called Anderson, while his wife counter-claimed that the admiral had misbehaved while posted to Malta with a Mrs Watson. The admiral was deeply suspicious of Emily, believing her to have helped his wife arrange meetings with her lover. Perhaps worse, he'd become aware that during his absences, Emily and Lady Codrington had shared a bed – a practice which, his wife had attested, helped with her asthma.

His wife's lawyers had intended to call Emily as a witness. She had signed an affidavit that said that one night when she and her friend were in bed together the admiral had entered the room and attempted to make an assault on her, offering the explanation that he'd come in to look for the poker. But when the day came to testify, Emily could not be found. There were various fevered speculations as to the reason. The most prevalent, and the one advanced by the poet Robert Browning, who took a close, not to say prurient, interest in the proceedings, was this: that the Admiral had entrusted his brother, a general, with a sealed package, to be opened if things went badly, casting fresh light on what had been going on during Emily's tenancy of the marital bed. In time, the missing witness returned from her flight abroad, but she now caused a further sensation by appearing as witness not for the wife but for the husband, saying the affidavit to which she had put her name was prepared by Lady Codrington and her lawyer, a Mr Few, and she'd signed it without even reading it.

This was a queasy moment for the Victoria Press. The case had been widely and lipsmackingly reported and it was feared it might cost the press its royal endorsement. That fear was misplaced, but the episode lost Emily some of her friends, and may have been the reason why, as the information about the Codrington menage came to light, Adelaide too now broke with her. Yet it could not be said that Adelaide took a high-handed moral approach to imputations of lesbian practice. One of her closest friends from the Langham Place days was a woman called Matilda Hays, a Creole, who was known as Max or Matthew, and who, as Elizabeth Barrett Browning put it, 'dressed like a man down to the waist'. Matilda had earlier been involved with a famous American lesbian actress called Charlotte Cushman, in a relationship that ended in 1857 in messy litigation.

Some of Adelaide's poems, notably 'A Parting', quoted above, suggest close relationships with men that might have led to marriage, only to end in betrayal, and at one point Thackeray told his daughters that Adelaide was engaged. Precisely what she felt for Max/Matthew/Matilda Hays is likely to remain forever a mystery. But she dedicated *Legends and Lyrics* to her, quoting Emerson: 'Our tokens of love are for the most part barbarous. Cold and lifeless, because they do not represent our life. The only gift is a portion of thyself. Therefore let the farmer give his corn; the miner, a gem; the sailor, coral and shells; the painter, his picture; and the poet, his poem.' A poem of Adelaide's called 'A Retrospect', formally addressed to Hays, reads, as subsequent critics have noted, much like a love lyric. All of which seems to have brought us a long and surprising distance from the woman imagined by most of those in Victorian England who so reverently sang 'The Lost Chord'.

As she neared her late thirties, Adelaide's health began to decline.

Friends, Dickens included, feared she was overtaxing herself, but she would not listen. From the autumn of 1862, she was confined to bed, suffering from tuberculosis. In his introduction to her *Legends and Lyrics*, Dickens described her death:

> At length, at midnight on the second of February, 1864, she turned down a leaf of a little book she was reading, and shut it up...
>
> She quietly asked, as the clock was on the stroke of one:
>
> 'Do you think I am dying, mamma?'
>
> 'I think you are very ill tonight, my dear.'
>
> 'Send for my sister. My feet are so cold. Lift me up!'
>
> Her sister entering as they raised her, she said: 'It has come at last!'
>
> And with a bright and happy smile, looked upward, and departed.

She was thirty-nine. After all, as Dickens, no stranger to sentimentality, noted, she had once written:

> Why shouldst thou fear the beautiful Angel, Death,
> Who waits thee at the portals of the skies,
> Ready to kiss away thy struggling breath,
> Ready with gentle hands to close thine eyes?
>
> ...
>
> Oh, what were life, if life were all? Thine eyes
> Are blinded by their tears, or thou wouldst see
> Thy treasures wait thee in the far-off skies,
> And Death, thy friend, will give them all to thee.

The Victoria Press had by now left Great Coram Street for Farringdon Street in search of premises where it could install a steam press. Although it had won the public approval of the Queen, its finances were never secure. In the year of Adelaide's death – which was also the year when the Codrington divorce case came to court – Emily was reluctantly driven to share its ownership with a printer called William Head, who bought her out three years later. It continued to confine employment to women, but a further takeover in 1881 put paid even to that.

Emily went on to a celebrated career as a lecturer both at home and in the United States. She championed a kind of qualified feminism, esteeming marriage as the highest state a woman could aim for, even if she herself, as obituarists like to say, 'never married', and ended her life in Chorlton-cum-Hardy with a companion called Charlotte Robinson, described as 'home art decorator to Her Majesty', to whom she left almost all her possessions. Curiously she also maintained that women should not play any musical instrument that did not allow them to make some display of their lips, a doctrine that if universally honoured would have precluded women seating themselves at organs and possibly rediscovering Adelaide Procter's lost chord.

Male compositors continued with great success to resist the employment of women. When I worked at the *Guardian* in the final days of hot metal printing, the management made occasional futile efforts to get rid of this barrier, but these were always opposed by union representatives, often on the grounds that no suitable lavatories existed that women could use. Other more realistic objections – the consequent need to abandon the practice where the unions controlled admission to the job on almost dynastic lines, and the need it implied for men working in the presence of women to temper their language – were not, for some reason, cited.

15

BLACKBURN

*This had, said the borough's Conservative MP Mr
Coddington, been the greatest victory that the people of
Blackburn had ever achieved. Gentlemen who had
everything they needed in life to assist them had finished
second best to working men.*

THE HOLE I'TH WALL PUBLIC HOUSE, Shear Brow,
at the top of a very sharp hill out of Blackburn, on a Sunday afternoon in February 2010. At one end of the bar,
with half a dozen men clustered around it, there's a monster TV
screen showing a match in which Tottenham Hotspur – a team
worth millions of pounds, including players from Brazil, Croatia,
Honduras, Cameroon and Russia – are taking on Everton – also
worth millions of pounds, with stars from the Netherlands, France,
Spain, Nigeria, South Africa and the US. Next to the screen, in
modest obscurity, you might just make out two small plaques,
commemorating a far greater football occasion, plotted more than
a century back in this pub, and practised for on a ground which
was then alongside the Hole i'th Wall, but is now buried under
college buildings: a defeat of the South by the North, of toffs by
humble toilers, of gallant amateurs by gutsy local virtual professionals as, against all the odds, Blackburn Olympic defeated the Old
Etonians in the FA Cup final of 1883.

Association football in England had two separate origins: the

Football Association (founded 1863) and the Football League (1888). The game as presided over by the Association was overwhelmingly southern and overwhelmingly gentlemanly. You played with the people you'd known at school or in your regiment rather than those drawn from the place where you lived. The pattern of play was individualistic as opposed to collective: a player was expected to take on the opposition with his clever dribbling skills rather than depending on interplay between team-mates threading the ball around. Though clubs often began paternalistically, with the efforts of churches to find sinless occupations for potentially sinful young men, the game in the North was essentially working class, rugged, firmly moored to particular towns, full of collective endeavour, and unshocked by the thought that people who showed exceptional skills and whom people were willing to pay good money to watch might quite decently be paid for their efforts.

The record of early cup finals charts the origins of the southern gentleman's game: in the first, in 1872, the Wanderers versus the Royal Engineers; in the second, the Wanderers against Oxford University; in the third, the University against the Engineers. Thereafter, it was the Engineers against the Old Etonians; then the Wanderers against the Etonians; then the Wanderers against the University; then the Wanderers against the Engineers. In 1879 the Etonians defeated the Clapham Rovers, but few of these Rovers came from the back streets of Clapham. Next year, the Rovers beat the young sprigs of Oxford; the year after that, 1881, the old boys of Charterhouse had a thumping win over those who had emerged from the playing fields of Eton.

Contrast that with the earliest years of the League, the creation of which for the season 1888–9 was directly linked to the events at Kennington Oval in the final of 1883. Half of its dozen clubs came from the North, the other half from the Midlands. When at the start of the 1892–3 season the League was split into two divisions, nine of the top sixteen came from the North, seven from the Midlands. It was ten years before a team from the South appeared as Arsenal benefited from the expansion of the lower division from twelve to fifteen clubs. They were still the only team from the South at the start of the new century in 1901; it was not until 1905 that a second club from the South was admitted – Leyton Orient – and they finished bottom. Indeed, as late as the league's 25th season in 1913–14, only six of the participants (Chelsea, Spurs, Arsenal, Orient, Fulham, all from London, and Bristol City, from the south-west) came from the south of England, against ten from the Midlands and twenty-four from the north.

The first northerners to break the southern monopoly of the FA Cup final came from Blackburn: the town's premier side, the Rovers, finalists in 1882, a team with a solid contingent of grammar school products, a much more socially privileged outfit than that which emerged from the Hole i'th Wall, but not quite good enough for the Old Etonians, who beat then 1-0. Blackburn Olympic, the finalists of the following season, were not even rated the best team in Blackburn, let alone in the county of Lancashire, where they were hardly to be mentioned in the same breath as such local giants as Darwen and Preston North End. They had played since their formation in 1878 on a rough and ill-equipped ground with a meagre and muddy pitch close to the pub they were born in. But that was before the team was taken in hand by the owner of a foundry in Birley Street, Sydney Yates, who was willing and able to finance the club. 'It is a sobering thought', says Blackburn Olympic's historian, Graham Phythian, 'that the FA Cup run of 1882–3 would have rendered the club bankrupt if not for him.' Yates, one might say, would prove to be Olympic's Roman Abramovich.

Olympic now began to recruit players from outside the town. One crucial signing was Jack Hunter from Sheffield, seven times capped for England and one of the new breed of footballers who thought they deserved to be paid. He had crossed the border from Yorkshire, mainly, it was suspected, because the rules against paying players were so strictly enforced in Sheffield. He became in effect the side's player-coach, teaching them the passing game, which was already well developed in Scotland but less so south of the border and hardly at all in the South. Additionally, he took over as landlord at a pub called the Cotton Tree, close to Yates's foundry in Birley Street. Olympic also acquired at this time a thunderous goal-scoring centre forward, George Wilson.

Though they prospered in the preliminary games of the 1883 Cup competition, few thought they had any chance of succeeding where the Rovers had failed against the privileged top teams in England. In the semi-final round they were drawn against the Old Carthusians. These lordly alumni of a school that numbered among its old boys such eminent figures as Lord Liverpool the prime minister, John Wesley the father of Methodism, Blackstone the jurist, and such writers as Addison, Steele and Thackeray, were on average, it was noted, a head taller than the Olympic side (the northern side's goalkeeper was only five foot six inches tall and weighed less than nine stone); and they demonstrated their sense of innate superiority by strolling on to the rugby ground where the game was staged dressed in expensive coats, drawing on their cigars.

And then they got thrashed. Olympic were two goals up at half-time and added two more by the finish. The Carthusians had failed to allow not just for the Blackburn men's football expertise but also for their assiduous preparation. Yates and the secretary of the Blackburn Olympic club, William Bramham – the nearest thing they had to a manager – had, unprecedentedly, taken the side for training sessions at Blackpool.

This victory put them into the final, to be played at Kennington Oval on 26 November. Their opponents were the Old Etonians, five times finalists, twice winners, and fielding eight of the team that had conquered the Rovers the previous year. The Oval, 230 miles from Blackburn, was the OEs' home ground. These teams came not just from two regions but from two different worlds. The Old Etonian captain, Arthur Kinnaird, thirty-six years old, immediately recognizable by his huge red beard and playing his ninth Cup final, would end up a knight, then a baron, the owner of some 12,000

acres, with homes in London and Perthshire, president of the Football Association, a director of Barclays Bank, and Lord High
Commissioner of the Church of Scotland. He continued to turn
out as a player until he was forty-seven. 'I believe', he once said,
'that all right-thinking people have good reason to thank God for
the great progress of this popular national game.' The goalkeeper,
John Frederick Peel Rawlinson, with a first-class degree from Trinity College, Cambridge, was the son of the Lord Chief Justice of
Madras. He would later become Recorder of Cambridge and
Unionist MP for the University.

Percy de Paravicini was the son of a baron, an accomplished
cricketer and later a magistrate and a Commander of the Victorian
Order. T. French had a first in mathematics from Oxford. He taught
for a time at Wellington College before being signed up as tutor to
the children of the Maharaja of Baroda. C. W. Foley, a graduate of
Cambridge, emigrated to India too, where he practised as a solicitor.
John Barrington Trapnell Chevallier, who would become a schoolmaster, married into the Cobbold family and was prominent in the
agricultural life of Suffolk. W. J. Anderson, who had scored the goal
that sank Rovers in the final of the previous year, served in the war
in South Africa and died there in 1903.

H. C. Goodhart would progress from a lectureship at his old college, Trinity, Cambridge, to the chair of Humanity and subsequently
that of Latin at Edinburgh University. Reginald Heber Macaulay,
who collected a first-class degree at King's College Cambridge, made
his name first as an athlete and then as a merchant in London and
Bombay. H. W. Bainbridge, another Cambridge man and a cricketer
for his university and for Surrey and Warwickshire, joined an iron
and steel company in the Midlands. Arthur Tempest Blakiston Dunn,
also of Trinity, Cambridge, ran a prep school, Ludgrove, which
prepared boys for Eton, until his premature death in 1902. He's
commemorated in the competition for the Arthur Dunn Cup for
which public school sides still compete, though with less attention
than they did when the London newspapers still covered their finals.

There could hardly have been a more arresting contrast with the players of Blackburn Olympic. One of them, the captain, was known as Squire Warburton, but Squire was his given name, not an indication of status; he was a plumber, pub landlord and poulterer. The rest were a dentist (the tiny goalkeeper, Hacking – though some accounts call him a dental assistant), three weavers, a spinner, a cotton mill operative, a foundry worker, a licensee (Hunter), a picture framer, and a clerk. Most would never have been to London before.

Through the week before the final, Blackburn was in a ferment. 'Telegrams will be received every few minutes at Hunter's Cotton Tree Inn', an advertisement in the *Blackburn Standard* promised, while the Sun at Astley Gate offered updates every twenty minutes. Yet, confirming the suspicion that the F A Cup was a southern invention, the *Standard's* football writer 'Free Kick' discerned an even more avid interest in the Lancashire Cup final, Rovers v. Darwen. Part of that came from people's awareness that Olympic were destined to lose in London. Free Kick thought Blackburn ought not to be too disconsolate: 'though the Olympians may fail, as did the Rovers, to wrest the Cup from the Londoners, the honour achieved by running into the final should be sufficiently great as to ensure for the light blues a class of fixture next season as will bring the Olympic exchequer an amount of gate money which will preserve them from the unpleasant position of being in debt.'

Eight thousand spectators, of whom perhaps 700 had travelled by special train from the North, made their way to Kennington to witness the confrontation. The Etonians dominated the early stages, effectively locking out the dangerous goalscorer Wilson, and took a half-time lead with a goal by Goodhart. It looked every bit like Cup final business as usual. Yet the second half saw the Etonians no longer looking invincible, and three minutes after the restart Olympic levelled the game with a goal by Matthews. Perhaps what did most to turn the outcome was an injury to Dunn, whose refusal to part with the ball had irked some spectators. He was tackled out of the game by the young Blackburn full back Ward, leaving the favourites, in these days long before the admission of substitutes, to hang on with ten men. With Goodhart developing cramp and Macaulay jarring a knee that made them even more vulnerable.

At the final whistle the score was one-all. Some of the Old Etonians expected a replay, but it now transpired that Kinnaird had promised Olympic that the match would go into extra time, so as not to drag Olympic's players away from their work yet again. It appears that his players had not been consulted: Reginald Macaulay said many years later he'd learned of it 'to my horror' only after the whistle blew for full time. It was not, even so, without precedent. The finals of 1875 and 1876, in both of which the Old Etonians featured, and in both of which Kinnaird played, went to extra time before a replay, and extra time was played again in 1877 when the Wanderers defeated Oxford University. But this time it was fatal for the Etonians. With their men labouring, Jimmy Costley of Blackburn coasted through the southerners' defence to achieve a historic victory.

Some of the gentleman supporters of Eton did not trouble to hide their resentment. 'So great was their ambition to wrest the Cup from the holders', the next edition of the *Eton College Chronicle* complained, 'that they introduced into football play a practice which has excited the greatest disapprobation in the South.' The *Chronicle* had heard of their seaside excursions. Yet in its view it was their own team's overwhelming superiority that probably cost them the match. It made them take things too casually, an error for which they paid dearly when Dunn left the field, Goodhart got cramp in both legs and Macaulay received 'a nasty kick in the knee'.

The crucial reason for the defeat, however, as the *Chronicle* judged, was the playing of extra time, for which by implication it blamed Kinnaird for his weakness and Olympic for their unsportingness: 'Neither side should have agreed to this, as there is no rule to force a Club to play an extra half hour when only one day is fixed for the match; but the Northerners naturally did not object, knowing that their course of training would stand them in good stead, while the Old Etonians did not care to rebel against the decision of the superior body... Considering that after half-time the Old Etonians played with ten men, and that Goodhart and Macaulay were practically *hors de combat* in the last half hour, they did not do so badly.'

Fifty years on, when Macaulay discussed the game with the writer Shane Leslie, who included a chapter on Arthur Dunn in a book called *Men Were Different: Five Studies in Victorian Biography*, the humiliation inflicted by these rough working lads from the North still rankled:

> Blackburn Olympic were not really first class and ought not to have reached the Final. We had every expectation of winning and were on the way to do so, having already scored the first goal, when in the middle of the first half Arthur Dunn put his knee out and we had to go on with ten men. We nearly pulled it off in spite of this. The Blackburn Olympic equalised but we only just failed to get a winning goal before time. I felt no doubt we should win on a replay but to my horror we were told that it had been arranged that in case of a tie we should play an extra half-hour. Our men were pretty well cooked, while the Blackburn men were in strict training and they just managed to get a winning goal.

The Old Etonian gripe was not just that their team had lost their match by being reduced to ten men: what offended them even more was the preparation that Olympic's players had done for the game. Having taken his team to Blackpool before the semi-final, Yates had compounded this unsporting procedure by taking them there again and also to Bournemouth before the final, and also by having them entertained in a hotel in Richmond, Surrey, before the day of the match. Some of those who came to cheer at the Oval had been even more vehement in their condemnation of such north country malpractice. According to the *Blackburn Standard*, 'college and cockney sympathizers of the defeated eleven... with an unwonted exhibition of bad taste, vented their disappointment by openly hissing the Olympic team'. With what was presumably irony, the paper added that such conduct 'was not indulged in, one may fairly presume, by any Etonians'.

The proud town of Blackburn had no time for such nonsense. This, said the *Standard,* had been an event that set not only Blackburn a-talking, but the greater part of the United Kingdom too. It was said that Olympic were lucky, but they had not won by luck, but by superior play and condition. It had been alleged, in the *Sporting Life* and elsewhere, that Olympic had been guilty of brutal play: yet Matthews of Olympic had had his jaw broken by one of the Eton players. These whingeing southern complainers could not justify their slanderous statements.

On the Monday after the match, the players toured the town in a wagonette drawn by eight horses. Thousands came out to cheer them. It was, said the *Standard,* 'one of the grandest sights ever witnessed in Blackburn'. There had been, as ever, this being Victorian England, a banquet to mark the victory, in this case in a restaurant in the West End of London. This had, said the borough's Conservative member Mr Coddington, been the greatest victory that the people of Blackburn had ever achieved. Gentlemen who had everything they needed in life to assist them had finished second best to working men. The captain, Warburton, loudly cheered on all sides, declined to speak, simply bowing to the applause; their worthy skipper, secretary Bramham explained, not being much of a speaker, had asked him to address them instead. A Mr Lund, described as 'an old Blackburn man', said nine tenths of the crowd at the Oval had belonged to Eton, Winchester, Harrow or some other public school. These people had been astonished to find the Olympic side – young, agile, invincible men – belonged to the working class. The absence of Sydney Yates, who had missed the final, was much regretted. He was said to be indisposed.

No doubt Kinnaird and his team-mates consoled themselves with the thought that this had been only one match and their dominance might be reasserted. In fact, what Yates and Bramham, with Yates's money, and Hunter, with his experience, skill and canniness, had done late in 1883 changed the shape of the game in England for ever. The Old Etonians never appeared in a final again, nor any side remotely like them, and no further southern side reached the final until Tottenham Hotspur got there in 1901.

These were good times for the cotton trade of the north-west and the manufacturing towns of the Midlands, and Blackburn was not the only place where men were appearing equipped with the money to fund local teams and eager for the success they might bring to their towns, themselves and their companies. The coming of the professional game, still regarded by some in the South as a form of irreligion, would from here on become irresistible, and on 22 March, 1888, a meeting at Anderton's Hotel in London gave official approval to the paying of players. From now on, professionals would dominate the top of the English game. And one of the casualties of this development would be Blackburn Olympic.

Lancashire clubs commanding even more money than Yates's, notably Preston North End, began to set their sights on Olympic's players. The very methods that had set Blackburn rejoicing did for them before long. It was Rovers, fielding a former Olympic star Joe Beverley, who won the cup the following season, beating Queen's Park of Glasgow by two goals to one, and they won the next two finals as well. Olympic, meanwhile, were sliding towards oblivion. Sydney Yates pulled out in 1884, and although he later returned for a time, his health was no longer good enough and his pockets no longer deep enough to sustain the club he had done so much to promote. By 1886 there was only one player – the dentist-goal-keeper, Hacking – left from their Cup final side, and even he appeared only intermittently. Having earlier cut players' wages, Olympic gave up paying their players altogether in January 1889, and became the genuinely amateur side they had been before Sydney Yates took command. In their last serious fixture, in May, against Everton at Anfield, they had to play Hunter in goal; they lost by six goals to one. They won their last home game by one goal to nil, but that was against a visiting team of soldiers from Ireland. They gave up for good in the following September, bequeathing their ground to a team of railway clerks.

Sydney Yates did not live to see their collapse. In December 1886 the local press reported: 'Mr Sydney Yates, of Wilpshire and formerly of Blackburn, died in Manchester on Sunday aged forty-five' (though in fact the registration of his death says he was thirty-nine). 'He was a prominent patron of the Olympic football club, and when they won the Association Cup the trophy was kept by him. The deceased retired from any part of the business some years ago.' It all seems sadly peremptory. A mere three years on, the memory of 'the greatest victory that the people of Blackburn had ever achieved', and 'one of the grandest sights ever witnessed in Blackburn' was fading already.

16

GILLINGHAM, KENT

❦

*New Brompton could hardly miss the Jezreelites
now. There were concerts in the grounds of Woodlands,
with crowds of up to 2,000 attracted by the quality of the
performances in which the students were prominent. Mrs
Jezreel conducted an orchestra of harpists, piano, piccolo,
and violin; she and James Jershom addressed the audience
on characteristic Jezreelite themes. There would, the
advertisements for such occasions promised,
be NO COLLECTION…*

AT THE TOP OF Canterbury Street in Gillingham, Kent, just off what used to be Watling Street and is now the A2, there's a bus stop sign saying: 'Jezreels'. Why Jezreels? 'Mummy,' one can imagine small children asking, 'what's a Jezreel?' No explanation is offered. But just round the corner, where the A2 begins its descent towards Chatham, there's a building that offers a clue. 'Jezreels Tower Works', says a signboard. This used to be the home of a firm that specialized in worm drives and hose clips, though when I was there in the spring of 2009 they seemed to have given it up, and the place was for sale.

Before that famously destructive decade, the 1960s, this spot was the site of Gillingham's most famous landmark, indeed, some would say the only landmark in a town that offers little to gasp at: an event in those days to make you pause and wonder as you drove down the hill. 'A vast area of urban congestion, with homes, shops and amenities for 73,000 people and practically nothing to look at,' Pennethorne Hughes said of the town in his *Shell Guide to Kent.* 'Architecturally it is a desert...' He did single out the tower – 'a now derelict temple of alarming yellow brick erected but not finished by the Jezreelites, the New and Latter House of Israel'; but by the time the book appeared, it had already gone.

So who was Jezreel? One answer to that can be found in the book of Hosea, where the Lord tells Hosea to go and take a wife of whoredom and the children of whoredoms, and he picks out Gomer, daughter of Diblaim, and she bears him a son, and on the Lord's instructions they call him Jezreel. But so far as is known, that Jezreel never set foot in Gillingham. The Jezreel who did was a man who, when he arrived, was known as James Rowland White, though even that may not have been his real name. White was a soldier, stationed in Chatham, and initially a devotee of Joanna Southcott, the prophetess who in 1814, at the age of sixty-four, made it known that she would shortly bear the child of the Lord, who would be called Shiloh. A succession of doctors examined her and several declared her claim to pregnancy genuine. But two days after Christmas, she died. She left behind a vast number of writings, many in fairly wretched verse, asserting that the redemption that orthodox Christians believed had been brought about by the death of Christ was in fact incomplete. It remained for a female descendant of Eve to challenge the devil to mortal combat. Only then would Satan be finally vanquished.

After her death a succession of men appeared claiming to be her true successor or even to be the son who should have been born to her. One of these, John Wroe, established himself at Ashton-under-Lyne, Lancashire, where he recruited a band of followers. His particular preoccupation – not part of the teachings of Southcott – was with the lost tribes of Israel, who were now, he maintained, to be found in England. He demonstrated his commitment to this belief by having himself publicly circumcized. In 1830 he had to be hustled out of Ashton as the result of a scandal involving three young girls in his flock.

For a time, James Rowland White, the future Jezreel, regarded himself as the new John Wroe, with such conviction that he went to Ashton and told them that this was the case; but they threw him out with contempt, and burned his writings. Posted to Chatham as a soldier with the second battalion of the 16th Foot – the Bedfordshire Regiment – White began attending meetings of the Christian Israelite sect in New Brompton, as Gillingham was then called, announcing that he was James Jershom Jezreel, messenger of the Lord, and requiring the little congregation to listen to him reading extracts from a work he had written in the space of twelve days and twelve nights called the 'Flying Roll' – a title that occurs in chapter five of the penultimate book of the Old Testament, Zechariah, where the prophet reports:

> Then I turned, and lifted up mine eyes, and looked, and behold a flying roll.
>
> And he said unto me, What seest thou? And I answered, I see a flying roll; the length thereof is twenty cubits, and the breadth thereof ten cubits.
>
> Then he said unto me, This is the curse that goeth forth over the face of the whole earth: for every one that stealeth shall be cut off as on this side according to it; and every one that sweareth shall be cut off as on that side according to it.

A roll, not specified as flying, also occurs in the book of Ezekiel, where the prophet is instructed to eat the roll.

New Brompton's Jezreel had deduced that 144,000 people among the remnants of the tribes of Israel, and they alone, would be saved, and that the English would be first in the queue. This, he had calculated, using Archbishop Ussher's then widely trusted chronology of the creation, would be happening pretty soon. The sect's trustees rejected these doctrines and tried to expel him, but most of the membership transferred their allegiance to Jezreel. That he was then posted abroad failed to diminish his hold on them; he simply sent his further instructions from India. And from November 1881, when he was discharged from the army, he was able to devote himself continuously to his mission, which included taking the message to distant lands. In the spring of 1881, a young woman called Clarissa Rogers had been sent to proselytize in America. In December White married her. She was twenty-one; he claimed to be thirty-two, but was probably over forty.

Together, James Jershom Jezreel and Clarissa, who from now on called herself Esther, embarked on a missionary tour funded by American benefactors. Here, and subsequently in Australia, devotees were told to sell all their possessions and come to New Brompton to join them in the order he now called the New and Latter House of Israel. A mission hall was opened, a substantial house called Woodlands was acquired in a road on the edge of the town, and in March 1884, James Jershom opened what he called Israel's International College, where students would be given a Jezreelite education.

New Brompton could hardly miss the Jezreelites now. There were concerts in the grounds of Woodlands, with crowds of up to 2,000 attracted by the quality of the performances in which the students were prominent. Mrs Jezreel conducted an orchestra of harpists, piano, piccolo, and violin; she and James Jershom addressed the audience on characteristic Jezreelite themes. There would, the advertisements for such occasions promised, be NO COLLECTION. But you didn't have to go to Woodlands to meet them. With their idiosyncratic dress and the hairstyles the movement ordained for men (where hair was grown long and then rolled up across the back of the head), Jezreelite devotees became familiar figures in and around New Brompton.

There were also Jezreelite shops scattered around the town. Advertisements among their publications – to be found nowadays in a collection at the Medway archives in Strood – demonstrate their range and variety: a wholesale and retail provision and tea merchants at 152 and 154 High Street; a coffee and cocoa restaurant at New Buildings, Chatham Hill; a boot and shoe manufacturer, a printer, a shoeing and general blacksmith, a purveyor of milk and butter, and a German bakery specializing in 'Vagos' bread. 'We would draw attention', said one of their publications, 'to our Pure Wheat Meal "Vagos" Bread which contains a large proportion of the germ of the wheat and is therefore full of nutrition… also to our delicately flavoured delicious "Mab cakes"…' To which was appended a verse:

> If one *Mab Cake* you should try,
> Soon you'll come again to buy.
> For its flavour is supreme –
> Named from Shakespeare's fairy queen.

Also on offer were 'Jezreel's Magic Polish!! This excellent furniture cream will prove a boon to all cleanly housekeepers'; 'Jezreel's pure orange marmalade'; 'Devonshire cream!! Jezreel's noted clotted cream… supplied daily at Jezreel's Refreshment Room, top of Canterbury Street…' They had infiltrated the West End of London too: Jezreel's stores and tea and coffee restaurant at 126 Great Titchfield Street; travelling bags and portmanteaus at 73-75 Oxford Street.

Most of the hymns at their open services were lifted from other hymnals already in print, but others were clearly their own compositions, on characteristic Jezreelite themes, such as this:

> Oh England! Happy favour'd isle,
> Where God's bless'd will is now reveal'd,
> On which the God of Hosts doth smile,
> *Here* God's elect will *first* be sealed.

Or this:

> Thy promises, blessed Lord, we claim,
> We have all signed the Roll;
> We've signed for Christ, man to redeem;
> We've signed for Satan's fall.

Sometimes they could be quite racy:

> Here is Shiloh, long expected,
> All his children to collect;
> Jesus was at first rejected,
> Now they'll give him due respect.

Or even vengeful, as in a hymn that must have been the work of Jezreel himself, recalling his humiliation at Ashton:

> Woe to the four who sought to destroy my Word,
> Their eyes were holden, they sought not their Lord;
> They hear not the voice, they see not the vision bright,
> Their day is turned into night.

And a few must have been barely singable (try it!):

> O ye remnant of the seed of woman,
> Who have disannulled your cov'nant with death and hell,
> An open door is set before thee, which no man
> Or power of darkness can close against Israel;
> 'Tis the door of immortality, through which
> The three Hebrew children have passed unscathed…

But above all, New Brompton was transfixed by the tower.

★

The tower, like most things in his organization, was a work of James Jershom Jezreel's own unassisted devising. He had aimed to build on the highest point of the hill at New Brompton, but was foiled in this ambition apparently because of objections from the army, and had to settle for a spot just below the summit. He specified its dimensions in the minutest of detail, basing them on the account of the new Jerusalem in chapter 21 of the Book of Revelation. This was not as eccentric an enterprise as it might sound: when Christopher Wren and his colleagues rebuilt the City of London after the Great Fire, they based their designs on so-called 'sacred geometry', some of it taken from the prophecies of Zechariah. It was, however, a cause of constant anxiety and frustration for Jezreel's Kentish builders, who had to persuade him to modify those aspects of his design – even the requirement that the building must be a perfect cube each side of which should measure 144 feet – which they considered impracticable.

It remained, even so, a very grand aspiration indeed, with the outer walls covered in Jezreelite symbols including the Flying Roll, though also incorporating the Prince of Wales's feathers. The heart of it, and Jezreel's finest conception, according to P. G. Rogers, whose book, *The Sixth Trumpeter, the Story of Jezreel and his Tower*, published in 1963, is the essential text for any Jezreelite study, would be a vast and lavish assembly hall, seating a thousand people, with a glass dome and a circular platform which could rise majestically from its moorings, a bit like the Wurlitzer organs which would one day be installed in the grandest of cinemas, and begin to revolve. Jezreelite shops would be clustered around it, and his international college would be relocated close by. By the end of 1884 he was ready for work to begin, in the expectation that it would be ready for use in 1887, the year of the Queen's Jubilee. The cost was estimated at £25,000 (around £1.2 million by 2009 standards) and since even the fund that Jezreel had accumulated over the years from his devotees could not meet that, it would need to be built stage by stage.

And then James Jershom Jezreel quite suddenly died, having broken two blood vessels. It was said in New Brompton's newspapers, and with even more confidence no doubt in New Brompton's shops, streets and pubs, that this was a dreadful blow to the faithful membership of the New and Latter House of Israel who had believed him to be immortal – a suggestion that was also aired in the national press, earning the *Daily News* a fierce rebuke from his widow, who insisted this had never been part of their doctrine. New Brompton turned out in force for the funeral. Little else, the *Chatham and Rochester Observer* reported, had been talked about in the town throughout the previous weekend. Some 4,000 people turned up, only to find themselves shut out, though they hung about until the late afternoon. As it was, the local press reported, the last rites were a modest affair, attended by no more than a dozen of the dead man's followers.

Though the community had until now been treated with a fair amount of respect, there followed a period of turmoil. Some of that was sparked by attacks on the reputation of the dead leader. He was said to have been a dictator – 'the most tyrannical man I ever saw', according to one defector – guilty of subjecting even his wife to his arbitrary discipline. A family where the father had joined the sect described their subsequent sufferings in detail to the *Observer*. It was even claimed that Jezreelite hymns were 'lewd and libidinous', a charge that a plough through their hymnals scarcely confirms.

The movement was destabilized by a struggle for the succession. A man called James Cummings rushed back from the US to address a packed and turbulent meeting, but even his venerable and impressive figure and mighty white beard, much admired by reporters, did not save him from being heckled. Yet Esther was always certain to win. She was still only twenty-four but strong willed, confident and resolute – more so, perhaps than her late husband – and a woman of style and swagger. She saw off Cummings so utterly that he gave up the fight and slunk back to America.

Esther's accession seems to have led to some refurbishment of the prevailing Jezreelite doctrine. To those who had expected that James Jershom would lead them to the promised land, it was now explained that, for all his merits, he had not been quite perfect enough. New emphasis was placed, as it had been by Joanna Southcott, on the role of The Woman who would complete the Christian redemption by expiating the original failings of Eve. There was also speculation that the birth of Shiloh, whom Joanna Southcott had failed to produce, might now somehow be back on the cards. Esther began to conduct herself with notable ostentation, riding around the town in an eye-catching carriage and treating herself to expensive clothes.

She also took charge of the tower. In September 1885 its cornerstone was laid in a four-hour ceremony that gave a prominent place to a woman called Emma Cave who had put up much of the money. The town turned up in fair numbers and reporters were much impressed, especially by the performance of Esther's choir and musicians. The *Chatham and Rochester News* remarked on the elegance of Mrs Jezreel ('under thirty years of age, I would say'). The secretary of the New and Latter House of Israel, Thomas Coope, told the afternoon's visitors that they little knew what was now at their very door. Time, and a very short time, would prove all things. A Mr Mihan, whose long and flowing white beard 'gave him a venerable appearance', explained that the plan of the Tower had been dictated by heaven and begged the attendance to study the Flying Roll.

But the public tolerance, even sometimes affection, which such public occasions fostered for this strange sect in New Brompton's midst, was not going to last, and in June 1887 a prolonged altercation occurred that reached the national press. It involved an American convert called Noah Drew. He had first encountered Mrs Jezreel on her visit to the US before she was married, when he invited her to his Michigan home and paid her expenses. He had joined the Jezreels on their subsequent US tour, and in time had heeded James Jershom's call to sell up and join him in Britain, giving the proceeds of his sale to the movement's funds. For a time he served as nightwatchman at Woodlands. Rooms were found for him and his family over a shoe shop owned by Esther's father in New Brompton High Street. But the unexpected death of Jezreel disturbed him and left him disillusioned. He asked for his money back.

Esther ignored him. Noah Drew took her to court, but the court found for Esther, who now resolved to evict him. The Drews were ordered to leave the premises where they had lived for the past ten years and move to a tiny room in another house in Mill Road. They refused. Other Jezreelites who lived in their house tried to expel them, but Mr and Mrs Drew barricaded themselves in. Noah Drew described to a sympathetic reporter from the *Observer* how he'd been standing guard inside his door armed with a keen-edged American hatchet – a weapon the Jezreelites would have known and feared, he explained, since he'd carried it around in his night-watchman days. A Jezreelite who tried to force his way in had his knuckles smartly rapped with it.

Eventually, an agreement was reached that the Drews should move to Mill Road on better terms than at first had been offered. But that night as he walked down the high street, Noah Drew saw a group of Jezreelites assembled for an open air service. As the *Observer* reported, 'seizing the opportunity which presented itself, the venerable-looking patriarch at once commenced to address the crowd assembled at the spot, and whose numbers rapidly increased as the probability of witnessing "some fun", as it is generally termed, became greater.' Someone brought the old man a chair and he climbed aboard it to continue his outburst. The crowd now became incensed and attacked the Jezreelites, tearing their flag, damaging their musical instruments, and mussing up the men's hair while uttering shouts of 'Who robbed the poor man of his money?' The windows of the house from which the Drews had been ousted were broken, and 'hooting and yelling of every description' rent the air of New Brompton. Eventually – and before a force of police had arrived from Chatham – the crowd went contentedly home. But next morning and throughout the following day, gangs of school-boys gathered around the Jezreelites, some shouting at the tops of their voices and 'heaping many uncomplimentary epithets' on such adherents as dared to show themselves.

The *Observer* interviewed Mr Drew, and – although this was not its intention – his 'very loquacious' wife. Why, he was asked, were Esther's people persecuting him? 'Because,' replied Mr Drew, 'we came out against their delusion, and since then they have treated us as slaves.' 'When we came out from them,' Mrs Drew interrupted, 'it was because of their wickedness and evil ways.' Would Mr Drew care to specify the practices that had so shocked them? No, he could not bring himself to speak of such things – they were too disgraceful. He could say, however, that at the previous Christmas Mrs Jezreel had spent fifty guineas on a sealskin jacket. 'I say it is fanaticism,' he said of the sect he had now forsworn, 'aye, and religious insanity.'

A year later, on 30 June 1888, Esther was dead. She died suddenly and mysteriously – so mysteriously that her doctor had to deny that she had been pregnant, with Shiloh or with some lesser child. The death certificate said it was peritonitis. She was twenty-eight. Some of the sect refused to believe that a second sure source of eternal redemption had now been taken from them, and when they could no longer deny her death, began to forecast her resurrection. As with her husband's funeral, few Jezreelites attended the ceremony, and though the police came in force to try to prevent the crush of that earlier occasion, not many turned up this time from the non-aligned of New Brompton either.

The obloquy that had welled up on the death of James Jershom did so even more fiercely now. Surely this was the time, said the *Chatham and Rochester News*, for this wicked nonsense right on its doorstep to cease. 'It is to be hoped', it declared, 'that the Gillingham absurdity will no longer continue to destroy the peace of families, seduce men from important, useful positions, and produce, as it has done, incalculable evil.' The paper reported the case of a Jezreelite member who, it said, had sold up and given the sect £1,000, only to discover too late its real nature. He had seen naked girls flogged by Mr and Mrs Jezreel, and children flogged also. Other adherents, the rival *Observer* claimed, had been ousted for failure to follow Mrs Jezreel's instructions to fast when her husband died.

Esther, the paper's informants had told it, had been harsher than James Jershom, spying on members and extracting confessions from them. That led to letters defending the recently dead Mrs Jezreel, and extolling her above James, whose role, believers argued, had been to prepare the way for her to occupy the supreme position. When Noah Drew died soon afterwards, the denunciations broke out all over again. Jezreel had been a heavy drinker; Esther had been made miserable by his infidelities; Esther had been a merciless bully, under whose regime life for the faithful had become ten times worse than before. The *Observer* condemned the couple as 'designing rogues'. This time, no one replied. New Brompton was left to assume the worst.

Again there were disputes over who should succeed, with Esther's father and one of her aunts in contention (a nephew whom Esther had favoured was left unconsidered) as well as outsiders, one from notorious Ashton. Work on the tower came to a halt. The walls were complete, but the roof had yet to be added. The venture had cost £30,000 so far, and some of the bills had never been paid. At least £20,000 more would be needed, and the coffers were all but empty. The builders won a court order giving them possession. The increasing rate of defections further eroded the movement's income. The house called Woodlands had to be sacrificed. The builders employed on the tower concluded a deal with a shadowy group of buyers who saw no purpose in saving it. Supporters gathered, the women weeping, as demolition began in July 1905.

Jezreelism was not done for yet. There now appeared out of the west a man from Detroit called Michael Keyfor Mills. While working through the tenth and twelfth chapters of the book of Daniel, he had recognized himself as Prince Michael, that great prince who was to deliver Israel out of its manifold troubles. His first wife had left him after his conviction in the US for seducing a girl of fifteen, though also because of his closeness to a woman called Eliza Court, whom he married on leaving prison. She now became Princess Michael, a character unmentioned in Daniel. He promised to save the tower and reopen the college. Asked how that might be paid for, he said that God would provide. But he fell behind with his rent on the tower and again its doors were closed to the Jezreelites.

It was occupied next by a school of dancing, with which the prince concluded a deal to gain readmission. More trouble followed. When the sub-lease ended, the school closed its doors on him, only to be besieged by a crowd of Michael's supporters who attacked the school's proprietor, a Mr Worrall. His wife's screams attracted a crowd of several hundred, which surged in to rescue her. Prince Michael posted a notice on the door of the studio, which stated that Mr Worrall had started the trouble by tearing down notices that carried the word of God, and trampling on them, and replacing them with posters advertising his dancing school. 'It rests with the people, not simply of New Brompton, but also of England and the whole planet', the prince proclaimed, 'to state whether they will stand for God, His Word, and his Ambassadors, Prince and Princess Michael, or whether they will take the responsibility of justifying that satanic power that will disregard, tear down and trample upon God's Word and thus cause his judgments to descend.'

In court, the defendant told the magistrates he would not remove his notice until ordered to by the Powers. Asked what Powers these might be, he replied that they were the Powers that had given him his authority and the name of Prince Michael. The stipendiary magistrate, Mr Alick J. Tassell, told the defendant to address the court in 'ordinary, not religious, language'. Fining him forty shillings with costs of £1.15s 6d, he said the assault on the Worralls had not been severe, but it had been unjust. If people had strange and extraordinary religious beliefs, that did not entitle them to deal with other people in ways they ought not to. The prince, however, continued to post his notices, including one that said the sinking of the *Titanic* had been prophesied by James Jershom Jezreel and foreshadowed the fall of Babylon. He also ordained 'on orders from the God of Israel' that all Jezreelite shops should from now on close on Saturdays rather than Sundays.

The prince and princess remained in the town for a further ten years, without many further excitements. It was still their intention, they said, to complete the tower just as Jezreel had intended. The prince, according to P. G. Rogers, was well known and well liked in Gillingham, instantly recognized by his exotic clothing, which 'invariably made him the centre of attention as he strode along the streets of the town, followed at a respectable distance by awestruck little boys'. He also owned one of the town's first motor cars, and could be seen enthusiastically working on it in the grounds of Woodlands, which he had somehow succeeded in reoccupying, even though the council, who owned it, had rejected his claim that God wanted him to have it rent-free.

And then, in the Jezreelite tradition, both the prince and the princess somewhat abruptly died. She was seventy-five, and went first; he was sixty-five, and followed her three days later. No doctor had been called to him: the reason for death was given as heart failure. This time the succession hardly mattered, since so few devotees of the cult of Jezreel remained. The tower, however, survived the death of the prince and princess by some forty years. During the Second World War there were rumours that it would be pulled down because it was such a helpful landmark for German bombers, but nothing transpired. Then the Co-op, which now owned it, offered it to the council, saying it should be preserved as a unique historical relic. The council, contemplating the cost, was unpersuaded.

The only option left now was demolition. That began in January 1960, and proved unexpectedly tricky. 'Never before,' the *East Kent Gazette* reported, 'has such a difficult demolition job been undertaken in East Kent.' A lorry driver was killed by falling masonry, an event which, had he still been around, would surely have impelled Prince Michael to put up one of his notices. The job was not completed until early the following year. When Philip Rogers completed his book there were still a handful of Jezreelites in the locality. By now, death has surely removed them. 'Though aesthetically speaking, the tower was not an architectural masterpiece,' Rogers wrote, 'it had, nevertheless, a grim, brooding majesty that was all its own. It was, also, in the truest sense of the word, unique.

Gillingham had within its confines something of which there was no like anywhere in the world.' There may be few in Gillingham now who know why the bus stop in Canterbury Road bears the name that it does; and soon, perhaps, there may be none left at all.

17

SPITALFIELDS, LONDON

MOSES ANGEL, FORMERLY ANGEL MOSES, IS
IDENTIFIED AS AN AGENT OF THE GREAT
CLANGING BELL OF ANGLICIZATION.

*'And they came in a great straggling procession recruited
from every lane and by-way, big children and little children, boys in blackening corduroy, and girls in washed-out
cotton; tidy children and ragged children; children in great
shapeless boots gaping at the toes; sickly children, and
sturdy children, and diseased children... with great
pumpkin heads, with oval heads, with pear-shaped heads;
with old men's faces, with cherubs' faces, with monkeys'
faces... all hastening at the inexorable clang of the big
school-bell to be ground in the same great, blind,
inexorable Governmental machine...'*

ON FRIDAY MORNINGS, the faithful trudge down
Brick Lane and Fournier Street much as the faithful of
Spitalfields have done week by week since the middle
years of the eighteenth century. But not the same kind of faithful.
When 59 Brick Lane first became a place of worship in 1743 the
congregation were Calvinists, refugees from Catholic persecution
in France: Huguenots, as they were called – a word of uncertain
provenance but probably loosely related to a Swiss German word
meaning confederate. They came, encouraged to do so by British
kings, in search of religious freedom, but in the hope too of rich
returns for their productive skills, above all in the weaving of silk,
but also as hatters, gunsmiths, makers of clocks and watches, and

craftsmen in gold and silver; and settled as close as they could to the city of London, in the area once called Hospital Fields and now known as Spitalfields. In those days the building was known as La Neuve Eglise. Over its door was inscribed the legend: *Umbra sumus.* We are shadows. It is still there today.

Later the immigrant population here were Jews from Russia and Poland, whose freedom to live as Jews, or in times of pogrom even to live at all, had been savagely diminished by Tsarist governments. Still later, Brick Lane and streets around it became the domain of Muslims from Bangladesh. And number 59 Brick Lane was transmogrified too, from Calvinist and later Wesleyan, Christian church to Jewish synagogue to Muslim mosque: not yet with a minaret added, but that had planning approval by the summer of 2009, though only on the condition that muezzins would not be permitted to use it to summon the people to prayer. All that, according to the great modern chronicler of the capital, Ed Glinert, in his *London Compendium*, establishes this as the only building outside the Holy Land to have housed the world's three major monotheistic faiths – Christianity, Judaisim and Islam. Which makes it, though the architecture is humdrum, a place to marvel at.

When the sect known as Machzikei Hadas V' Shomrei Shabbas – a name that proclaimed their strict observance of the laws of the Sabbath – consecrated their synagogue here in September 1898 there must have been a particular cause for rejoicing in view of the purpose to which the building had been dedicated before. When the Huguenots abandoned it, their community having drifted away from their first Spitalfields sanctuary and dispersed across London, it came for a time into the hands of organizations whose sometimes aggressive purpose it was to convert the Jews to Christianity, a pitch they seasoned with generous financial inducements. From 1819 it served as a chapel for Wesleyans. By the end of the century it was unused again. The Machzikei Hadas Society had been founded in 1891 by ultra-orthodox Jews who found the regime of the then Chief Rabbi too lax. They took the chance to move from the mission hall they had previously occupied to a place of their own, and refurbished it at a cost of around £6,000 (equivalent to almost £400,000 in 2010) to accommodate 1,000 men and 750 strictly segregated women. Here, said the *Jewish Chronicle,* reporting the consecration ceremony, was a people's synagogue, built from the mites of the many. The many Jews in the street were 'bubbling over with happiness', while the Gentiles of the locality looked on, half in mute astonishment and half with a feeling of reverence.

And yet the previous week the *Chronicle* had recorded an occasion of grief and historic loss in Spitalfields. This was the funeral at Willesden of perhaps the most remarkable figure in the story of Spitalfields Jews, though one strikingly uncommemorated there today: Moses Angel, for fifty-five years the almighty headmaster of the Jews' Free School in Bell Lane. For those who knew his difficult beginnings, his achievements seemed all the more astonishing. He had started life not as Moses Angel but as Angel Moses – son of the landlord of the Black Lion, Vinegar Yard, in one of the direst patches of Covent Garden. His father, Emanuel Moses, more familiarly known as Money Moses, was transported to Australia in 1839 for his part in the audacious theft of a consignment of gold dust valued at more than £4,000, with the help of his widowed daughter – the sister of the man who became a headmaster – Alice Abrahams.

Moses had been notorious even before this event. The *New Newgate Calendar*, reporting the case, noted that Money Moses's role in trying to dispose of the loot was very much what was expected of him. 'It was pretty generally known,' it observed, 'that he was one of the most daring and successful "fences", or receivers of stolen goods, in the metropolis. The ramifications of his business were well ascertained to extend to every species of roguery which existed in London...'

Angel was well out of the way by the time this happened. A prodigious scholar, admitted to London University at fourteen, he had caught the eye of a gentile benefactor who was training him for the law until his firm collapsed. He next found work as a bank clerk in Dublin. So when his mother Sarah and some of his brothers and sisters followed his father to Van Diemen's Land (now Tasmania), Angel did not go with them. The *Calendar* had noted that during his time awaiting trial, a remarkable change had come over Money Moses. Imprisonment awaiting trial had reduced him to a mere shadow of his former sturdy confident self. Five months after disembarking, Emanuel Moses was dead.

So too, in a sense, was his son. Angel Moses now reinvented himself as Moses Angel, under which name he applied in 1840 for a post as teacher in the Talmud Torah, the religious school that was part of the Jews' Free School in Spitalfields – also taking on in the following year the joint editorship of the newly founded *Jewish Chronicle*. In August 1842, when still only twenty-four, he was installed as the school's headmaster on a salary of £140 a year plus a rent-free house and free coal; at which point he abandoned for good his interest in journalism, and indeed in almost any activity outside the life of the school.

The school had first opened purely for religious instruction in 1732 – a reminder, this, that Jews were settled in this sector of London well before the great influx in the later decades of the nineteenth century – but in 1817 it expanded to offer more general elementary teaching, adopting the name of the Jews' Free School. In 1822, to allow the admission of girls, it moved from Ebenezer Square to Bell Lane. One of Moses Angel's former pupils recalled at the time of the old headmaster's death that when he took over the school, the standard of education had been such that one government official had called it 'a sink of ignorance'. There was only one master: instruction was otherwise left in the hands of the older pupils. The school was open to all those children in Spitalfields who were Jewish and poor. That guaranteed an intake which might have reduced most heads to despair. Once the great East European influx began, almost a third were newly arrived in England, and came from homes where the languages of their homelands persisted and English had never been spoken.

In evidence to an official inquiry in 1871, Angel described some of the local parents as the refuse population of the worst parts of Europe, whose first object in sending their children to school was to keep them out of the way. The population around Bell Lane lived 'quasi-dishonourable' lives by selling things that were not what they seemed, and the children contracted from them many objectionable habits. The school governors came under pressure from formidable figures in the London Jewish community to censure him for these comments; they refused.

Understandably in such circumstances Angel maintained the practice of keeping on beyond the age of eleven only such children as showed appropriate promise. Yet year by demanding year, working with Anthony Rothschild, a scion of one of the country's richest and most powerful Jewish families, who was president of the school, he rebuilt its reputation to a point where government inspectors, Matthew Arnold among them, had nothing but praise for it. As Dr Gerry Black establishes in his history of the school, nothing moved without the head's authorization and scrutiny. He was first to arrive in the morning – on Mondays he came in early enough to set and wind every clock in the school, of which there were more than a hundred. He was last to leave in the evening, having seen his charges safely out into the crowded streets. He kept meticulous log books on pupils and teachers alike. And, despite the demands of administration, he always continued to teach.

He was, as he no doubt needed to be, famously strict and austere. The tributes paid to him on his death are strangely equivocal. Some described him unconditionally as a lovable man – you could not help loving him, the rabbi who gave the address at his memorial service declared, while women teachers who had worked for him were in tears at the funeral. Yet the *Chronicle*, in saluting one who had briefly once been its editor, evoked a reserved and distant figure, regretting that most who dealt with him had never got close to the man; few knew, it said, that what to so many who approached him appeared to be 'a severe, almost repellent character' was but part of the outer man, 'the hard shell covering much generous feeling and even weakness of character'. It linked that with the circumstances – which it did not spell out – of his earlier association with every species of London roguery: 'Proud of having been the architect of his own career, he never could – even in his declining years, when his nature had greatly softened – quite shake off the memory of what he had lived through and had lived down from the days when he stood on the threshold of his promising life.'

There's a glimpse of the softer Moses Angel in Liza Picard's glorious book *Victorian London*, where she describes how he treated deserving boys to a day out at the British Museum and the Surrey Zoological Gardens. They picnicked on a grass verge: 'the children and their bearded, revered headmaster sitting on the grass by the road enjoying their meal together must have been a remarkable sight.'

And the gathering around the grave testified to his unparalleled role in the life of Jewish East London. The Chief Rabbi could not be there – he had gone to Leicester and Leeds to open new synagogues – but other eminent figures were gathered, some of them head teachers whom he had trained. And though, for reasons the *Jewish Chronicle* was unable to understand, the school had permitted only a small contingent of senior boys to attend, there were present, unusually for a Jewish funeral, a number of women, teachers who had served under Angel in the fifty-five years before ill-health at last persuaded him to relinquish his headship. He had built Bell Lane through these years into the largest elementary school in the kingdom, perhaps in the world. He had started with 500 pupils; by the end of his term in office there were more than 4,000. His teaching staff, mostly recruited from former JFS pupils, was now a hundred strong.

On Dr Black's calculations, a third of all Jewish children in London came into his care and under his shaping influence. And his reach across the Jewish community spread even wider than that. 'At a time,' the school's historian writes, 'when it was difficult for a religious Jew to obtain teacher-training experience, JFS operated as a teachers' training college, providing qualified teachers not only for itself but for almost every other Jewish school in England, and indeed for schools throughout most of the British Empire. It produced more recruits for the Jewish ministry than Jews' College. It played a significant part in countering the efforts of Christian missionaries seeking to convert the East End Jews, and made an important contribution to the fight to obtain emancipation for English Jews. It furnished thousands with an escape route out of poverty.'

The influence of Moses Angel was nowhere more discernible than on the crucial issue that helped to shape this community: whether the children who grew up in and around Spitalfields were to remain first Jewish, and then, and only then, English, or whether the balance should be tilted the other way. In the jargon in which these matters are discussed, Moses Angel, reserved, unradical Orthodox Jew though he was, lined up with the Anglicizers. In particular he wanted to extirpate Yiddish, then still the commonplace language of the streets, which to him seemed demeaning and unintelligible. The authorities were impressed. A Board of Trade report in 1894 declared: 'A far more powerful influence [than adult evening classes] for Anglicizing the foreign Jewish community is the great Jews' Free School in Bell Lane, Spitalfields, which, in the spring of 1893, was attended by 3,582 Jewish children... They enter the school Russians and Poles and emerge from it almost indistinguishable from English children.'

Others were less enthusiastic. 'It was the bell of the great Ghetto school,' wrote one of its products, looking back from the 1890s to his own childhood, and nostalgic for a culture that he perceived to be dying, 'summoning its pupils from the reeking courts and alleys, from the garrets and the cellars, calling them to come and be Anglicized. And they came in a great straggling procession recruited from every lane and by-way, big children and little children, boys in blackening corduroy, and girls in washed-out cotton; tidy children and ragged children; children in great shapeless boots gaping at the

toes; sickly children, and sturdy children, and diseased children;
bright-eyed children and hollow-eyed children; quaint sallow for-
eign-looking children, and fresh-coloured, English-looking children;
with great pumpkin heads, with oval heads, with pear-shaped heads;
with old men's faces, with cherubs' faces, with monkeys' faces; cold
and famished children, and warm and well-fed children; children
conning their lessons and children romping carelessly; the demure
and the anaemic; the boisterous and the blackguardly, the insolent,
the idiotic, the vicious, the intelligent, the exemplary, the dull—
spawn of all countries—all hastening at the inexorable clang of the
big school-bell to be ground in the same great, blind, inexorable
Governmental machine.'

The Huguenots of Spitalfields, for whom not many records
survive, are elusive. Little, too, is specifically recorded of the Irish
immigration, especially after Waterloo, which again transformed the
sights and sounds of Spitalfields streets and once more, as with the
Huguenots as they became established, aroused suspicion, envy and
fear in the host community. That is not so with the Spitalfields Jews.
Their lives are documented in biographies and memoirs and in
modern academic studies, notably those of William J. Fishman and
Anne J. Kershen, whose *Strangers, Aliens and Asians: Huguenots, Jews
and Bangladeshis in Spitalfields 1660–2000* is an essential text for
uncovering the successive layers of Spitalfields life. In a book edited
by Kershen, *London – the Promised Land?* Fishman evokes the
coming here of the Russian and Polish Jews:

> Slowly, the narrow streets and cobbled alleyways, once Irish habita-
> tions – their previous inhabitants pressured by the newcomers to
> move towards the docks – filled up with the *landmanschaft* families
> emanating from the same town or village *shtetl* [a word meaning a
> settlement inhabited by Jews, but not necessarily exclusively so] in
> Russia or Poland. They formed their own self-contained street
> communities with workshops located in the once stately homes
> constructed by bourgeois Huguenot merchants and despoiled by
> the 19th century transient slumfolk. On Fridays, the even of *Shabbat*

(Jewish Sabbath) the cloistered thoroughfares came to life as candles blazed from the front parlours of the surrounding shabby, three tiered tenements and congested rookeries. During the week they laboured at the tailor's bench or behind the machines of the sweatshops geared to the production of cheap clothing and boot making: the newcomers, *greeners*, sometimes sleeping on those very benches and breathing in the fetid air accumulated during the day.

You can also find the story of Jewish prevalence in the dry pages of street directories for Spitalfields in the second half of the nineteenth century. Here is Bell Lane in 1891, as the headship of Moses Angel was drawing towards its close:

> Jews' Free School
> London General Omnibus Co. Limited
> Netherlands Musical and Dramatic Club
> 6–7 Goldberg, David, shoemaker
> 7 Haimsohn, David, baker
> 8 Angel Wolff and Simon, butchers
> 7a Goldberg, Davis, chandler's shop
> 8a Jacobs, Ezra, butcher
> 11 Freedman, Solomon, glasscutter
> 12 Goldman, Solomon, chandler's shop
> 13 Phillips, Isaiah, pastry cook
> 15 Simmons, George, confectioner
> 16 Reed, Leonard, butcher
> 16a and 17a Frost, Nathan, flour factor
> 17 Heiser, Abraham, china etc dealer
> 18 Bernel, David, butcher
> 22 Davis, Moss, egg dealer

In neighbouring Wentworth Street, with its Abrahams, Solomons, Hyams, Goldbergs and multiple Cohens, the pattern is much the same.

Yet to get the fullest sense of those times you need even more the rich epic novel by Israel Zangwill, product of the Jews' Free

School, the writer for whom a few pages back the Anglicizing notes of the bell seemed to toll for a culture that would soon be no more. Here, in his *Children of the Ghetto*, are the noise and the clamour of the streets, the vivid and thrustful markets, the noisy, packed-full, unsalubrious houses once occupied by single Huguenot families and now by what seems like swarming congregations of Jews. Number 1, Royal Street, for instance, where at the start of the book we meet the twelve-year-old Esther Ansell, doing her anxious best to cope with the role of mother to the motherless family of her father Moses – a figure whom, like Zangwill's own father, cannot make much of his life:

> Yet Moses always made loyal efforts to find work. His versatility was marvellous. There was nothing he could not do badly. He had been glazier, synagogue beadle, picture-frame manufacturer, cantor, pedlar, shoemaker in all branches, coat-seller, official executioner of fowls and cattle, Hebrew teacher, fruiterer, circumciser, professional corpse-watcher, and now he was a tailor out of work.

The Ansells – father, children and elderly, querulous grandmother – live in the attic at the top of the house:

> No. 1 Royal Street had been in its time one of the great mansions of the Ghetto; pillars of the synagogue had quaffed *kosher* wine in its spacious reception rooms, and its corridors had echoed with the gossip of portly dames in stiff brocades. It was stoutly built and its balusters were of carved oak. But now the threshold of the great street door, which was never closed, was encrusted with black mud, and a musty odour permanently clung to the wide staircase and blent subtly with far-away reminiscences of Mr. Belcovitch's festive turpentine.
>
> The Ansells had numerous housemates, for No. 1 Royal Street was a Jewish colony in itself, and the resident population was periodically swollen by the 'hands' of the Belcovitches, and by the Sons of the Covenant, who came to worship at their synagogue on the ground floor. What with Sugarman the Shadchan on the first floor, Mrs. Simons and Dutch Debby on the second, the Belcovitches on

the third, and the Ansells and Gabriel Hamburg, the great scholar, on the fourth, the door-posts twinkled with *Mezuzahs* – cases or cylinders containing sacred script with the word *Shaddai* (Almighty) peering out of a little glass eye at the centre... Thus was No. 1 Royal Street close-packed with the stuff of human life, homespun and drab enough, but not altogether profitless, may be, to turn over and examine; so close packed was it that there was scarce breathing space.

Zangwill knows that the ghetto is doomed, and recognizes that it should be, but like Esther, who escapes it, only to find herself driven back to it when trapped in adulthood in the milieu of enlightened prosperous Anglicized Jewry, he still feels its strange allure. He is fascinated by the scholarly disquisitions and debates of otherwise humble men living cramped and discomfiting lives and often scraping what money they can in the sweatshops of Jewish tailoring. He seems even to envy the pleasure they find in the rituals of religion, sometimes more crucial and satisfying than the religion itself – the prescribed rules of worship, of diet, of dress. That emerges most vividly in his account of the informal synagogue created on the ground floor of 1 Royal Street by a group who style themselves The Sons of the Covenant:

> They prayed metaphysics, acrostics, angelology, Cabbalah, history, exegetics, Talmudical controversies, menus, recipes, priestly prescriptions, the canonical books, psalms, love-poems, an undigested hotch-potch of exalted and questionable sentiments, of communal and egoistic aspirations of the highest order... And the method of praying these things was equally complex and uncouth, equally the bond-slave of tradition; here a rising and there a bow, now three steps backwards and now a beating of the breast, this bit for the congregation and that for the minister; variants of a page, a word, a syllable, even a vowel, ready for every possible contingency...

The most devout of the Sons of the Covenant will not even cross his Ts when he writes a letter, for fear that he might seem to be making the sign of the Cross.

Older Jews like these remained resistant to the pressures of Anglicization applied by an Anglo-Jewish establishment desperate to keep its poor and needy brothers and sisters in line in the hope that the host community could thus be brought to see them as assets rather than some undesirable pestilence. That anxiety grew so great that when the great influx began they sought to deter potential arrivals by warning that life in London was scarcely to be preferred to the standard privations of Russia and Poland; but they were not believed.

For the children of such households, however, educated, like Esther in Zangwill's novel or Zangwill himself, out of their class and family context, there were tensions to be resolved, which in the case of Zangwill's protagonists, as indeed for the writer himself, led to a break with the constraints of both the Orthodox and the Reform traditions, and indeed with the sense of pure Jewishness too.

> Esther led a double life, just as she spoke two tongues. The knowledge that she was a Jewish child, whose people had had a special history, was always at the back of her consciousness; sometimes it was brought to the front by the scoffing rhymes of Christian children, who informed her that they had stuck a piece of pork upon a fork and given it to a member of her race.
>
> But far more vividly did she realize that she was an English girl; far keener than her pride in Judas Maccabaeus was her pride in Nelson and Wellington; she rejoiced to find that her ancestors had always beaten the French from the days of Cressy and Poictiers to the days of Waterloo; that Alfred the Great was the wisest of kings, and that Englishmen dominated the world and had planted colonies in every corner of it, that the English language was the noblest in the world, and men speaking it had invented railway trains, steamships, telegraphs, and everything worth inventing. Esther absorbed these ideas from the school reading-books. The experience of a month will overlay the hereditary bequest of a century. And yet, beneath all, the prepared plate remains most sensitive to the old impressions.

As the Huguenots had done, the Jews in time drifted away: not as the Huguenots to scatter through the wider community, their sense of Frenchness almost entirely lost, but to settle in the outlying areas that the expansion of the railways, over and under ground, now opened up to them: Hackney, Stoke Newington, Dalston; Golders Green, Finchley and Hendon; Ilford; and later, even further afield, Stanmore and Pinner – places where, an adventurous few having settled, others were ready to join them. There were no more Huguenot communities; there would always be clearly identifiable Jewish communities, here as in provincial cities like Manchester and Leeds.

That pattern was well established in the first two decades of the twentieth century and accelerated thereafter until by the 1950s Spitalfields might seem to the casual visitor to be barely Jewish at all. There are organized Jewish walks that point out the relics: not the Bell Lane school, since that was largely destroyed by wartime bombs (the school persists as the JFS Comprehensive, in the north-west London suburb of Kenton) but the synagogue-turned-mosque in Brick Lane and the house at 19 Princelet Street where, when it is open (which rarely happens) you can still see the part that served as a synagogue. The itinerary also takes in one or two surviving shop fronts (including that of N. Katz, a shop that sold only twine) and the building in Brune Lane that still bears the inscription 'SOUP KITCHEN' though it's now refashioned offices; and what used to be the Yiddish theatre until someone in the audience, over-convinced by the special effects, yelled 'Fire!', and the audience panicked, and seventeen people died. In the autumn of 2009 one could still find one Jewish shop in Brick Lane: Epra Fabrics, dealing, traditionally, in textiles.

Now, part of that swathe of east London that used once to be called Little Jerusalem (and before that, Petty France) is officially recognized, though not formally yet renamed, as Banglatown – colonized over some fifty years by people from the Bangladesh province of Sylhet. The first were men who came to work for a while and make enough money to build grand lives for themselves back home. When that dream faded, families came to join them, finding themselves burdened with similar troubles to those that the Jews from Russia and Poland had encountered half a century earlier.

Here again, the accounts of diligent academics are filled out and enriched by novels from such writers as Monica Ali. Here again is the poverty, the brutal overcrowding; the wretchedly ill-paid work in cramped and unhealthy surroundings; the comforts and reassurance of the rituals of religion, the distinctive rules about diet (where kosher once ruled it is now halal) and dress, and the institutional subordination of women. Where once the Gentiles wandered in to patronize Jewish markets, now inquisitive outsiders congregate in and around the Sylheti restaurants that punctuate Brick Lane, from the ceremonial arch marking the entry to Banglatown at the southern end to that other Jewish survival, the all night bagel house at the northern. And again, as with the Jews, so with the Bangladeshis: here are the tensions that come from a double identity, and the rival aspirations for an integrated or a multicultural society.

Yet to see Spitalfields as a Jewish ghetto reinvented as Bangladeshi ghetto misinterprets what is happening here. Brick Lane and the streets to the east of it are Bengali Muslim territory, genuine Banglatown. But west of Brick Lane, another immigration is well advanced, of a quite different kind to those before it. Substantial money, often City money, has moved into reclaim and refurbish, restoring the houses of Huguenot weavers in the best of their streets to levels of grace and opulence unknown since they left.

It's too early yet to see whether the Bangladeshi presence here, like that of the Huguenots and the Jews before them, will end in progressive departure. Some more prosperous families are relocating to Essex, but as the first decade of the new century ended it still seemed hard, walking these streets, to envisage the Bangladeshi community being dislodged from its Banglatown. Yet once big money has colonized the streets west of Brick Lane, it will look for new territory to inhabit and to improve. Already the clustered

'Indian' restaurants of Brick Lane, nearly fifty of them now, once largely serving a local clientele, are priced up and pitched at the tourist trail. We may in coming years see an Anglicization of Spital-fields of a kind undreamed of in Moses Angel's day.

And what might then become of 59 Brick Lane? When they left, the Huguenots specified that the building must be used only for the worship of God. That rubric accommodated the Jews and there-after the Muslims. Yet the process one can observe in Spitalfields now might seem logically to predicate a new and entirely different role for it – as some kind of temple of Mammon.

18

CRADLEY HEATH,
STAFFORDSHIRE

MARY MACARTHUR UNSHACKLES THE CHAINS OF
HER MESMERIZED STAFFORDSHIRE WOMEN.

৪৯

'She whirls from meeting to meeting, strike to strike, congress to congress; the street shouting behind the dust and rattle of her car. It is a strike that gives her most congenial theatre for her gifts. She comes to help a huddle of cowed and injured girls and gives them her own confident and indomitable spirit...'

IN CRADLEY HEATH, as black a place as any in the Black Country, they made chains: from the humblest that latched a gate to the chains that held the anchors on the *Titanic*. The great chains were made in factories, under the eyes of employers; the more modest, to the orders of middlemen, known as foggers, in the backyards of meagre cottages, where husband, wife and such children as were old enough to assist would labour away at the roaring, roasting forge. Often the men worked in the factory and the women at home: some of them no more than children, some, because of their poverty, still at work in their eighties: the only retirement for them would be death. Such women worked even in the latest stage of their pregnancies. The son of a backyard chain-maker told the local historian Ron Moss that his mother worked on her chains from six in the morning until six in the evening, gave birth, and went back to work until ten. This was a rough, tough place where people lived rough, tough lives. It seems as one reads of their circumstances chillingly appropriate that the first Staffordshire bull

terriers, born to fight and to kill before crowds, were bred in
Cradley Heath.

From time to time concerned strangers came to the place and
were outraged by what they saw. 'The best forges,' said a parliamentary report of 1843, 'are little brick shops of about 15 feet by 12 feet,
in which seven or eight individuals constantly work together, with
no ventilation, except the door and two slits... but the majority of
these work places are very much smaller, filthily dirty, and on looking in upon one of them when the fire is not lighted, present the
appearance of a dilapidated coalhole. In the dirty den there are commonly at work a man and his wife and daughter; with a boy or a
girl hired by the year. Sometimes the wife carries on the forge with
the aid of her children. The filthiness of the ground, the half-ragged,
half-naked, unwashed persons at work, and the hot smoke, ashes,
water and clouds of dust, are really dreadful.'

They were scarcely less dreadful half a century later when in 1897
Robert H. Sherard published his book, *The White Slaves of England*.
He had found 'a town of the Black Country, where in smoke and
soot and mud, men and women earn their bread with the abundant
sweat not of their brows alone; a terribly ugly and depressing
town...' One saw few old men in Cradley, he noted; lung disease
carried them off at an early age. Yet the circumstances of the women
distressed him still more. 'One may come across sheds with five or
six women,' he wrote of his visit, 'each working at her anvil; that
are all talking above the din of their hammers and the clanking of
their chains, or they may be singing a discordant chorus; and at first,
the sight of this sociability makes one overlook the misery which,
however, is only too visible, be it in the foul rags and preposterous
boots that the women wear, or in their haggard faces and the faces
of the frightened infants hanging to their mothers' breasts, as they
ply the hammer, or sprawling in the mire on the floor, amidst the
showers of fiery sparks... The impediment of children, to mothers
to whom motherhood is here a curse, is nowhere more clearly defined. The wretched woman, forging link by link the heavy chain,

of which she must make 1 cwt. before her weekly rent is paid, is at each moment harassed by her sons and daughters. There is one child at the breast, who hampers the swing of the arm; there is another seated on the forge, who must be watched lest the too comfortable blaze in which it warms its little naked feet prove dangerous; while the swarm that cling to her tattered skirt break the instinctive movement of her weary feet...'

Such conditions are thought of today as 'Dickensian', though Dickens had been in his grave almost thirty years when Sherard wrote, and forty when a new clamour of affronted observers arrived in Cradley Heath to witness the strike of women chain-makers in 1910, in the days of the greatest and most prosperous empire the world had known. The *County Express for Worcestershire and Stafford-shire* – a Conservative paper, but deeply sympathetic to the plight of the Cradley women – quoted someone whom it described as 'an interviewer':

I have been watching some of the work for which the chainworkers refuse to accept less than 2 ½d an hour. In all England you will find nothing to beat the sheer sordid squalor of Cradley Heath. In its slums practically every house has its chainshop, with forge and bellows, wherein men, women, and children toil feverishly forging chains. I went into one of these, where a woman was turning rods of iron into plough chains at the rate of 7s 6d per hundredweight. A baby hung in an improvised cradle from the ceiling, and two other children, sickly and stunted, sat on a heap of cinders on the floor. The chainmaker, without stopping her work for an instant, contrived to keep an eye on her children, and to answer the questions I put to her.

By working 10 or 11 hours a day she could make about 8s. a week, but out of that she had to pay 2s. and sometimes 2s.6d. for fuel... Then she had to pay 6d. a week in rent for the forge, which was not her own. Altogether it was rarely that she cleared 5s. 6d. a week. She began work at seven in the morning, taking an hour for dinner and half-an-hour each for breakfast and tea, and never knocked off until after seven. All the time she was talking she went on busily with her work, beating the rod, bending it into the shape of a staple with two or three quick hammer strokes, and then, having cut off the staple and passed it through the last made link of the chain, hammering the two glowing ends together. Sweat poured from her face and arms as she laboured. Her hands and arms were covered with burns from flying sparks. Occasionally she would straighten herself, gasping for a fraction of a second to let a little air into her congested lungs. I asked her why she did it. 'To pass the time and keep mysel' warm.' She laughed bitterly, and added more seriously, pointing to the children, 'I've 'em to keep and feed some-how, ye know.'

The perpetuation of such conditions was all the more deplorable in that Parliament believed that they had to some degree been remedied. Union agitation about the paltry wages that workers like these were paid had persuaded the editor of the *Daily News* to pro-mote an exhibition on the evils of sweated labour. Makers of arti-ficial flowers, hook and eye and button carders, sewers of sacks and furs, and makers of chains from places like Cradley were paraded, and statistics of their wages and their family budgets displayed. Large numbers came and were duly shocked and horrified. That had led to a Bill being passed that established a kind of rudimentary mini-mum wage for specified occupations. Trade boards were created, with both sides of industry represented, to fix figures for the chain trade, the lace trade, paper-box making, and wholesale and bespoke tailoring.

Conditions were added, however, which had the effect of deny-ing the chosen beneficiaries their promised relief for a time, and in some cases, even for good. Employers were given six months to im-plement the new arrangements. More ominously, they were also given the right to invite their workers to contract out and continue to work for what they'd received before. Forms were enthusiastically prepared, and the women invited to sign them – or rather, since many, perhaps even most, were illiterate, to make their marks; which they did, in substantial numbers, often having very little idea of what they'd agreed to.

The local union leadership in Cradley Heath was quick to mobilize against these practices. Thomas Sitch, now almost fifty, had left school at eight to work in the chain trade. He was now general secretary of the Chainmakers' and Strikers' Association. His son Charles, who had spent two years at Ruskin College, Oxford, was his father's assistant and chief local organizer of the women's campaign, along with Charles Homer, a skilled chain-maker and the Association's treasurer. These two men, the *County Express* reported, were 'hard at it from early morn till dewy eve and a long while after that.' Julia Varley – originally from Bradford, now based in Birmingham – had started work at thirteen as a sweeper in a woollen mill, and had served terms in jail for her part in campaigns for women's suffrage. But none of them, experienced and dedicated though they were, was equipped to give the women of Cradley Heath the kind of dynamic leadership needed to lift and sustain their spirits and capture the nation's attention. Their campaign would never have been so compelling without the energy, drive, and sheer mesmerizing charisma of a woman called Mary Macarthur.

★

Hers, one friend and fellow-warrior later said of her, had been 'a panting, breathless life, sustained with unfaltering verve, courage and determination to achieve'. She had been, from her earliest days, a whirlwind: ambitious ('I must, I will be famous,' she wrote in a childhood diary), too strong-willed and restless to do well at school, and feeling herself trapped in the home of her father, a draper who because of ill-health had moved from Glasgow to Ayr.

After school she had little notion of what to do with herself. She had founded a school magazine and at her father's suggestion offered to write for a local newspaper. Like her father, the paper was strongly committed to Conservative causes and hostile to trade unions. It despatched her to report on a meeting of the shop assistants' union, with strict instructions to write something mocking. But Mary had done some book-keeping at her father's shop, and had made friends with some of her fellow employees, and as the meeting progressed, she found that, far from wanting to mock, she was eager to join. Her feelings, it seems were reciprocated. The union organizer addressing the meeting, a man called John Turner, had spotted her in the audience. 'I noticed an animated group of young ladies in the centre of the room,' he wrote later, 'with a laughing, vivacious, fair-haired girl in their midst.' He invited her to sign up with the union and, despite her father's expressed displeasure, she did.

Within a few months she was chairing its local branch and fighting her first campaigns against the tyrannical practices of the worst employers in a largely unregulated industry – as the protection given to other workers through the Factory Acts did not apply in shops. Mary rose rapidly through the ranks, becoming president of the union's Scottish section and then in 1903, the year she turned twenty-three, a member of the national executive, serving alongside a woman seven years her senior, Margaret Bondfield, who would one day become Britain's first woman cabinet minister.

She first met Bondfield at a union conference in 1902, when the older woman was immediately taken with this 'tall, slim, radiant girl… gloriously young and self-confident'. Her association with Margaret was crucial in what happened next. Because of tensions at home, Mary resolved to move to London, where she took a job as a book-keeper. Margaret told her she ought to aim higher than that and persuaded her to apply for the post of secretary of the Women's Trade Union League. Gertrude Tuckwell, its honorary secretary and editor of its journal, would later remember Margaret Bondfield introducing 'a tall slip of a thing, dressed in black, very silent, but intensively attentive, with that air of subdued excitement which made one feel the air alive all around her, and herself mentally holding out both hands to adventure, adventure which always came'. Margaret Cole, the Labour historian and politician, says in a memoir of Mary Macarthur that she went through the League's sleepy London headquarters 'like a tornado'.

A union activist called J. J. Mallon observed this whirlwind at work through many campaigns. 'Breathlessness is indeed her dominant characteristic,' he wrote. 'She is always at top speed. She whirls from meeting to meeting, strike to strike, congress to congress; the street shouting behind the dust and rattle of her car. She loves movement for itself and deeds for themselves. In her world life is not contemplated or mused over; it is lived; lived in new hurries, acute emotions, and an ever broadening and intensifying activity. It is a strike that gives her most congenial theatre for her gifts. She comes to help a huddle of cowed and injured girls and gives them her own confident and indomitable spirit… the secret of her oratorical success lies in her power to put herself into elementary communion with her audience.' In two years of haranguing, persuading on platforms, leading deputations, and supporting and counselling women involved in industrial confrontation, Mary was crucial in achieving a 20 per cent lift in union membership, to a total of 70,000.

Most of such women's unions, though, were too small and fragmented to give them the clout they required. Something more comprehensive, and more threatening to their opponents, was needed. 'Women,' she said, 'are badly paid and badly treated because they are not organized, and they are not organized because they are badly paid and badly treated.' The result of that perception was her creation in 1906 of the National Federation of Women Workers, of which she became general secretary. It was from this base that she had campaigned for the legislation, so vital for the women of Cradley Heath, which set up the trade boards and opened the way to a minimum wage.

Her evidence to a Commons committee that considered the Bill drew specifically on her visits to the town, during the first of which she had noted: 'The red glow of the forge fires and the dim shadows of the chainmakers made me think of some torture chamber of the Middle Ages.' The committee asked her to bring exploited women to London as witnesses. In searching for suitable candidates she traced a woman in Nottingham employed in making lace-trimmed garments for which she was paid one penny each. Too poor to buy bedclothes, she would cover herself at night with the baby linen she was stitching. She had incipient diphtheria; and through handling some of the garments, Mary developed it too. But that was a price she willingly paid, for her testimony was seen as instrumental in persuading the committee to come out in favour of trade boards.

It was from this base that she persuaded A. G. Gardiner, editor of the *Daily News*, to commit himself to the London exhibition that had awakened so many to the ugly truth of what sweated labour entailed. Her biographer Mary Agnes Hamilton describes the occasion: 'She broke in on (Gardiner), who had never seen her before, and, white-faced with burning eyes, poured forth her story and appealed for his help. He listened, greatly moved; when, however, he began to suggest some difficulties in the way of the course of action she wanted him to pursue, she disarmed and alarmed him by bursting into tears.' It was then that Gardiner suggested putting the weight of the *News* behind the exhibition that would do so much to propel her campaign to eventual success. So the cause for whose promotion she journeyed to Cradley Heath in the autumn of 1910 was very much Mary's cause.

She had just turned thirty. Margaret Bondfield said of her at this period of her life: 'in the throes of a strike, she seemed aflame, but in preparing and planning her brain was cool and critical'. It is sometimes hard to discern, as it is with those tears in the editor's office, how much in her make-up was purely spontaneous and how much was calculation. One of her notable qualities, as even admirers agreed, was her gift for infuriation. She could be stubborn and difficult, and wounding to those around her. She was headstrong, ill-tempered, imperious. Some with whom she negotiated found her intolerable, notably David Lloyd George, who had to deal with

her in his role as Munitions Minister during the First World War –
though the ill-feeling there was reciprocal: he treated her, she
complained, like a girl.

Her rants and rages did not last long. Both sides forgave and
forgot; even those she'd maligned usually thought these affronts a
mild price to pay for such brilliance of leadership. She had built up
during the London years, and even before, an impressive range of
contacts: Keir Hardie was a friend and admirer, as was Ramsay
MacDonald (whose wife Margaret was until her early death in
1911 an especially cherished friend). She could coax money out
of fat wallets, even those on the other side of the social and
political divide. During the Cradley Heath dispute she managed to
conjure contributions even out of Conservatives in the employer
class such as Joseph and Neville Chamberlain. That enabled the
union to offer a level of strike pay which ensured that the women
were better off than they had been when working.

She had, too, an incomparable gift for getting her way with the
press. At Cradley she offered for interview a woman called Patience
Round, who was seventy-nine, a chain-maker and the daughter,
wife and mother of chain-makers, and had her photographed with
a placard that read: 'England's disgrace! Locked out after 67 years
chain-making'. (The dispute was sometimes portrayed as a lock-out
rather than a strike because some employers refused to give work
to women who would not sign away their rights under the new
legislation.) Patience hugely enjoyed the attention and became an
iconic figure in Cradley. Despite her ravaged life she lived to the
age of one hundred and three.

Yet even above her talent for effective contrivance, Mary
Macarthur offered to a matchless degree vitality, unflagging commitment and perhaps above all a sense of theatre. On the pit heap
from which she preached the cause to the crowds in an area called
Lomey Town west of Cradley Heath High Street, on the marches
and demonstrations she loved, with the Cradley Brass Band in the
forefront, she enthralled and excited crowds and left them bursting

for battle. You can see it all in a photograph now in the possession of the Black Country Living Museum at Dudley. A great crowd of men and women and quite a few children, some of whom have turned away to make sure they are photographed, is gathered outside the premises of W. C. Barker and Sons. The men wear caps and the women bonnets. Someone is flourishing a Union flag. And there in their midst, on her soap box, the cynosure of all eyes, is Mary Macarthur, serene and smiling, under a rather grand hat.

Some of her meetings, J. J. Mallon noted after attending one in Nottingham, 'were the most remarkable I have ever known. Mary Macarthur hypnotized them. The women would devour her with their eyes. Their faces would reflect all the changes in her moods. When she told a funny story their laughter was loud and unending. When she struck a tragic note they were tense and full of apprehension. On one memorable evening – she was feeling the strain of her continuous exhortation, and was a little over-emotional – she plunged a large audience of home-workers into tears and kept them there. Though they wept they were happy. Poverty and suffering had cut them off from the world, but Mary Macarthur had re-established communication and made them feel they were still members of the human family. "Keep on, miss," cried a voice from the crowd when she paused for breath on one such occasion, "it's better than t' seaside." '

John Galsworthy, on an excursion that took him into a world immeasurably distant from that of his well-heeled Forsytes, was present at one of these meetings, and left an unexpectedly emotional, indeed overwrought, account of it in a book called *The Inn of Tranquillity*.

> The morning had been spent at the forges: but at two o'clock began fulfilment. The forges were stilled, and from court and alley forth came the women. In their ragged working clothes, in their best clothes – so little different; in bonnets, in hats, bareheaded; with babes born and unborn, they swarmed into the high street and

formed across it behind the band. A strange, magpie, jay-like flock; black, white, patched with brown and green and blue, shifting, chattering, laughing, seeming unconscious of any purpose. A thousand and more of them, with faces twisted and scored by those myriad deformings which a desperate town-toiling and little food fasten on human visages; yet with hardly a single evil or brutal face... A thousand or more of the poorest-paid and hardest-worked human beings in the world...

The band played; and they began to march. Laughing, talking, waving flags, trying to keep step; with the same expression slowly but surely coming over every face; the future was not; only the present – this happy present of marching behind the discordance of a brass band; this strange present of crowded movement and laughter in open air... For an hour the pageant wound through the dejected street, pursuing neither method nor set route, till it came to a deserted slag-heap, selected for the speech-making. Slowly the motley regiment swung into that grim amphitheatre under the pale sunshine... Silent now, just enjoying the sound of the words thrown down to them, they stood, unimaginably patient, with that happiness of they knew not what gilding the air above them between the patchwork ribands of their poor flags... It seemed to me that in those tattered, wistful figures, so still, so trustful, I was looking on such beauty as I never beheld. All the elaborate glory of things made, the perfected dreams of aesthetes, the embroidery of romance, seemed as nothing beside this sudden vision of the wild goodness native in humble hearts.

The eyes of the world were upon them, Mary Macarthur told the ranks of the mesmerized. She could not recall any strike that had so seized the attention of the newspapers. (Or indeed, in this case, of the cinema: an item on the dispute had found its way, at her prompting, on to the Pathe News.) This had been an essential part of the calculation: to muster public opinion against those who declined to pay a decent and justified wage. And negotiations well away from her vibrant theatre of protest showed how well that had worked.

Most of the big employers conceded from the outset that the

money ought to be paid, though emphasizing the danger that those who agreed to pay would be straightaway undercut by those who did not. The problem was with shopworkers and middlemen – known locally as foggers – who required a sharper persuasion. One, who wrote to the *County Express* complaining that they were being unjustly attacked, suggested that the real trouble at Cradley Heath was that so much was spent on drink. And indeed a great deal was spent out of tiny incomes on alcohol, by women as well as by men; but as Robert Sherard had noted a decade before, the conditions of work made that necessary. The beer they drank was usually a variety known as Burton Returns – 'that is to say beer which has been returned to the brewers as undrinkable by customers more fastidious than the chain-makers'. Before long, though, even the foggers were falling into line as the employers compiled what was called a 'white list', effectively ruling out all further dealings with those who declined to honour the trade board agreements.

That was the breakthrough. The women of Cradley Heath had unconditionally won. It's your triumph, Mary Macarthur told them (though they said it was hers). They had lit a fire that was going to spread all over England. The women working in the brickfields, the nailmakers of Bromsgrove, the lacemakers of Nottingham and all such women workers were going to take heart and encouragement because of the stand made by the women of Cradley Heath.

The continuing effects of what happened at Cradley could be seen the following year when Mary was involved in the prosecution of twenty-one separate disputes in Bermondsey, south London, several over conditions in jam-making factories. Reporters dispatched to the battlefront complained that many of the women employees smelled strongly of jam. When the disputes ended, the headquarters building used for the strike had to be fumigated. Again, impressive sums of money were raised to sustain the women. In eighteen of the disputes, they won.

The following year Mary Macarthur married Willie Anderson, son of a blacksmith from Banff, an ILP stalwart, and one of those who had brought her to socialism. He had first proposed three years earlier, in 1908, only to be rejected on the ground that Mary's causes (and her career) must come first. He persisted, and she gave in. They established themselves in a house in Mecklenburgh Square in Bloomsbury, which served both as home and office, with no one being quite clear where one ended and the other began. An amiable chaos prevailed. Mary continued to work at her usual unsparing pace, even when she found she was pregnant; the child, a son, was stillborn. A daughter, Nancy, was born in July 1915.

Through the war, Mary Macarthur campaigned for decent pay and treatment of munitions workers, in defiance of a chorus of disapproval that contended that women ought to be thankful for a chance to play their part in the war effort, instead of complaining. She was undeterred. 'The methods of the Ministry (of Munitions) in dealing with the whole question of wages,' she wrote in the *Daily News*, 'seem to be simply part of its deliberate policy of placating whatever may be the most powerful interest at the moment. In cases where, driven desperate by over-fatigue and under-payment, women munition workers engaged in vital work have revolted and refused to continue, it has been found possible to do more for them in a few hours than has been done for the mass of silent, uncomplaining women in a year.'

When, after the war, most women were given the vote and the doors of the House of Commons were opened to women MPs, Mary Macarthur was the first to be nominated – as Labour candidate for Stourbridge, just down the road from Cradley Heath. Willie Anderson was already installed, having been elected unopposed in December 1914 as Labour member for Sheffield Attercliffe. The returning officer refused to let Mary be nominated under her maiden name, familiar in Stourbridge; she had to appear on the ballot sheet as Mary Anderson. She lost to a Liberal. To her greater disappointment, Willie lost too. Both suffered for their pacifist sympathies; opponents accused them of having been soft on the Germans. The only woman elected in 1918 was the Countess Markiewicz, who was at the time in prison and who as a Sinn Fein candidate was in any case pledged not to take her seat if elected. No Labour woman would reach the Commons until Margaret Bondfield, Dorothy Jewson and another close friend of Mary Macarthur, Susan Lawrence, arrived there in 1923.

Even so, there seemed every likelihood that, despite her setback at Stourbridge, Mary would be one of the first to succeed. But now she sustained a blow from which she never recovered. The year 1919 brought an epidemic of Spanish flu that is nowadays thought to have killed at least fifty million people across the world. On 16 February 1919 Willie Anderson made an open-air speech in Bradford. The weather was dire. He caught a chill, developed influenza and then pneumonia, and died on the 25th, twelve days after his forty-second birthday.

It was part of Mary's philosophy that even in the face of such a dreadful event one must continue to fight for one's cause. But her friend, the maverick Liberal MP and minister, Charles Masterman, was not deceived by the show she put on. At first, he said, she seemed less bereaved than a hunted thing. She tried to sustain the usual relentless pace of her work, but was taken ill on her way home from a tour in America. Told that she urgently needed an operation, she put it off to fulfil a Labour Party engagement. She appeared, plainly unwell, at the trade union congress at Portsmouth in September 1920, but by now it was clear that her cancer would kill her. She died on the first day of January 1921. She was forty.

There is no way of knowing what she might have achieved had she lived. So clearly outstanding among women trade union leaders, she would probably have surpassed the most successful of the first contingent of women politicians too, including Margaret Bondfield, the first woman Cabinet minister in the Ramsay MacDonald government of 1929. Only Jennie Lee, born in 1904, and above all Barbara Castle, born in 1911, commanded attention as she did. Cradley Heath has every reason to honour her. Not only was the women chain-makers' strike the most celebrated event in its history;

it owed to Mary Macarthur its grand Workers' Institute of 1911-12, built with the funds left over from the money she raised for the strike.

But that building was swept away in a programme of 'improvements' in 2006: struck down with others, including the Christ Church Methodist New Connexion of 1884 and the Whitley Memorial Sunday School of 1911, from the modest collection of buildings that gave some sense of presence and style to the town. They were sacrificed to make way for a bypass, long demanded in Cradley Heath, and a giant Tesco. 'There's a Tesco there,' said a woman I met in the Dudley archive at Coseley when I said I was heading for Cradley Heath, 'and that's just about it.' Redevelopment has taken not just the traffic out of the high street but much of its purpose too. In the summer of 2009 the place had recession written all over it. Some of the charity shops had abandoned hope; even the Lidl store looked deserted – though sure enough the Tesco was packed and bustling.

There's a Mary Macarthur memorial garden in Lomey Town on the site of the slag heap that was her platform, but it's sad and neglected, and its noticeboard offers no information about the woman for whom it was named. A list of 'local attractions' outside Tesco's was chiefly concerned with attractions elsewhere – including her Workers' Institute, which with the help of millennium money was dismantled and taken brick by brick to be rebuilt at the Black Country Living Museum in Dudley. What Cradley Heath needs today, and what every realist knows it is not going to get, is someone or something to clean it up, cheer it up, galvanize it, and give it back something of that uncomplicated pride in achievement that so moved the heart of John Galsworthy a hundred years ago. Even the mightiest Tesco cannot do that.

19

SHOREHAM BEACH,
SUSSEX

MARIE LOFTUS'S INFANT BOHEMIA BECOMES
SIDNEY MORGAN'S LOS ANGELES.

❦

*'The quaintest feature of Shoreham are the bungalows,
most of which consist wholly, or in part, of disused railway carriages. They extend along the beach for about two
miles. Some are arranged with taste, and with their
tall flagstaffs and fluttering pennants present
a gay appearance...'*

THE FIRST TIME THE people of Shoreham glimpsed it over the harbour wall, the sight must have mystified, even alarmed, them: a procession of dutiful, toiling horses haul-ing a railway carriage straight into the sea. Where on earth did they think they were heading for – France? But in time such scenes became quite familiar. The carriages were on their way to join a growing accumulation on the mile-long spit of shingle that cuts Shoreham-by-Sea, at the mouth of the river Adur, off from the sea. Here, as time went on, the carriages would be skilfully tacked to-gether to make bungalows, on a scale that would one day ensure that the place became known as Bungalow Town – a name that ac-quired enough official sanction for it to be bestowed on a nearby railway station.

Precisely how this process began is nowhere recorded. It's usually said in Shoreham that it started with a fisherman who acquired a railway carriage as a place in which to enjoy a quiet break in be-tween bouts of angling. A history of such spontaneous plotland developments – *Arcadia for All: the Legacy of a Makeshift Landscape* by Dennis Hardy and Colin Ward – suggests that the pattern began with a holiday-maker who, having pitched his tent there one summer, returned the following year with a railway carriage. In neither version is the pioneer named. Through the 1880s and 1890s, others appeared with their rolling stock at the ready and set up at intervals down the spit. But what gave this developing colony the distinctive Bohemian flavour for which it was later famous was the arrival, on a date sadly unrecorded, of a decided celebrity: a great music-hall queen of the day – the Sarah Bernhardt of the Halls, as some enthusiasts called her – Marie Loftus.

Loftus was a Glasgow girl, born in 1857, who first appeared on the stage at around the age of seventeen and became a leading attraction in London at twenty, singing sentimental songs ('One Touch of Nature makes the Whole World Kin') interspersed with naughtier numbers. She married Ben Brown, one of a comedy team called Brown, Newland and Le Clerq, and at nineteen gave birth to a daughter – Cecilia, usually known as Cissie. Cissie's career on and off the boards would one day eclipse her mother's. An accomplished performer from early youth, mainly as an impressionist, at sixteen she was entrancing the young Max Beerbohm, and at seventeen eloped with the novelist, playwright, historian and former Westminster MP Justin Huntly McCarthy (described by the *New York Times*, which reported their wedding in Edinburgh, as 'writer of light literature, frequenter of green rooms, and admirer of prima donnas and well known actresses'). She is said to have been painted by Toulouse-Lautrec, and in later days in America played roles that ranged from Desdemona to one of the elderly ladies in *Arsenic and Old Lace*.

Having set herself up on Shoreham Beach, Marie invited gangs of her showbiz friends down from London, some of whom were so impressed that they wanted railway carriage-bungalow homes of their own. The Shoreham historian N. E. B. Wolters, whose book *Bungalow Town*, first published in 1985, preserved much of what we nowadays know about the colony, says that at the Royal Command Performance of 1912, no fewer than twelve of the selected artists had bases here. At least one – the comedian Will Evans – saw a commercial opening, and built not just for himself but for customers, giving his bungalows names like 'Puss in Boots' and 'Sleeping Beauty' after productions he'd played in. Elsewhere some enthusiast for the works of Henry Wadsworth Longfellow had named his bungalows 'Hiawatha', 'Nokomis' and 'Minnehaha'.

The first homes had been rudimentary, and the whole new settlement on Shoreham Beach, with wooden boards slapped on top of the mud to serve as its roads, was primitive too. Even into the 1920s, according to Hardy and Ward, there was no piped water and no sewers; gas and electricity had to wait until after the war. The main access from Shoreham town was by ferry. Gradually, though, a variety of ingenious devices had come into use to disguise the humble origins of the buildings: gable roofs, balconies, elegant cladding, modest extensions upwards and sideways.

The editor of *Arts and Crafts* magazine lived in one of them, and in 1904 described it thus:

> The quaintest feature of Shoreham are the bungalows, most of which consist wholly, or in part, of disused railway carriages. They extend along the beach for about two miles, in some places a hundred yards or so apart, but generally they are pretty close together, and occasionally two rows deep. Some are arranged with taste, and with their tall flagstaffs and fluttering pennants present a gay appearance... The bungalow occupied by myself is a very ingenious affair. There are several coaches to each wing, which at one side open on to the beach, and at the other into a large saloon or lounge, an extension of which to the rear gives a second sitting-room, off the kitchen. To go to your bed-room you open the carriage door. It reminds me of the saloon of an American steamboat with 'state-rooms' right and left. The inside windows of the carriages are covered with mirrors, which greatly increase the apparent size of the apartment, but they rather suggest the idea of a hair-dresser's saloon. The

bedrooms which get the afternoon sun are rather hot then, but those on the other side are always cool, and so is the lounge, which is protected by an attic, which serves as an air chamber...

Will Evans was one of the links between the fashion Marie Loftus began and a new invasion of Shoreham Beach, which made it even more talked about in the town. The Sussex coast, especially Brighton, had been home to the beginnings of British cinema. The light here was good, the air unpolluted, there were all the landscapes and seascapes a director could hope for, and trains ran regularly and decently fast from London. The first company to produce here was the Sunny South Film Company, in which Will Evans was one of the partners, along with a West End set designer called Francis Lyndhurst. They took over Shoreham's Old Fort, established under Palmerston for repelling the French, and still there today – though in the summer of 2009 so pathetic a sight that one wonders how it could ever have daunted invaders. They made their first movies here in 1913: brief knockabout comedies directed by Lyndhurst and featuring Evans and friends engaged on enterprises – building a chicken house, moving a piano – where things could be guaranteed to go wrong. In 1915 Lyndhurst took over Sunny South and renamed it the Sealight Film Company. On a stretch of shingle close to the newly built church of the Good Shepherd, he erected a purpose-built studio made of glass.

The great days of Shoreham cinema, though, only arrived in 1919 when an outfit called the Progress Film Company set up in Bungalow Town. It had been created by an accountant and newspaper owner from Lytham St Anne's called Frank Spring, who served as producer for most of its work; but the animating genius, as director and writer, was Sidney Morgan. Most of his output – seventeen productions over three summers (since they had to rely on natural light, no filming was possible during the winter) – is lost. Even his most celebrated and successful production, his own adaptation of Dickens's *Little Dorrit*, survives only in fragments. His essential adjutant during these years was his ever-resourceful cameraman Stanley J. Mumford; the star of most of the films they made together was his daughter Joan.

Like Cissie Loftus, Joan's talent flowered and was recognized early. Her blonde good looks and wide-eyed ingenue charm delighted audiences, and ensured she would catch the eye of rather bigger companies than her father's. The Progress Company had advertised Shoreham Beach in its prospectus as 'undoubtedly the Los Angeles of British production', but Joan had the chance of the real Los Angeles too. After *Little Dorrit*, she was offered a Hollywood contract, but her father – without consulting her – turned it down. 'You could see a complex motivation,' she said much later, 'the break-up of the family, the loss of his star and a certain amount of jealousy. And… I was only 15 – and not a pushy 15. Some girls of that age today would jump in a taxi and go. I didn't.'

Instead she stayed to take starring roles in *A Lowland Cinderella* and her father's adaptation of Hardy's *Mayor of Casterbridge* – mostly filmed in the nearby downland town of Steyning, but with some scenes shot in Dorset, where Hardy, in his wheelchair, came to watch them at work. Some of Morgan's actors, especially those who had plenty of opportunities in the West End of London, commuted to Sussex, but others, who had yet to make their names in the capital, shacked up in a lively and often hilarious communal building called Studio Rest, where the young Sybil Thorndike, star of *Moth and Rust* (1921), used to wake her colleagues up in the morning as she practised singing her scales on the beach outside their windows. Yet despite the success of Morgan's Dickens and Hardy adaptations, the operation was always precarious. Tiny companies like these saw themselves as the victims of big American money, which kept their work out of US cinemas while dominating screens across Britain.

In 1922, new management took over the Progress company, with ambitious plans for new buildings, including a studio where they could process film instead of having to despatch it, as previously, to be dealt with in Thames Ditton, Surrey. At this point Morgan left, and took his star-daughter with him. To lose its principal assets must have shaken the new Progress company, but what followed was still more disastrous. In the winter of 1922–23 a fire destroyed Studio Rest. Stanley Mumford and his brother were there at the time and were able to rescue precious negatives stored under the beds; having done so, Stanley, a professional to the last, grabbed his camera and recorded the conflagration.

That was not, says N. E. B. Wolters, the final act of the drama: a few more films were made at Bungalow Town, one starring Florence Turner, 'the Vitagraph Girl'. All else thereafter was a mere epilogue. The colony, however, continued for another decade, though with conventional seaside homes increasingly advancing across all available space and the old, raffish culture of railway carriage accommodation beginning to fade away. By 1937, there were 600 homes, a church, some clusters of shops and a pub on the spit.

What did for the place was the war. The site was deemed to be vulnerable to German invasion, and therefore commandeered by the military. Most of the occupants were given forty-eight hours to get out of their homes, which the army then demolished with high explosives – a scene that, sadly, Stanley Mumford was no longer around to record. As the war ended, one observer described the wretched state to which the island had been reduced, with rabbits scurrying over a devastated plain. Much of the territory, overgrown and deserted, was back to where it had been before Marie Loftus discovered it. Though the church and perhaps a hundred homes remained, most of the once neat streets had been obliterated, and their bungalows with them. Abandoned military gear littered the place; barbed wire was everywhere.

A battle now began over this blighted spot, which Hardy and Ward record with their customary sympathy for people deprived of homes that they loved by imperious authority. Those who had lost their bungalows wanted their territory back; but local government at county and district level had other ideas. They were strongly opposed to the return of the plotlanders: they envisaged a community far more tidy and orderly, a place of polite and responsible full-time homes rather than free and easy holiday billets. A Bill to bring that about was introduced in the House of Lords, where, to the consternation of bureaucrats, it was rejected. Charles Clive Bigham, second Viscount Mersey, chairman of the Lords committee that examined the case, thought the plotholders had a better case than West Sussex County Council allowed for. 'I am talking,' he explained, 'about the little man who has been content perhaps to live in a railway carriage. I should not care to live in a railway carriage myself [Lord Mersey lived in style at Bignor Park, near Pulborough in West Sussex], but there are people who are quite content with that.' Those who felt they were claiming to have their citizen rights restored may have found that a little patronizing, but at least it was well intentioned and liberal – and, above all, it meant they had won.

Yet their victory did not last long. The sweeping powers of the Town and Country Planning Act of 1947 gave the local authorities the opening they needed to purchase the spit. This meant another inquiry, which this time went the government's way, though not before some odd attitudes had been uncovered. One senior civil servant advising the minister admitted that he'd changed his view of Shoreham Beach once he'd actually gone there and seen it. His previous extirpationist views had been based, he confessed, on a visit some twenty to twenty-five years earlier. The resolve at all levels of government to reinvent Shoreham Beach struck Hardy and Ward as strange, perhaps even sinister. This was not a beautiful stretch of coast defaced by development such as Peacehaven, or a health risk like Camber Sands. 'In retrospect,' they conclude, 'the impression emerges that Shoreham Beach lent itself as a convenient test-bed for new, post-war town planning procedures… Though Shoreham Beach was, in one sense, of no more than local importance, as a nursery for new procedures its significance was national.'

Though the radio presenter Chris Evans is reputed locally to have a place on the Beach, there is little of the tingle of showbiz left. Marie Loftus died at eighty-three in 1940, and her daughter Cissie, after difficult years with drugs and alcohol in both Britain and the US, three years later, at sixty-six. Sidney Morgan died a further three years afterwards. Joan continued her acting career until the 1940s, when she turned to the writing of film scripts, plays and novels and finally, at an advanced age, to property development. In 1995 she came back to Shoreham after an absence of seventy years to open an exhibition celebrating the film-makers of Shoreham Beach at the town's small but excellent Marlipins Museum. When she died in 2004 at the age of ninety-nine, the film-maker Kevin Brownlow wrote an affectionate tribute to her in the *Independent*, describing her as 'the last star of British silent cinema'.

Today, as you cross over the bridge from the town, and walk beyond its tall twin blocks of apartments, Atlantic Court and Pacific Court, to its seaside parades of smart houses with names like Breakers, Windrush, Caprice and Sea Breeze, Shoreham Beach looks exactly the decent, tidy, untroublesome kind of place that the post-war planners wished it to be. Yet it's also overwhelmingly bland. There's a sense that not just the old raffish, Bohemian flavour but almost any perceptible flavour has been drained right out of it. Hardy and Ward, whose book was first published in 1984, include a photograph of one of the early bungalows in which you can still clearly see the side of a London Brighton and South Coast railway carriage, first- and third-class compartments plainly delineated, down one side in the yard. I have looked for this building in vain, and even the Shoreham Society, whose help I solicited, was unable to trace it. No doubt the old woodwork has fallen prey to the cladders. There are still, though, here and there, bungalows with a hint of a railway origin. I would hesitate, for instance, to whistle in the vicinity of 97 Old Fort Road, Shoreham Beach, in case it began to move.

20

EYNSFORD, KENT

%

'When I arrived, on the morning of Easter Sunday, the celebration had been going on since Good Friday. On the sitting-room table was the largest bottle of port that I had ever seen... The guests had begun the day with doses of Eno's Fruit Salts and gin, which they assured me gave the most refreshing and invigorating feeling on which to start the day.' As had become traditional, they then crossed the road to the pub...

INTO THE PRETTY HIGH STREET of Eynsford in the Darent Valley of Kent, a village that seems to the innocent eye to drip with decorum, at a point almost opposite the Five Bells public house, an ingenious developer inserted in 2008 a tidy development of houses where before there had been a run-down car repair site. The parish council, asked to consider a suitable name, drew up a short-list of nine, from which it chose Warlock Court – 'as an acknowledgement', the chairman explained in the council's annual report, 'to our association with this internationally renowned composer, who lived close by'. 'We hope,' he added optimistically, 'that this will be a refreshing departure from our usual naming after a previous incumbent of the land, or the previous name of the land itself.'

But here he was rather too confident. At the point in the next council meeting where the proceedings were opened up for public discussion, Mr J. Alexander senior presented an argument in favour of naming the development after Gibson's Foundry, rather than after Warlock. He felt the name Gibson better represented Eynsford's history, as the site had been owned by the Gibson family for over a century, whereas Peter Warlock had only been a village resident for a few years. He also noted that Gibson drain covers still existed in many places throughout the village. Mrs Newbold and Mrs Cremer, the minutes of this meeting record, also supported the use of the name Gibson, 'and did not like Warlock, who already has a blue plaque in the village'. Much of the village had found the goings-on at the cottage that Warlock and friends occupied in the mid-1920s not much to their taste. Eighty years on, it seemed, old discontents were still unburied.

Warlock arrived in Eynsford at a difficult time in his difficult life. His attempt to establish himself as music critic of the *Daily Mail* had lasted only a matter of months. He had lost his job as editor of a musical newspaper called *The Sackbut*. If he was ever to find employment other than his composing, he needed to be close to London, but he longed to leave the flat he was renting in Bury Street, just off Piccadilly – which he would leave in a state of such squalor that the landlady wrote to his mother in Wales to complain. What his mother thought was always important. She was a domi-nant – and his friends thought domineering – presence in Warlock's life. Apart from all other considerations, he needed her money to keep him afloat.

His friend Hubert Foss had rented the cottage in Eynsford from Mr Munn, the grocer. Having another cottage nearby, Foss offered it to the composer. It met several of his requirements. The Five Bells was across the road and, close beside it, another pub called the Cas-tle. It was twenty minutes or so from a station where trains ran to Victoria – an easy journey, except when he fell asleep on his way home and woke up at Maidstone, and had to walk nineteen miles back to Eynsford. That these accidents happened came as no surprise to his friends, who were well aware of what he got up to in London. Indeed, according to the local historian Gwen McIntyre, who charted Warlock's adventures in the village in a booklet published by the Farningham and Eynsford Local History Society, they used when appropriate to ring the stationmaster at Eynsford to ask him to wake Warlock up, haul him out of the train, and set him out on the road to the village. On especially fraught occasions, they would meet him themselves, and wheel him home in a barrow.

Though it's as Warlock that he's remembered now, most of all for his *Capriol Suite* and his song series, *The Curlew* – a work of a grace and delicacy that seems barely reconcilable with the drunken rois- tering life that he led for so much of his time in the Darent Valley – he was still at this stage known to most of the world by his birth name, Philip Heseltine. His father, a solicitor, died when Philip was two; his mother, Edith, remarried and moved to a house at Llandyssil, just west of Montgomery. The young Heseltine – shy, diffident, introverted, a product of Eton who had failed to acquire an Etonian sheen and self-confidence – was so sharply different from the subsequent boisterous, often riotous Warlock that the legend developed that he'd simply dumped one personality for an- other – a thesis popularized, to the disgust of some of those who knew Heseltine/Warlock best, in a book published in 1934, four years after Warlock's apparent suicide, by his regular collaborator and companion, the music critic and minor composer, Cecil Gray.

Warlock's menage at Eynsford quickly made him the talk of the village. The house was running with cats, one of Warlock's untidy passions. He took in a second composer, the Anglo-Irishman E. J. Moeran, who was going through a phase where he wrote so little that he seriously contemplated giving up composition and going into the motor trade. Moeran was known as Old Raspberry because of his redness of face, a condition much attributed to his fondness for drink. The writer on music Lewis Foreman says that while serv- ing in the First World War – which Warlock escaped, having fled to Ireland when he feared he might be conscripted – Moeran sustained a severe head injury that had the unfortunate effect of making him appear drunk even after very small quantities of alcohol. It seems clear, even so, that the quantities involved were not always small. Their long sessions in the Five Bells – Warlock would sometimes turn up in his pyjamas – were one demonstration of that. Moeran owned an old Renault car that was subject to misadventures, especially when there were fellow drinkers on board. Despite his unreliable driving, the services of the Renault were much in demand, not least because there were thought to be twenty-seven pubs within four miles of the cottage.

The two composers were supported by a kind of factotum, a man called Hal Collins, whose mother was a Maori and whose grandmother, so he liked to claim, had been a cannibal. He was noted for his vast consumption of stout, after which he liked to perform frightening Maori war dances. Collins had a wide repertoire of practical skills and made some additional income by painting pub signs. Sending a bookplate produced for him by Collins to his friend Colin Taylor, once his teacher at Eton, Warlock wrote, a little inaccurately: '(It was) drawn for me by a strange man whose mother was a cannibal, and used, within his memory, to lament the passing of the good old days when she could feast upon her own kind.' There were various women present for much of the time, some regular, others transient, including his principal mistress Barbara Peache, who although she confided to friends that she always knew the relationship to be doomed, remained close to him after Eynsford and was living with him in Chelsea at the time of his death.

Sometimes their bed was shared by a woman called Judith Wood, but whether for reasons of lust or cramped accommodation is not resolvably clear. Certainly the place was aswamp with visitors at the weekends. According to Hubert Foss, 'The inmates were… brilliant, eccentric, passionately alive (but aware of death), hedonistic, utterly unselfish in the cause of music, enthusiastically scornful, friendly, quarrelsome, drunk and sober by erratic turns, but always with the fixed idea of genius as their guide.' Cecil Gray's account is notably more sardonic: 'There was a constant stream of visitors, some of whom stayed only for the day or for a night, others indefinitely, for months on end, and others until they had to be forcibly ejected – poets and painters, airmen and actors, musicians and maniacs of every description, including pyrophils and claustrophobes – everyone who was in any way unusual or abnormal was sure of receiving a ready welcome at Eynsford.'

The composer Constant Lambert, at twenty-three some ten years younger than Warlock and Moeran, was often there: his biographer Andrew Motion accepts that Warlock introduced him to composers like Boyce whose music he did not know, but thinks he nurtured the taste for strong drink, which in time would be Lambert's downfall. The young Anthony Powell was another Eynsford visitor, introduced by Lambert. Warlock, the novelist writes in his memoir, *To Keep the Ball Rolling*, 'had turned himself into a consciously Mephistophelean figure, an appearance assisted by a pointed fair beard and light-coloured eyes that were particularly compelling. His reputation, one not altogether undeserved, was that of a *mauvais sujet*, but I always found him agreeable and highly entertaining, though never without a sense, as with many persons of at times malign temper, that things might suddenly go badly wrong.' William Walton too was invited, but tired of the place's relentless conviviality and according to his widow, Lady Susana, found Warlock himself hard to take.

In her wild knockabout memoir, *Is She a Lady?*, the artist Nina Hamnett records a fun-filled, booze-fuelled, visit one Easter (Warlock did not like Christmas, and made Easter a kind of rollicking surrogate Yuletide.) Though in fact she was closer to Moeran, Hamnett says it was Warlock who asked her to Eynsford (which curiously she places in Hertfordshire): 'When I arrived, on the morning of Easter Sunday, the celebration had been going on since Good Friday. On the sitting-room table was the largest bottle of port that I had ever seen. It must have been a teraboam. I tasted some of it and it was very potent...The guests had begun the day with doses of Eno's Fruit Salts and gin, which they assured me gave the most refreshing and invigorating feeling on which to start the day.'

As had become traditional, they then crossed the road to the pub, returning some time later for musical festivities.' "*Penitence, Pardon and Peace cantata*," a fine piece of music of a Divine nature, by a Victorian composer, J. H. Maunder, had been discovered and someone had found a passage into which fitted the limerick about the "old man from Newcastle"... We sang songs of all kinds and drank beer the whole evening. As the Spring was beginning, and as I had nothing to do in London and was very bored, I spent a great deal of my time at Eynsford. They were the most sympathetic and intelligent company I had ever been in. Heseltine was a man who really should have lived in about 1400. At any rate, he did his best to put a real English spirit into life in Kent, and he was adored by all the farmers and yokels.'

Mr Munn, the ultimate landlord of the cottage, seemed in no way displeased by the uses to which it was now being put. He even composed a premature epitaph for his tenant and neighbour:

> Here lies Warlock, the composer,
> Who lived next door to Munn, the grocer.
> He died of drink and copulation,
> A sad discredit to this nation.

(When this was reprinted in a collection called *The Weekend Book*, 'copulation' was replaced by 'dissipation'.)

What the villagers would not have known, nor the farmers and yokels, was that, when he was sober and not sunk in gloom – as according to Munn he might be for days on end – Warlock worked diligently for much of the time, sometimes composing (his *Capriol Suite* was written at Eynsford) and sometimes writing on music, on which he had firm opinions, vehemently expressed. In his youth a devoted admirer of Delius – he had a long correspondence with the composer and Jelka, his wife – he revered many ancient composers, especially the Elizabethans, some of whose work he rescued from near obscurity, and such later figures as Liszt, Berlioz and Bartók. He was one of the first in Britain to appreciate the genius of Bartók whom he visited in Hungary and invited to London and Wales, during which time he took him out on a motorbike and deposited him in a ditch. He despised, with an equal fervour, the music of Gustav Holst, and was sniffy about Stravinsky. Warlock also engaged while at Eynsford in a somewhat one-sided feud with the music critic Percy Scholes ('that stinking bag of putrescent tripe') who had written disparagingly of the music of Liszt, pursuing him by letter, obscene postcard and even by telephone until the critic threatened legal action; though Scholes did not go through with it, explaining that he did not want to be responsible for a genius being jailed.

For too many in Eynsford, however, Warlock was less a fine modern composer than a booze-fuelled nuisance. That applied even to those who had never actually witnessed the naked midnight motorbike rides he was said to take with his equally naked girlfriends. Motor cycles were almost as much an obsessional taste as cats. 'Whenever he was in funds,' wrote Gray, 'the first thing he would do would be to buy a motor cycle … he must at different periods have possessed at least a dozen of them, each of which, however, came to a disastrous end after only a very short time. The first of the series, I think, was an exceptionally powerful and wicked specimen at Eynsford on which, accompanied by a friend in a side car, he once spectacularly charged through the doors of the saloon bar of a public house, the throttle having refused to close and the brakes to act, appropriately enough just on opening time.' There was also talk of black magic, which may well have been justified: certainly his adopted name Warlock did little to dispel such suspicions.

Both the joy and the pain of having Warlock as one of your neighbours is quite easy to imagine as you walk through Eynsford now. This was a place that valued its peace and its respectable reputation, and Warlock and his menage were unconducive to both. Indeed, had such a system existed then, he might very well have been made the subject of an ASBO for his persistent upsetting of neighbours – often simply out of high spirits but sometimes intentionally.

The household may have been, as Hubert Foss submitted, devoted to art and beauty, but there was clearly a matching addiction to what used to be called *épater les bourgeois*. Their self-indulgence was particularly hard on their next-door neighbours, the Eynsford Baptists. Nina Hamnett has an account of that too. 'Next to our house was a chapel. It was surrounded by a small garden and on Sunday mornings we ran a rival show. When the service started, we began with several works by Max Reger, the noisy German composer some of whose music sounds completely drunk. These were played on the pianola. The "Fairy Queen" [she means Purcell's *The Faerie Queene*, I imagine] was then played, and we ended up by roaring sea songs, ending up with an unexpurgated version of "Nautical William". I heard only recently that the congregation said a prayer every Sunday morning for us.' Gwen McIntyre reports an incident in which as children were leaving the Baptist Sunday school, Warlock came across the road from the Five Bells pub and said: 'I will be your God.' The children were shocked and went off in search of the superintendent, a Mr Pocock, who was 'quite angry, and so were other church members'. Understandably – and one might think, justifiably – so.

But these constantly eventful, high-spirited, frequently raucous, days were too good to last. Though Warlock's first two years in the village went better than most of his troubled life, by 1928 the arrangement looked doomed. Only his mother's subventions had sustained him there for so long, and he'd now reached the point where, with his income dwindling and no immediate prospect of better times, he had to accept that the game was up. He wrote to his friend Bruce Blunt: 'I can no longer sell even the exiguous amount of trash and drivel that I have hitherto been turning out, sullying the name of music in the press. So I shall endeavour to find some other, humbler, activity.' Moeran and Collins stayed on for a while without their master of ceremonies, but Collins fell into decline. He ate less and less and, though he denied it, was clearly extremely ill. 'Collins has tuberculosis,' Warlock wrote to a friend.

'He has wasted away to a skeleton and seems to have lost all his vitality. But he insists obstinately that there is nothing the matter with him, and refuses to take proper medical advice. He is very much more Maori than European, and the fatalism of his race makes him difficult to handle in a matter of this kind.' He died in September 1929, at forty-seven.

Moeran moved to the Cotswolds, recovered his talent for composition, and wrote a symphony and a sinfonietta and concertos for the violin and cello. (The symphony had a conspicuous success when revived for the 2009 promenade concert season.) He was working on a second symphony when he died in the river Kenmare in Ireland, where he had now made his home. Though an accident or even suicide was initially suspected, it was found he had died of a massive stroke. Moeran had outlived his old Eynsford housemate by sixteen years. Warlock took his own life in London in December 1930 (an open verdict was recorded, but the evidence of suicide is overwhelming – not least, that he characteristically put out his cat before he switched on the gas). 'I see constantly,' Jelka Delius wrote, 'the beautiful, lovable incredibly intelligent and artistic boy of twenty – and that tragic figure lying in a gas-filled room with his face to the wall in the early morning.'

In the Eynsford of 2008, Mr J. Alexander senior got his way. The parish council reconsidered the naming of the Apex development and reverted to the practice it had earlier sought to repudiate: in the words of its chairman, 'our usual naming after a previous incumbent of the land, or the previous name of the land itself'.

Sevenoaks council, which had the last word on the subject, concurred. So today the development right by the cottage where Warlock and Moeran set Eynsford's tongues busily wagging, and so handy for the Five Bells on the other side of the road, is Gibson Close. The maker of many drain covers has prevailed over the man who left us *The Curlew* and the *Capriol Suite*.

21

DRAYTON MANOR, STAFFORDSHIRE

SIR ROBERT PEEL, PERFORMER ALONG WITH HIS
HARMONY BAND OF 'HOW CAN YOU SAY WE'RE
THROUGH', RECALLS — IF ONLY BY DYING — THE
GREAT DAYS OF THE PEELS OF DRAYTON.

❧

*Given his past exotic career, his time in this love-nest
had been unwontedly placid. 'At night', Mrs Draper
told the* Daily Mail, *'Sir Robert would sit with me,
making coloured rugs, while I crocheted tea cloths.'*

O N AN APRIL DAY in 1936 a crowd of well over a
thousand people — some put it at nearer three
thousand — including a greedily gawped-at bevy of
theatrical celebrities, gathered at St Peter's church, Drayton Bassett,
near Tamworth, for the funeral of a man who at various times had
made his living as a fisherman, cowboy, used car salesman,
bandleader, and manager of a dance hall in one of the better
Birmingham suburbs. The explanation for such an apparent
mismatch lay in his name. The dead man was Sir Robert Peel, 5th
baronet, the latest, but not quite the last, of a sequence of Robert
Peels who had once brought excitement and pride to this village
and the neighbouring village of Fazeley. For some eighty years the
line had succeeded and prospered. This Sir Robert's great
grandfather, the 2nd baronet, twice prime minister, had been one
of the most eminent men in England. Yet from the moment he died,
in a fall from his horse while riding down Constitution Hill in
London, the Drayton dynasty began to fulfil that pattern that

people liked to categorize as rags to riches and riches to rags in three generations.

Sir Robert Peel, who was to become the 1st baronet, had come to this spot on the Staffordshire-Warwickshire border in the 1790s. His own father, also a Robert Peel but known to all as 'Parsley Peel' after his most famous pattern design, had established himself as a manufacturer and printer of calico at Blackburn, Lancashire. Though a plain man and proud of it, he acquired a family coat of arms with the motto '*Industria*'. 'My father,' wrote his third and most successful son, the first Sir Robert, 'can be truly said to have been the founder of our family.' This second Robert established a mill, powered by a lively stream, at Fazeley, two miles out of Tamworth, and bought the big house at Drayton from the aristocratic Thynnes – a family brought low by wilful extravagance – which he had rebuilt to meet his own grander standards. From 1790, as he must have always intended, he was MP for Tamworth. He spoke rarely at Westminster, and never conspicuously well. But his faithful adherence to Pitt, and his timely raising of money for military operations, was rewarded in 1800 with a baronetcy.

This Sir Robert's allegiance to his father's watchword '*Industria*' was matched by his sons. Five became Members of Parliament, two of them reaching the Cabinet; one son became a dean of the Church of England. But his hopes for his eldest son were the highest. 'Bob, you dog,' he was said to have told him, 'if you are not prime minister some day, I'll disinherit you.' Bob went from Harrow to Christ Church Oxford, where he prepared for his finals by working, so one of his brothers recorded, eighteen hours a day – a level of industry rewarded when he emerged with a double first (classics and mathematics). At twenty-one he was a Tory MP (his father, now a very rich man, had purchased for him the Irish rotten borough of Cashel), at twenty-two a minister, at twenty-four Chief Secretary to the Lord Lieutenant of Ireland, and at thirty-three Home Secretary, for the first of two terms in this office. In December 1834, when he was forty-six, he began the first of two terms as prime minister.

Having built a fine house in Whitehall Gardens, close to Downing Street, he was able in the 1830s to replace the house at Drayton, which his father had built only forty years earlier, with something more splendid still. From the death of his father in 1830 he was also the local MP. Though in some senses still a plain man, like his father and grandfather – he never surrendered his accent, and his table manners were notoriously rough – this Sir Robert had a taste for fine arts. Over the years he assembled an envied collection – some kept in London but some at Drayton – of pictures, mainly Dutch and Flemish, to which he added a series of portraits of his family and of eminent people he liked and admired, commissioned from the pre-eminent portrait painter of the day, Sir Thomas Lawrence, and including two paintings, exhibited in 1825 and 1827, of his Julia, his beautiful wife. In time he remodelled the gallery in which his Drayton collection was housed and named it the Statesmen's Gallery. He also accumulated a notable library.

His political eminence gave the people of Drayton Bassett the sense of having a truly great man in their midst. Queen Victoria herself came with Prince Albert in 1843, arriving by train at Tamworth and being borne in a carriage past excited crowds to Drayton with her prime minister on his horse at her side. He loved the place: 'my heart is set upon home, and not upon ambition,' he wrote to his cherished wife Julia. Douglas Hurd's biography, published in 2007, finds him at Drayton in the sunny summer of 1846, feeling liberated at the end of his second spell as prime minister. The days, he says contentedly, 'are too short for my present occupations, which consist chiefly of lounging in my library, directing improvements, riding with the boys and my daughter, and pitying Lord John (Russell, his Whig successor) and his colleagues.' 'We had a glorious merry-making yesterday,' he recorded in that same summer, 'all my labourers and their wives, 125 in number, dined under a tent – their children were feasted at the Inn at Drayton. The evening was just past in Bowls – skittles – quoits— cricket – football – and above all dancing – which was kept up by old and young on the green sward in front of our windows till long after it was dark. It was a very pretty sight.'

The pleasure and pride that the people of Drayton took in having him among them was poignantly evident in the way they turned out for his funeral after the chilling news of his death at sixty-two, three days after his accident, on 2 July 1850. Queen Victoria, who usually got her way, had wanted a state funeral in London, which few local people could have attended. But Peel had been clear that, in death as in life, his preference was for Drayton, where he asked for a funeral 'without ostentation or parade of any kind'. François Guizot, a historian who had become a government minister and at one point prime minister of France and was now in exile in England with his master, King Louis-Philippe, describes the occasion in the first biography written of Peel:

On the 9th of July, at about one o'clock in the afternoon, the body of Sir Robert Peel was carried from Drayton Manor across the park and fields, to the parish church. His family, his principal political friends (who had come down from London to attend the funeral), his household servants, and the farmers and labourers on his estate, formed the procession. The weather was gloomy; the rain fell in torrents; a thick fog, blown hither and thither by violent gusts of wind, covered the face of the country. A numerous multitude from Tamworth and the surrounding villages, had nevertheless assembled near the church, at the entrance to the graveyard. On the arrival of the coffin, all stood uncovered, motionless and mute; slowly it was carried through the tombs to the portal of the church; at the head of the procession, the Bishop of Gibraltar read aloud the prayers of the liturgy; and when it had entered the church, the crowd pressed eagerly, but noiselessly, into the edifice. The bishop ended the funeral service. The desire of Sir Robert Peel was religiously fulfilled; his body was lowered, without parade or ostentation, into the vault in which his father and mother were interred – followed by the regrets and prayers of the humble population among whom he lived when he was not engaged in governing the state.

Few would have thought at that moment that the great days of the Peels of Drayton were already over. But now the slide began. The old saying about quick money – one generation to make it, one to enjoy it, one to lose it – was about to be confirmed at Drayton Manor.

★

The architects of decline, and so of the 5th baronet's severely reduced inheritance, were the great Sir Robert's son and above all his grandson. '*Industria*' might appear on the family arms but this was not a concept to which Sir Robert, 3rd baronet, ever subscribed. Where his father had come out of Oxford with a double first, he left without a degree. Succeeding to the baronetcy and to the house and estate at Drayton at twenty-eight, he abandoned his fitful career as a diplomat and took his father's place as MP for Tamworth. His performances at Westminster disappointed, even dismayed, his father's old friends. He was gifted, unquestionably: blessed with a powerful, musical, resonant voice and cutting a more striking figure – though a somewhat dandified one – than his father had, but with little of substance to say. Edward Stanley, MP, later to become 15th Earl of Derby, observing Peel's first parliamentary performances, thought him 'half-insane', his undoubted talent drowned in his affectation and eccentricity.

In 1855, he was given a place in Lord Palmerston's Liberal government; six years later he was occupying a post his father had filled with distinction on his way to the premiership – Chief Secretary to the Lord Lieutenant of Ireland. But his ministerial career conformed to the general picture of self-indulgence and waywardness – remarkably so in a man who had once been a diplomat. As a *Times* obituary would say of him: 'He thought he had solved the Irish question when he made excursions *incognito* through the country on a jaunty-car and interviewed the peasants in the style of a modern Haroun-al-Rashid. But Fenianism was raising its head and his way of dealing with its parliamentary apologists was not calculated to promote peace… His career in Ireland was a failure…' His political masters were required to rescue their headstrong subordinate from a series of scrapes, including a threatened duel and an altercation with a fellow passenger in a railway carriage, which ended with the police being called and the Chief Secretary being summoned to face charges of using abusive and insulting language. Soon afterwards he resigned his ministerial office, and was never offered another.

Though they may not have been fully aware of his reputation as MP and minister, there were other occasions closer to home about which the people of Drayton Bassett and Fazeley would certainly have heard, not least because the *Tamworth Herald*, established in 1868, so assiduously chronicled the family's adventures and misadventures. Where the early Peels had a talent for making money, their successors demonstrated an equal flair for squandering it. Partly because he and Emily Hay, daughter of the 8th Marquess of Tweeddale, whom he married in 1856, had lost substantial sums of money as breeders, trainers and gamblers on horses (he used the pseudonym Robinson for these activities) and partly because of their many other extravagances, including grand social entertainments in London and the building of a villa in Switzerland, the 3rd baronet began to sell off his father's collections, recouping £75,000 (more than £3 million today) in 1871 through a sale of pictures to the National Gallery. He also disposed of Fazeley Mill, once the very foundation of Peel prosperity but now hit by the decline of the cotton trade. Local Liberals grew impatient with his habit of voting more with the Conservatives than with his own side and as the 1880 election approached began to look for an alternative candidate, at which point he stood down.

In his final decade he rarely appeared at Drayton. At his death in May 1895, the *Herald* recalled his last years, 'passed for the most part in the St James's Club Piccadilly where he frequently spent many hours in the afternoon, reclining his gouty foot upon a sofa, reading either a French novel, or a volume of the *Racing Calendar*, or a speech delivered by his father which he had exhumed from *Hansard*'. The village, even so, turned out for him when he died as it had for his father. Though the service had been announced as private, several thousand people crammed into Drayton Bassett, among them many who had been there for the great Sir Robert's funeral forty-five years before. Peel tenants lined the route to the church, falling in behind the procession as it passed them.

★

Worse was to follow. The arrival of the 4th baronet, yet another Sir Robert, and like his father succeeding at twenty-eight, at first suggested that the Peel connection with Drayton and Fazeley would now be renewed. He promised to settle at Drayton within a few weeks. The district would find him, he pledged, a true and trusted friend. But a steady corrosive improvidence unpicked all his good intentions. When he left Oxford, it was stated at one of his bankruptcy hearings, he had debts of £50,000 (the best part of £3 million today). After his father's death, he published two novels. The first, *An Engagement* (1896), intended as social comedy, is a flimsy affair that has barely begun before it is over. The second, *A Bit of a Fool* (1897), casts rather more light on the 4th baronet, since here he dealt with a theme he knew all about: the perils and torments of debt. 'Summonses, writs, petitions in bankruptcy, poured in upon me, until I did not know which way to turn,' says his novel's hero; and that was the fate in true life of his creator. Though he once broke the bank at Monte Carlo, netting £12,000, (some £700,000 in 2010 money), that merely diminished his debts – it was not enough to eliminate them; and in general his gambling produced the same degrading outcome that it so often did for spoiled sons of great aristocratic families.

His novels were never going to make money, and nor, with agriculture in steady decline, was the estate, while the cotton business that had once fed the family's fortune was no longer there to sustain him. His best chance now seemed to be to make an opulent marriage. His relations with women had been the subject of scandal on a scale that must surely have reached the ears of Drayton and Fazeley. He was known to have been the lover of the actress Lillie Langtry, an honour he shared with the Prince of Wales; another of Lillie's lovers beat her viciously after learning of her trysts with Sir Robert.

On a visit to Monte Carlo, he met Kitty Sanford, a nineteen-year-old girl from a famously rich American family. Allured by her prettiness, grace and accomplishment (her money, of course, may well have been an added attraction), he followed her to Paris, proposed and was accepted. But Kitty's tyrannical grandfather, Henry Sanford, proprietor of the Adams Express Co., knew all about the Lillie Langtry affair, and summoned Peel to New York, declared him to be a 'libertine' and banned any further relationship. In early 1896, Peel met, and swiftly became engaged to, Eleanor (Ella) Williamson, the twenty-five-year-old daughter of the powerful and extremely rich linoleum manufacturer Jimmy Williamson – ennobled in 1895 as Lord Ashton and owner of a Jacobean castle on the River Lune far surpassing in grandeur the Peel house in Drayton. But one day the bride-to-be received a package of letters, containing information about her intended husband of which, until then, she'd known nothing. The wedding was promptly cancelled and his hope of financial redemption lost. It must have been particularly galling for him that Ella then went on to marry his cousin Willie, making him one of the richest men in the land.

Peel's affairs seemed to take a turn for the better when in May 1897 he announced his engagement to Mercedes, daughter of Baron and Baroness de Graffenried of Thun, Switzerland, whose family, the *Tamworth Herald* – that unsleeping chronicler of all the baronet's tribulations – assured its readers, was 'the oldest and best in Switzerland'. Drayton Bassett was denied its hoped-for treat, a Peel marriage, since the civil ceremony took place in Paris and its religious version in Switzerland, but in early July the couple drove from Tamworth station to Drayton Manor, to be greeted with letters of congratulation from the two villages, accompanied in some cases by donations of poultry. Sadly, however, the same edition of the *Herald* had to report the issue of a bankruptcy notice against Sir Robert on a claim by Victor Honour, a money-lender, for £2,264, with costs. And sadly, too, the marriage was not to succeed. He celebrated his wife's arrival at Drayton by building a Swiss Lodge close to the gates, and in 1898 a son was born to them, who would one day be Robert Peel, 5th baronet. But he had not got rid of his debts. As the Tamworth historian, the late Mabel Swift, mordantly notes, Mercedes thought Sir Robert was rich; Sir Robert thought she was rich; each was mistaken.

The 4th baronet went bankrupt on seven occasions, and sometimes faced court proceedings of an even more embarrassing nature. He seemed to have quite a habit of not paying bills. After one such episode he appeared at Clerkenwell police court in October 1911, summoned for obtaining credit at the Midland Grand Hotel, St Pancras, while an undischarged bankrupt. Sir Robert, the court was told, had stayed two nights at this not inexpensive location, had borrowed some cash on account, and had got the hotel to pay for a parcel from Messrs Stagg and Mantle of Leicester Square, a women's fashion house. This left him with a bill for £32 17s for which he paid with a cheque for £40, pocketing the £7 3s difference. The cheque bounced. The hotel demanded its money, but got no reply. A cashier called on Sir Robert, who explained that he had expected a payment into his account of £3,000. He promised to send them the money. It did not arrive. The accused was committed to appear at the Central Criminal Court. But by the time the hearing was due he had settled. The Common Serjeant, presiding, said he accepted the agreement, though adding he was disturbed to note that a considerable part of Sir Robert's bill had been incurred for wine, spirits and liqueurs.

These were grievous days for those who had known the Peels of

Drayton at their greatest. 'The noble mansion of Drayton Manor, Tamworth', the *Herald* reported in February 1898, 'witnessed on Saturday one of the most curious and least edifying scenes in its history, when a quantity of the present Sir Robert Peel's personal property was brought under the hammer to satisfy a sheriff's execution.' First up, fetching sixteen shillings, were a pair of brown leggings, a silk cushion, some gloves and an assortment of ties. Later came three pairs of white duck trousers and three cricket jackets, and six fancy tweed suits, some never worn, said to have cost eight guineas apiece. In the final act of the day, the sale of nineteen goldfish in their marble fountain relieved the debts of the impoverished baronet by a further thirteen shillings.

But this was only a marginal prelude to a series of epic disposals. At the turn of the century, silver and plate worth between £5,000 and £6,000 were put up for sale, followed by much of the great Sir Robert's art collection and library. But that created a further problem. The 4th baronet, it was asserted by some of his relatives, had no right to dispose of these heirlooms. Much of what he was planning to sell was covered by one of the settlements that were commonly made among aristocratic families in Victorian England, designed to prevent the first-born son from frittering away a family's fortunes. Indeed, the trustees complained to the Chancery court, Sir Robert had already disposed of assets that did not belong to him, including the picture his grandfather had most of all cherished – Sir Thomas Lawrence's portrait of his wife Julia.

October 1909 saw the first of a series of sales in which he sought to dispose of land, farms, farm buildings, market gardens, houses and cottages across the whole Peel estate. Still more was put on the market in 1917–18, including more Lawrence portraits and the last of the library. Sir Robert found himself ever more isolated. As Drayton was progressively denuded he became alienated from most of his family. His uncle, Viscount Peel, former Speaker of the Commons and a nationally eminent figure, had several times taken legal action against him. At one point he was committed for trial at the Old Bailey for a serious libel against his brother-in-law. Binding him over, the judge said he took a serious view of Sir Robert's behaviour, but concluded that for a man who bore such an honoured name, the mere fact of having to stand in the dock at the Old Bailey would be some little punishment. As before in his courtroom history, it seemed that the honoured name had saved him from something worse, not excluding imprisonment.

His wife Mercedes had returned to her native Switzerland. But hope remained that the son who had been born to them might bring back the glow that his father had largely extinguished and restore the old, proud Peel connection. His marriage in 1920 would prove to be the most colourful day in the lives of the people of Drayton Bassett and Fazeley villages since the day when the great Sir Robert brought the queen and her consort to Drayton Manor.

★

Bobby Peel, born to the 4th baronet and Mercedes in April 1898, had run away from Harrow to join the army, giving a false age. Recalled, he went to Christ's College Cambridge and then joined the Coldstream Guards, becoming a commissioned officer but then being discharged because of ill-health. On medical advice he left for Australia to work on a cattle station. He also had spells as a fisherman and a used car salesman. What seemed to attract him most, though, was the world of show business – a taste that fed the suspicion that, as gossip had long asserted, he was not in truth the son of his accredited mother Mercedes but the product of his father's affair with Lillie Langtry. Part of the lure of the stage, as so often with the sons of upper-class houses, was the presence of gorgeous show girls. In Australia, when only twenty, he met a British actress who used the stage name Maud Fane, with results that were later spelled out in a Melbourne divorce court, reported by one newspaper under the headlines:

Maud Fane's Marriage
Principal Girl Loses Affection for Hubby
She slips on Peel and falls
Theatrical drama behind the scenes.
Intrigue with an 'Infant' who has an estate.

Edgar Warwick Goodchild, a theatrical manager aged thirty-five, the paper explained, was seeking to end his six-year-old marriage on the grounds of his wife's misconduct with Robert Peel. The court was told that Maud had taken advantage of Edgar's absence on tour with his theatrical company, The Jesters, to decamp to live in a flat with the co-respondent. Alice Bindon, a former housemaid, remembered Maud entering Peel's room in July 1918. Sometimes she was in her kimono. The couple had breakfast together four or five times a week. There was evidence that the bed had been occupied by more than one person. Eventually a decree nisi was granted with costs against Peel. Some reports said that Maud and Peel were then married; more persistent stories said she had borne his child. But soon all thoughts of Maud Fane seem to have been swept away by his passion for another actress and dancer, even younger than he, Phyllis Monkman. She rejected him; he persisted. It was she who introduced him to the hugely successful Canadian entertainer, Beatrice Lillie. She instantly took to him – the prospect of one day bearing the title of Lady Peel may have had something to do with it – and soon they became engaged. Yet even at the engagement party, he told Phyllis he would not go through with this marriage to Beatrice if she would only relent.

Phyllis would not succumb. So, to the huge excitement of Drayton Bassett and Fazeley, a society wedding for Robert and his glamorous bride was fixed for January 1920 at Fazeley – Fazeley rather than Drayton Bassett, since the fourth Sir Robert had quarrelled with the vicar of Drayton Bassett, who accused him of neglecting his duties to the community. The old man declined to attend the wedding, saying he was unwell, though Beatrice Lillie says he sent her a diamond bracelet. In 2009 someone posted a picture on YouTube of the gathering outside the church after the ceremony. There is Sir Robert, tall and willowy, a good foot taller than Beatrice, who looks to be enjoying the moment more than he is. The principals are crammed together outside the church door since the space in front of Fazeley church was scarcely adequate for such an exotic occasion. The villagers came in their legions to the church gate to see not just Bobby and Beatrice but also the glittering supporting cast of show business stars they had invited.

The reception, held at the Manor, was a surreal affair. There were notices of sales by auction plastered all over the building and inquisitive people opening doors found most of the rooms crammed with packing cases. If that set the tone for the Peel–Lillie marriage, the honeymoon seemed to confirm it. After a first night at Drayton, the couple departed for Monte Carlo, where the young baronet seemed to be set on repeating his father's achievement of breaking the bank. On their first night they set off for the casino, where Bobby settled himself at the table playing number seventeen. After a while Beatrice went back to their hotel, expecting her husband to join her. She woke at six next morning to find she was still alone. She waited for him in mounting disquiet for much of the day. Eventually he returned saying he was very sorry, but he thought in the circumstances she would forgive him. He had won them some £10,000.

The next night he went out again, and again he stayed out all night. When he returned next morning, she could tell from his face that the inevitable must have occurred. Had he lost the lot? Yes, all ten thousand, he told her – 'and a lot more'. They had to borrow money to pay their hotel bill.

Ten months into the marriage a son – yet again Robert, the destined 6th baronet – was born. But by then the chances that the marriage would last were remote. Four months after the birth, Beatrice went back to the stage, in Britain, but then increasingly in the United States. Bobby, as always looking for some fresh way of making, if not his fortune, at least some kind of remunerative living, returned to Australia, this time as a sheep farmer.

Old Sir Robert lived out a lonely few years in diminished Drayton. In his final months he was paralysed from the waist down. In February 1930 he died, and was buried at Drayton Bassett. Though the service was private, the congregation, the *Tamworth Herald* reported, 'filled the edifice'. But not one of his family attended the service: all were abroad, the paper explained. The new baronet returned to England to take up his dubious inheritance and started to look around for a settled career. But as so often with his plans, nothing came of it. For a time he managed a dance hall next to the Palace cinema in Erdington on the fringes of Birmingham, but his main ambition now was to establish himself as a bandleader. That involved a regular band – Sir Robert Peel and his Harmony Band, though sometimes Sir Robert Peel and his Bing Boys Dance Band – and also the leadership of a band of unemployed miners, in appearances for which he recruited such West End stars as Gertrude Lawrence and Jack Buchanan. That people found such an avocation surprising in the great grandson of a celebrated prime minister seemed to him pure snobbery. 'To be frank,' he said when his band first appeared in Birmingham, 'I am just an ordinary human being anxious to entertain and make a little money... I will not allow my title to hinder me in my aspirations.'

There was little, however, that the new Sir Robert could do for Drayton Manor. He opened a social club, ran the Fazeley cricket club, which played in the grounds of the Manor, and captained its Saturday team. But even the house was now doomed. In February 1926, the announcement was made that the family home, together with that portion of the estate which remained, had been sold privately and would shortly be put on the market in lots. Sir Robert retained the Swiss Lodge and a portion of the estate, which in 1929 he designated a parkland for the people of Tamworth and the surrounding villages. The house and the land around it were sold in April that year and, soon afterwards, most of the house that Prime

Minister Peel had built with such pride was demolished. In a small museum at Middleton Hall, just south of Drayton, run by the Peel Society of Tamworth, I found the sheet music of one of Sir Robert's favourite numbers: 'Through (How Can You Say We're Through)', – lyrics by Joe McCarthy, music by Jimmie Monaco, as featured by Sir Robert Peel, Bart, and his Harmony Band. That seems a suitable epitaph for this last stage of Drayton Manor.

By the early 1930s the 5th baronet was fading out of the life of Drayton, Fazeley and Tamworth, though, as events would show, he was not forgotten. The news briefly supplied in the *Tamworth Herald* on 7 April 1934 was as grievous as it was unexpected. The 5th baronet had died the previous day, the day before his thirty-sixth birthday, in a nursing home at Tunbridge Wells, Kent. His death seems to have resulted from an operation for peritonitis that somehow went wrong. His mistress of several years, Doris Draper, was at his side. The couple had been living in a house called Westfield, set in some sixty acres at Penshurst, south-west of Tonbridge. Given his past exotic career, his time in this love-nest had been unwontedly placid. 'At night,' Mrs Draper told the *Daily Mail*, 'Sir Robert would sit with me, making coloured rugs, while I crocheted tea cloths.'

It was some indication of the decline of the house of Peel that the 5th baronet was reported to have left a mere £2,012. The estate, however, had not been finally settled, and figures given in a subsequent bankruptcy hearing showed liabilities of £14,000 against assets of £1,600. Yet however diminished his circumstances, 'Darling Bobby' was still fondly remembered at Drayton, where people still liked to recall how their parents, their mothers especially, doted on him. His funeral produced the last great occasion to which the dynasty treated the people of Drayton Bassett. The *Herald* thought a thousand people were present but others, Beatrice Lillie included, claimed there were up to three times that number. Nearly all those who gathered for that occasion are dead, but a Fazeley man called Joseph Hunter, approaching ninety when I talked to him, remembered it well – remembered, too, seeing Sir Robert – 'a tall handsome man, a great womanizer' – with Beatrice at the Manor, and later on, with his mistress when he and Doris lived for a time at Swiss Lodge. His memories are recorded in a book, *My Memories of Fazeley and the Peels of Drayton Manor.* The late baronet was interred in a family vault, just behind the church, until now solely occupied by his great-great-uncle Edmund Peel of Bonehill, interred in 1850. Joe Hunter attributes this conjunction to the fact that Edmund, like this Sir Robert, had been exceptionally tall. No other grave would have been long enough for the 5th baronet.

Even then there was hope that the story that had begun with the first baronet's arrival at Drayton almost 150 years earlier was not yet over. Beatrice Lillie for one believed that her son had the qualities in him that might enable the family name to be rescued and restored. Like four baronets before him, the boy was at Harrow. At the outbreak of war he announced his intention to leave and enlist in the Navy. His mother, required to give her permission since he was not yet twenty-one, reluctantly decided not to stand in his way. He was posted to Colombo. On Easter Day 1942, his boat was hit by a bomb. He was killed, along with fourteen others.

Little of Drayton Manor now survives. Only one wing of the house and the clock tower still stand. In 1949 an entrepreneur called George Bryan saw an advertisement in a trade magazine that said the estate was for sale. The army had taken it over during the war, and Bryan found the place, as he put it, 'a total rubbish heap'. He began with one tiny restaurant, a tea room, three hand-operated rides, half a dozen rowing boats, some pedal cars and a set of second-hand dodgem cars picked up in Middlesbrough for £500. Over the years, he and Vera, his wife, built the place into today's Drayton Manor Theme Park, a kind of West Midlands Disneyland. Here and there, there's a minor obeisance to the great days of Drayton. The square in front of the remnant of the house that Robert Peel, Prime Minister, built is called Peel Plaza. On the way to the Bryans' pleasuredrome, you pass a sign that advertises a Sir Robert Peel's

Nature Trail and Duck Decoy Walk, that I dutifully explored without getting any numinous sense that the great man himself had once walked here. The Peel museum was here for a while, but its building has now been turned into Mrs Kindley's tea rooms.

In the church of St Peter at Drayton Bassett you will find memorials to most, though not all, of the six Robert Peels (there is none to the debt-strewn 4th baronet). As you'd expect, the commemoration of the second in line is the most imposing. For the 5th baronet, a plaque that bears the family coat of arms and Parsley Peel's motto '*Industria*' has been placed there by Beatrice, his widow, and Robert, his son. The sixth and last of the line, who rarely saw Drayton (though sometimes he came to stay with old family servants) has a grave 5,000 miles away in Colombo.

22

BOOSBECK, CLEVELAND

RUTH PENNYMAN AND MICHAEL TIPPETT BRING
CAPTAIN MACHEATH AND ROBIN HOOD TO
IMPOVERISHED CLEVELAND.

ટ&

*The clash of cultures that night must have constituted
a discord that little in the music of Tippett
could have matched…*

I N THE 1830s there was little more to Boosbeck, North Yorkshire, east of then insignificant Middlesbrough and four miles
or so from the sea at Saltburn, than a beck called the Boos.
Then came the explosive growth of the ironstone industry, propelled by such entrepreneurs as Henry Bolckow, John Vaughan and
Arthur Dorman of Middlesbrough, and a rash of houses began to
appear, run up at speed to accommodate a workforce that, though
mainly recruited from Yorkshire and Durham, contained quite
substantial contingents from work-starved places like Norfolk,
Lincolnshire and the south-western counties of England. East
Cleveland, of which Boosbeck was part, along with such burgeoning urban villages as Lingdale, Skelton, Brotton and Skinningrove
on the coast, developed a reputation as a tough, rough, hard-
drinking, hard-living place, scary to genteel visitors; and though the
course of the twentieth century tempered that, it remains a part of
the kingdom with a flavour all of its own. In 1997 the Teesside-born
writer Harry Pearson recalled it as it was when he was growing up
there in the 1960s: 'Weird places. The nearest thing in Britain to the
hillbilly towns of the Appalachians. Warm, good-hearted people,
mostly; but not entirely averse to fisticuffs after a drink or two…'

Almost the last place in England, then, one might have imagined, to have staged the premiere of a work by the gentle, pacifistic, homosexual composer later famous across the world as Sir Michael Tippett. Yet this was where the villagers assembled in numbers one night in 1934 to hear the twenty-nine-year-old composer conduct a performance by the people of Boosbeck (including a chorus of children who'd had to learn Latin to sing one of its songs), visiting students, and a scratch orchestra made up of Tippett's London friends and acquaintances, of a work for which he had written the music to a text which the programme attributed to David Michael Pennyless. In fact, it was the work of a troika of Tippett himself, his friend David Ayerst, a *Manchester Guardian* journalist who had reported on deprivation in Cleveland for his newspaper, and a woman whom much of Boosbeck might in most circumstances have been tempted to write off as an upper-class bigwig: Ruth Pennyman of Ormesby Hall.

The clash of cultures that night must have constituted a discord that little in the music of Tippett could have matched. Yet unlike the glamorous first night audience that assembled twenty years later for the premiere of what it regarded as the composer's long-awaited first opera, *The Midsummer Marriage*, only to reel out in late evening largely disappointed and baffled, this one was warm and approving; as the people of Boosbeck had also been when the year before Tippett conducted similar forces in a somewhat truncated version of Gay's *Beggar's Opera*, with a miner's daughter, Madge Tansley, as Polly Peachum and a local insurance agent as Captain Macheath.

The best way to get a sense of the circumstances that had brought the young Tippett to Boosbeck is to take the road that runs south from the eastern end of the main street (and the main street is most of Boosbeck), past the old mining site at Margrove Park down to the A171 as it makes its glorious way under the shadow of Roseberry Topping towards the coast at Whitby. At the village end of this road is the old Miners' Institute building, boarded up when I was there in the summer of 2009 though still in occasional use, with its

clock stopped, perhaps for ever, at a quarter to nine. The performance of Tippett's *Robin Hood* was staged in a building beside it,
Boosbeck church hall, which has now gone.

Half a mile or so down this road, on the eastern side, is a parcel
of land known as Heartbreak Hill, the location now of a sturdy collection of nibbling sheep with a derelict shed and a few small stone
buildings dating from Tippett's day, under a wooded hill. This was
one of three sites procured in 1931 by Major James Pennyman of
Ormesby Hall, husband of Ruth, in an attempt to find useful employment for the area's vast army of unemployed. Their jobs had
been suspended and possibly lost for good because of the steady
decline of the ironstone industry, which was severely diminished
and on its way to eventual extinction through general economic
uncertainty and an influx of cheap imports from Spain.

Portraits of James and Ruth Pennyman hang on the walls of
Ormesby Hall, twelve miles back towards Middlesbrough and
owned by the National Trust. With his serious glasses and neat
moustache the major looks like a perfect casting for the role of a
military man who in peacetime occupies a place on the local
hierarchical ladder that leads up towards the Lord Lieutenancy of
his county, while chairing the local Conservative Association. And
that is indeed what he was. His wife has the standard headscarf of
aristocratic county ladies, but there's just a hint in her face of the
unconventional; and Ruth – the major's second wife after his first
had died in childbirth, and ten years younger than Jim – more
than lived up to that indication. A producer of plays and stager of
pageants, she was also a writer, one of whose own plays was dash-
ing enough for the typing agency to which she sent it to have
complained about having its girls exposed to this kind of language.
She was, further, though she never belonged to the party, a
self-proclaimed communist. Books still on the shelves at
Ormesby give some flavour of the household's disparate interests: *The History of the Russian Revolution*, by Trotsky. *Problems in
Astrophysics. Noble Essences* by Sir Osbert Sitwell. *Soviet Communism:*

A New Civilization? by Sidney and Beatrice Webb. The *Collected Poems* of Austin Dobson. During the Spanish Civil War Ruth was instrumental in bringing Basque children to Britain and was eager to go out to assist the Quaker welfare operations in Spain. Though told not to go by the major, she managed to slip off briefly to Barcelona.

Malcolm Chase and Mark Whyman, authors of *Heartbreak Hill: a Response to Unemployment in East Cleveland in the 1930s*, published by two local councils, suspect the major's motives in starting the Heartbreak Hill project may have been partly political – to distance himself from the local Conservative MP, Commander Robert Bower, whose lack of evident feeling for the sufferings of his constituents threatened the party's hold on the Cleveland seat. There may have been another significant calculation too – owners of fine houses and lavish surrounding land, like the Pennymans, had reason to fear for the future if the mood of the unemployed turned from sullen acceptance to anger and then even perhaps to revolution. Yet in Mark Whyman's account of the couple, *The Last Pennymans of Ormesby: the Lives of Jim and Ruth Pennyman of Ormesby Hall, near Middlesbrough*, you can see a gradual change in Jim, which his wife above all must have wrought. From a privileged background, schooled at Eton, a basically decent but thoughtless and blinkered imperialistic military man, he begins to show a compassion for work-starved men and their families in places like Boosbeck, leading him, like the future Edward VIII in the South Wales valleys, to the conclusion that Something Must Be Done.

Jarrow, fifty miles to the north, may have caught the popular imagination, but the blight that encompassed East Cleveland went beyond Jarrow's. In three years from 1930, the number of jobs in the ironstone mines of East Cleveland fell from 4,361 to 1,076. The figure for those out of work in the labour exchanges of the two most easterly districts of East Cleveland was close to 90 per cent. 'There are probably worse villages and there are better,' Ayerst wrote in the *Manchester Guardian*. 'It is probably a fairly average village in the ironstone country.' He brought home just what that meant by itemizing the inhabitants in one street of fifteen houses. Two-thirds of its men who were able and willing to work were unemployed. Two of those still in work were employed to relieve unemployment.

Though ostensibly the creation of the Cleveland Unemployed Miners Association – a formula arrived at to allay trade union fears and apprehensions about what might otherwise seem the product of a patronizing lordly philanthropy – the scheme devised for East Cleveland was largely the work of the Pennymans. The major persuaded a sympathetic local landowner to make available three pieces of land: Heartbreak Hill; a second site at Charltons, just off the main Whitby road; and a patch close to Lingdale, at the top of the hillside above Heartbreak Hill, called Busky Fields. There was not much money to fund the venture, and the land that the major acquired was meagre and unrewarding. That was how Heartbreak Hill got its name. The land at Charltons, festooned with rocks, became known as Dartmoor, while 'busky' is a local word indicating gorse, which copiously flourished, impeding every attempt at cultivation, on the third of these sites – though here at least the digger could pause from his labours and take solace in the views of the sea.

The prospect of working this land was not attractive to those who had made their lives in ironstone mining. As one former miner told Malcolm Chase: 'it was all land that had to be reclaimed. It was all just moorland, rough ground, whin bushes, bracken, you know, anything, rubbish.' They'd have much preferred to have been assigned allotments such as those on which some of their number already worked with enjoyment and satisfaction, on an individual basis, rather than communally as the major insisted. But such choices were not on offer. So some sixty men were found to work the three sites, unpaid, but with the expectation that they would share in such profits as might accrue.

Some dropped out early on. The workforce fell to around about thirty men; but later the numbers climbed back to sixty. Part of the problem was that years of demanding physical work followed by poverty and inadequate food had left some of these men too weak for the effort the rough lands required. One solution for that, the progenitors came to conclude, was to recruit the kind of young, strong and healthy young men from prosperous homes who in other areas of England were already enlisting for work camps.

That aspect of the operation brought to Boosbeck a creator of work camps elsewhere, especially at his farm at Springhead in Dorset: the romantic dreamer Rolf Gardiner, who believed that the nation's salvation lay in the rejection of the ugly, inhuman, mechanical world of modern industry and a return to a life based on the rhythms and logic of nature. That could only be done by finding idealistic young people to share his dream, ready to content themselves with simpler forms of employment, to enrich their lives with music and especially dancing, and to turn aside from the temptations of material wealth and such low forms of art as American jazz. The apparent fascination of English youth with degenerate America left him repelled. He dreamed instead of an English alliance with its traditional partners in Germany and the Baltic; and he found inspiration here in the youth movements of Germany. These blue-eyed blond young men in their Lederhosen were models he longed for English youth to emulate. He had spent much of his own youth in Germany, and he tried to ensure that the work camps that he created were enhanced by the presence and infectious example of Germany's young idealists.

The first of the camps that came to be associated with the East Cleveland projects of Jim and Ruth Pennyman was based in tents at Marske on the coast. Here the programme followed the lines that Gardiner had developed at Springhead. An early reveille, a bracing march through the countryside along routes devised by himself with hymns that he had selected to be sung on the way. A morning and afternoon that interspersed exacting labour with time for rest, reflection and reading and lectures on suitable subjects, and choral singing to finish the day. Organized games, which the campers might have enjoyed, but which Gardiner regarded as demeaning, were discouraged.

Yet East Cleveland too had an aspect, outside its hard reputation, which had originally brought the area to his notice, and exemplified what he wanted to find and develop in England's national life. There was a tradition in the communities here of sword dancing. The village, or small town, of Skelton, next door to Boosbeck, had a lively and accomplished sword dancing group, with men who worked the ironstone mines through the day demonstrating a high degree of grace and skill. For Gardiner, music and dancing were as much a part of the *raison d'être* of these ventures as the agricultural labour. For the first of the camps the musical direction was entrusted to his German friend Georg Goetsch. But Goetsch was not available for the second. David Ayerst, the *Manchester Guardian* journalist who had written about the East Cleveland project, suggested that they should send for his friend Michael Tippett.

Tippett at this point was living in a village in Surrey, having finished a course of studies with the celebrated teacher R. O. Morris, unemployed and uncertain what to do next. He brought with him his closest woman friend, Francesca Allinson – she played Lucy in the production of *The Beggar's Opera* – and his first serious lover, Wilfred Franks. He was expected to dig, and Chase and Whyman suggests that his concentration on music helped him avoid that requirement. 'He lasted one morning,' they say, 'hated it, and devised the idea of an operatic production partly as a means of escaping the tyranny of the spade.'

It was never part of Gardiner's plans that Tippett should write himself: Gardiner's emphasis was on early polyphony, a diet to which Goetsch had adhered. Though it was Tippett himself who told Malcolm Chase of his reluctance to dig, he pictures his motives rather differently in his memoir *Those Twentieth Century Blues*.

At the 1933 Boosbeck work-camp, I joined in the digging of the land, living in a tent with the students. I thought ultimately the best

means of bringing everyone together would be a theatrical performance and decided to create for them a version of *The Beggar's
Opera*... The performance took place in the local welfare hall: entrance cost adults one penny and children one halfpenny. The audience that appeared was so considerable that I was crushed up against
the little orchestra I was conducting. One lady, arriving late, was
turned away by the local policeman. She waved her umbrella threat-
eningly, and said. 'I'll beat yer bloodie brains in, yer buggers, if you
don't let me in!'

At the next work camp, he says, he got even closer to the villagers,
since this time he stayed in the home of an unemployed miner.
What he found in Boosbeck – the poverty, hardship, and near-de-
spair of the miners, the lack of evident bitterness, the honesty and
warm-heartedness – had a lasting effect, converting the light left-
wing political allegiance with which he arrived to the Trotskyism
that soon after he began to profess. His *Robin Hood* – not really an
opera, as he said in a letter to his fellow composer Alan Bush, so
much as 'a musical and comfortably romantic operetta' – was a tale
of the triumph of poor over rich. The work's upper-class villain not
only loses his girl to the lower-class man that she loves but ends up
financially broken, while the money for which Robin has ransomed
him is distributed to the general populace. 'And every man and
every maid,' says the final chorus, 'shall freely live in peace. None
shall be rich nor any poor. The curse of hunger cease.' That might
not have been quite how Jim Pennyman would have expressed his
best hopes for the future of British society, but these were plainly
Tippett's aspirations for Boosbeck.

So what did rough unsophisticated Boosbeck, which could never
have seen anything like it before, make of this visiting gallimaufry?
Despite the success of these two entertainments, relations were
sometimes uneasy. Initially, the presence of Germans among the student labourers, essential to Gardiner's vision of things, was resented
in Boosbeck, more at this stage because of lingering memories of
the First World War than because most people already imagined and

feared a second. On one occasion the Boosbeck brass band refused to perform in their presence. For a time some of the out-of-work miners feared that the students might be too soft and effete to do their share of the digging, though in fact because they were stronger and fitter they often outdug the miners.

There was clearly some disdain and distrust for Gardiner with his airy-fairy theories of life and extravagantly eccentric behaviour – an opinion that Tippett shared. But there is evidence too of some resentment over the paternalistic role of Jim Pennyman, amounting even to a temporary rebellion. Wilfred Franks described an incident on one of the digging lines:

> There were these two groups, you see. Rolf came along, and he said, 'Well alright now, you line up there and we'll line up here, and we're going to roll the turf back'... We went on, we worked for about an hour, no contact between them, you see. Then one of the miners said, 'Here he is, here he is', and they all stopped work and looked. And there was a car coming down the road. And *he* was Major Pennyman... He came along: 'This won't work, it's no use. We must all dig together in a line. Now one miner, one student, one miner, one student.' And the miners were standing there like this, and one of them shoves his spade in and walks away, and another one did the same thing, and they all did the same thing.

In April 1934 the *Cleveland Standard* published a glowing report in which its representative, V. W. B. S., described the attempt to alleviate dreary hours of unemployment by what he called work on a communal farm. 'Assisted by University students of different nationalities, including Germans, Scandinavians, and even Egyptians,' he enthusiastically reported, 'they are reclaiming rocky moorland and turning it into productive agricultural plots... They possess 600 head of poultry, 30 goats, 30 pigs, and 14 hives of bees... although the profits are devoted almost entirely to meeting overhead charges and the expansion of the undertaking, the unemployed are breeding their own stock as far as possible, and making pigstyes, cucumber frames and henhouses on the model of those purchased for them in the first place by Major Pennyman.' Mrs Pennyman, meanwhile, had organized a work party for the women of the village.

'Some of the miners,' said the *Standard*, 'naturally thought that the young gentlemen, not being accustomed to manual labour, would be "duds"; but they took off their jackets – and even their shirts – and now everyone has nothing but praise for the way the students tackled that hard work.' The building of a swimming pool and recreation ground for the village was now being contemplated.

What finished the project for good was the expectation of war, with the long-delayed rearmament programme rekindling demand and allowing some of the closed ironstone mines to reopen. Those who had laboured at Heartbreak Hill, in the gorse of Busky Fields and among the stones of Dartmoor, returned to their real occupations with relief, pleasure and pride. The last camp was held in April 1935. It has long been asserted in Boosbeck that one participant then was William Joyce, the Lord Haw Haw of German broadcasts to Britain during the Second World War, convicted of treason and executed in January 1946; but no proof has been found for that. The Pennyman scheme had also included an attempt to create an alternative source of employment in Boosbeck – a furniture factory whose products were for a while despatched to posh London stores, especially Peter Jones in Sloane Square. But that collapsed after a mere three years of existence.

Rolf Gardiner continued right up to the outbreak of war to try to build bridges with Germany, a country he deeply revered even though he rejected Hitler, whom he found incurably vulgar, as he did Mussolini. There is no way of knowing how many of those who had gone on his morning marches, sung the hymns he had chosen for them, and gone to bed in their tents with the sound of Monteverdi still in their ears, died in the war fighting against each other.

23

NORTH END, HAMPSTEAD

LUCY HOUSTON, DAME OF THE BRITISH EMPIRE,
WHO USED TO BE POPPY RADMALL, IS ORDERED
BY GOD TO 'FIGHT ON'; WHICH SHE WOULD
HAVE DONE ANYWAY.

ঌ

*'I entered the room and found her lying on a divan cov-
ered with rugs. She wore a red gown, had a red white and
blue neckerchief tied like a stock, and a red bandanna
about her head from beneath which a little blonde curl
was allowed to peep – a plastered little curl. Her puffy
old face and her peepy little eyes were like a caricature of
her caricatures. This, then, was the famous millionaire
harlot – the child who at sixteen had married from a
chorus after running the streets as a gamin – who had
had three official husbands and had taken for the last of
them Robert Houston of Liverpool, who made his
fortune out of coffin ships…'*

ON THE EASTERN SIDE of the road that eases down
from Hampstead Heath towards Golders Green, behind the Old Bull and Bush pub, there's a cluster of
quiet roads that snuggle up to the edge of the heath. They make
up North End – once a rural village separate from Hampstead,
now a mere subdivision. On the southern side of this settlement,
where a road called North End joins North End Avenue, is a
house that through most of its life has been quiet, modest and
uncontentious. That was how things were before Lucy Houston
arrived here in 1908; and again in 1936 once she'd been trans-

ported away to her overdue rest in a cemetery at East Finchley.

Through the years in between, however, there was nothing quiet or modest about it. From here there would emerge at any time of the day or night, sometimes on foot, at others installed in her car and urging her chauffeur to drive faster, a woman, usually clothed in red, white and blue and carrying wherever she went an enormous handbag – sometimes two – bulging with banknotes, jewellery, documents to be read or distributed, and letters written in violent language in violet ink on purple or blue writing paper. Sometimes a troop of her tatterdemalion political infantry would muster in the grounds of Byron Cottage to prepare for one of her missions: to persecute, for instance, Sir Samuel Hoare, Secretary of State for – and in her bestiary, spineless seller-out of – British India, and latterly, Foreign Secretary, as he defended his parliamentary seat at Chelsea. 'Not a statesman,' she wrote of him, 'but only a pirouetting mountebank... What does Sir Samuel Hoare know about India? I believe that he once went there for a weekend.' For this expedition she had her forces dressed as what were known in those days as nigger minstrels, and before they left she rehearsed them in a song directed at Hoare, composed by herself.

Early morning walkers on Hampstead Heath might meet her marching along with her handbag, and often with her faithful secretary who was used to being wakened at any hour of the night and summoned out for a stroll, pausing, should she meet a rough sleeper, to delve deep in her handbag and fish out a wad of notes; though at least she would not be naked on these excursions, as she sometimes was when she took her early morning constitutionals on the deck of her boat, the steam yacht *Liberty*. On a Sunday or a bank holiday you might find her making a speech on the Heath, perhaps on the rights of women. 'That', people would say as she marched back to Byron Cottage, perhaps to greet some lieutenant or to welcome some favoured visitor – the Prince of Wales was among the eminent figures who were seen at some time being swept into North End – 'is Lucy Byron'; or as she later came to style herself, Lucy Houston, Dame of the British Empire.

She had started life in dramatically different circumstances: born, whatever she usually claimed, in 1857, as Fanny Lucy Radmall, but know as 'Poppy', seventh child and third daughter of a maker of boxes in Camberwell. At sixteen she was on the stage – some accounts say as a chorus girl, others, as a dancer – where one night she caught the eye of a millionaire brewer from Burton-on-Trent, sixteen years her senior, called Gretton. So besotted did he become that he abandoned his job and his family and took her off to Paris where they lived, apparently happily, as man and wife until his death at forty-two in 1882, leaving her £6,000 a year (£290,000 a year in 2010 values) for life. In the following year she married Theodore Brinckman, who sometimes used the name Broadhead, the heir to a baronetcy, which meant that the new Mrs Brinckman might be Lady Broadhead one day. He was twenty-one. She told him she was nineteen, though in fact she was twenty-six. The marriage was doomed not to last, and in 1895 (at which stage his expected baronetcy had still not arrived) she divorced him on the grounds of his adultery.

After a six-year interregnum, she was married again, this time to a baron, thus acquiring an even more enviable name than 'Lady Broadhead' could ever have been: Lady Byron. Her new husband, as she took pleasure in pointing out, was a relative (though in fact only a very distant one) of the poet and fighter for liberty who had long been one of her heroes. This must have made up for some less alluring aspects of the new match. Bankrupted two years earlier, Byron was commonly known in society as Red-nosed George. In 1908, seven years into this marriage, she bought Myrtle Cottage, North End, and renamed it Byron Cottage. If this was to honour her husband, that was exceptional, for in other respects she honoured him sparingly, if at all. Indeed, as the marriage began to disintegrate, she sent him to live in the servants' quarters, while she lorded – or ladied it – in the rest of the house, cut off by a green baize door.

George died in 1917, at the age of sixty-one. As with her previous marriages, there were no children. Five months later his widow became a dame, one of the first contingent of dames to be appointed, in recognition of her provision for nurses in Hampstead during the war. None of the rest of those chosen had come from a background remotely like hers. Apart from a former mayor of Oldham, Lancashire, all came from the peaks of society, with Queen Mary herself at their head.

Lucy's final conquest, and much the most prized, was Sir Robert Paterson Houston, whom she met in 1921 or 1922 and married two weeks before Christmas 1922. He was seventy; she must now have been sixty-seven. He was not to everyone's taste, any more than she was. Mightily rich, a shipowner who had made a fortune out of the South African war, and another out of the 1914–18 war, Sir Robert was a notably hard-faced Tory MP for one of the Liverpool seats, with a reputation, according to H. Warner Allen, one of Lucy's biographers, for 'downright brutality'. He lived in tax exile on Jersey, where his boat the SY *Liberty* was based. Hard though he was, Houston was clearly smitten. Friends counselled him against marrying her, suspecting the real attraction must be his money, but he shunned their advice and lavished presents on her – some of which she refused as not really worthy of her, and told him to spend even more. When his yacht was involved in an accident, the insurance claim for replacing her lingerie amounted to £4,000 – equivalent to around £85,000 in 2010. She further required him to change his will, bumping up the £1 million he had planned to leave her to £6 million.

Sir Robert's taste of late-life bliss was not to last for long. In their sixteen months of marriage he had two breakdowns, during which, both he and his wife agreed, she had saved his life. In April 1926, however, it was third time unlucky: this time, he died, leaving her, for the second time (the third, if you count her brewer), a widow, but a prodigiously rich one. On some estimates she was now the second richest woman in England. Whatever his friends had thought of her motives for marriage, she was deeply distressed by his death, becoming so distraught that the authorities of the island of Jersey

had her placed under restraint, from which she was rescued only by
the intervention of eminent figures brought expensively from London, including Lord Horder – physician to the royal family, to several
prime ministers and to a starry array of celebrities, who according
to *Time* magazine charged her $5,000 (around £40,000 now) for his
services. The religious visions she experienced at this traumatic time
remained a deep influence on her for the rest of her life.

There was never much doubt about what she would do with her
money. She had several homes to maintain – apart from Hampstead
and Jersey there was an estate in the Highlands of Scotland, which
she liked to describe as 'her fastness'. She kept on, though she rarely
used it, her husband's treasured boat, the *Liberty*, treating its captain
and crew with queenly imperiousness. She raced horses (her colours
were red, white and blue), whose trainers she ill-used in much the
same way. But she was, above all, a patriot, and she wanted her
money to serve her country. And the best way of doing that, as she
saw it, was to invest it in campaigns to restore the glory of England
– now, in her view, most dreadfully tarnished. She had for some
time been publishing political pamphlets that displayed an undoubted talent for vituperation coupled with a less than adequate
grasp of the libel laws, and now she contemplated founding a patriot
newspaper, which she wanted to call *The Pepperpot*. Reluctantly
brought to accept that the project was unlikely to work, she alighted
instead on a weekly magazine called the *Saturday Review*, which
became the principal passion of the last few years of her life.

The *Review*, before she laid hands on it, was a political and literary
journal, well to the right of centre but gently and innocuously so.
Its main mode of controversy was a series of debates in which one
writer commended a man or a cause while another argued against.
A piece headed 'Why I Like G. B. Shaw' was thus immediately
countered by a piece that condemned him. Hitler was dealt with
in the same even-handed fashion. Much of the rest of its space was
devoted to reviews of the arts and to poems by well-loved figures
like Alfred Noyes. But the last thing its new dominatrix wanted the

paper to be was innocuous. Noyes before long was out, and noise was very much in.

She announced herself in the edition of 11 March 1933: 'Knaves or Fools? by Lady Houston D.B.E.' – the byline she usually favoured, though sometimes she would sign herself Lucy Houston, Patriot, or Lucy Houston, Truthteller. 'Clumsy ineptitude,' she declared, 'is the Trade Mark of the "National" Government in every law they utter. The more stupid and senseless their "gestures", the more they chortle and chuckle and pat themselves on the back... Were I asked to put in the pillory England's three greatest knaves (or fools) I should name Ramsay MacDonald [the Labour prime minister heading the National government], Sir John Simon [the National Liberal Foreign Secretary] and Stanley Baldwin [the Conservative leader and number two to MacDonald]. And until these three false, fatuous, fuddle-headed self-illusionists are got rid of, England will go from bad to worse.'

From then on, ceaseless torrents of calumny poured out of the *Review*'s headquarters in the Adelphi, where Lucy used to be swept in style in fast cars that did not go fast enough for her liking. (Once under harassment her driver went the wrong way round a round-about and was caught by a policeman. 'I am Lady Houston,' his employer announced in terms that she clearly thought would settle the matter. 'Drive on!') For a time, the editor she inherited, Guy Pollock, remained in post. But although some of the ambience of the former *Review* remained – columns on fishing and drama and radio, a fashion feature from Paris, denunciations of the persecution of motorists – Pollock had little if any remaining influence over it. He also distressed her by refusing to publish some of her verse.

Lady Houston cranked up the vehemence week by week. Pollock was supplanted by an editor whose views were entirely in tune with her own and who did not recoil from her versifying. She gave the magazine a new cover. 'Under which flag?' it demanded. 'The Honoured flag of our Forefathers – when Britannia Ruled the Waves – and kept the peace of the world because Her Navy was

Supreme' – or – 'The Red Flag of Socialists, Communists, and Bolshevists – Three Names with but one Meaning – Disintegration
and Slavery – for all Britons.' Beneath this there appeared every
week the rubric: 'Cover designed by Lady Houston DBE.'

'Our new cover,' an editorial note explained, 'has been designed
by Lady Houston, who, probably more than any other individual
patriot, typifies and expresses the sturdy British independence of
thought and clarity of imperial wisdom which made our Empire.
To-day that Empire is being given away. Conservatism, the creed of
Empire, is being watered down with a base mixture of Liberals and
Socialists. Our prime minister, a Socialist whose record irrefutably
brands him as a traitor to this country, leads a government elected
on Conservative principles with the largest Conservative majority
on record. To us it is lamentable, suicidal…' This was one of several
occasions when the magazine appeared on the street with sections
blacked out because the distributors could not risk handling anything quite so libellous. The trade, her editor wrote, was frightened.
The one person who was never afraid was Lady Houston: 'the trouble is that Lady Houston *will* speak the truth – and all the King's
horses and all the King's men cannot muzzle her.'

She had sent the PM a telegram challenging him to sue her; he
had, of course, not responded. It was unmistakably clear, the *Review*
repeatedly stated, that the policies of the government were being
dictated to the traitor MacDonald by Communist Russia. She fitted out the SY *Liberty* with lights that spelled out the message: 'To
Hell with the traitor MacDonald'. On Remembrance Day 1933
she published one of those outbursts that caused the distributing
trade to tremble and refuse to deliver the paper: 'Our Prime
Minister today – Ramsay MacDonald – is the same man who –
when our soldiers were being mown down and could not defend
themselves for want of ammunition – preached for and wrote to
munition workers to play Ca-Canny – and to strike! How can any
of you – who read these words and mourn the irreparable loss of
the one you loved best – be sure that your dear one's life was not

sacrificed – through the TREACHERY OF THIS TRAITOR!!'

Yet Baldwin's offence in her eyes was scarcely less dreadful. A man who called himself a Conservative was colluding in treachery. After the 1935 election the Dame's twin traitors were joined in the pillory by the new foreign secretary, Anthony Eden – a mere mouthpiece, the magazine said, for the Russian foreign minister Litvinoff. Riled by the *Review*'s attacks, Eden was bold enough to inquire: 'Who is Lady Houston?' And who, the dame retorted, was Anthony Eden? 'A certain nancyfied nonentity. To Mr Eden – love of country – is anathema.'

These assaults were not the work of the lady alone. She surrounded herself at the review with a strange little coterie of loyalists, inspired in equal part by devotion to Houston and hatred of those whom she hated. J. Wentworth Day, a former PA to Lord Beaverbrook, who had negotiated her acquisition of the *Review*, was her choice to replace Pollock as editor. He listed among his hobbies in *Who's Who*, alongside shooting, fishing, riding and sailing, 'taking the left-wing intelligentsia at its own valuation'. The magazine's columnist 'Historicus' was Collin Brooks, right-hand man to Lord Rothermere and his editor for a time at the *Sunday Dispatch*. In his journals, recalling their first meeting, he refers to Lucy Houston as 'the famous millionaire harlot' and says he was warned before he made the journey to Byron Cottage that he might find her sexually predatory. Much more than Houston herself, he was anti-Semitic. Brooks was the author of pieces such as 'Is Britain to be the catspaw of Moscow?' and 'If I were King' ('If I were King, I would join hands with those states which have purged themselves of decadence and Bolshevism. I would tell them that Britain, too, is for purity of race and for the high traditions of the past.')

Its columnist 'Kim', author of such contributions as 'Betrayal of our Navy by the Lossiemouth Delilah [MacDonald]' was Comyns Beaumont, the man Lady Houston had had in mind to run her putative *Pepperpot*. A former *Daily Mail* journalist who had edited the *Bystander*, Beaumont wrote an extraordinary series of books based on the theory that the universe had been shaped and reshaped by a series of great catastrophes (there are curious echoes here of Hugh Miller's theory of successive catastrophes). He believed, among other things, that the great Egyptian dynasties had ruled in South Wales; that Jerusalem had been located in Edinburgh; that Jesus was born in Glastonbury and the events of his life occurred in Somerset; and that Francis Bacon, author of Shakespeare's plays, was the illegitimate son of Elizabeth I.

The life of Mrs Nesta H. Webster, whose popular work *The Surrender of an Empire* was serialized in the *Review*, had been irreversibly changed by reading a book about the French Revolution, in the course of which she realized that she was the reincarnation of a countess who ended her life under the guillotine. Her death had been brought about by a shadowy sect called the Illuminati, which, propelled by the Jews and Freemasons, was now dedicated to the destruction of Britain. Almost equally paranoid was another star of the Houston stable, Meriel Buchanan, supplier of such contributions as 'You are heading straight for Bolshevism, Mr Baldwin', and 'Communists plan to pervert England's youth'. What she wrote was inflamed by the experiences of her father, who was British ambassador to St Petersburg from 1910 through to the revolution.

The dame made endless telephone calls, often lasting an hour, at any time of the day or night that suited her. Those in her coterie were subject at any moment to imperious summonses to her Berchtesgaden at Hampstead, where, says Warner Allen, another faithful adherent, she greeted them in bed, wearing a pink turban and a bright red dressing gown and a priceless fur coat. Collin Brooks recorded a visit that he'd been asked to make by Warner Allen on 21 January 1935:

> I entered the room and found her lying on a divan covered with rugs. She wore a red gown, had a red white and blue neckerchief tied like a stock, and a red bandanna about her head from beneath which a little blonde curl was allowed to peep – a plastered little curl. Her puffy old face and her peepy little eyes were like a caricature

of her caricatures. This, then, was the famous millionaire harlot – the child who at sixteen had married from a chorus after running the streets as a gamin – who had had three official husbands and had taken for the last of them Robert Houston of Liverpool, who made his fortune out of coffin ships.

Her working methods were legendary. 'Lady Houston,' says Wentworth Day, 'read every word that went into the paper. She dictated her articles at top speed – in jerks and flashes. Punctuation was entirely foreign to her literary composition. She sprinkled dots and dashes through her paragraphs like pepper from a pepper pot. She underlined, rewrote, crossed out, asked for advice, ignored it, told you to mind your own business, and then, when the whole thing was going to press, rang up the printers and altered half of it – at overtime costs which made one shudder.' Having asked Warner Allen, to furnish her with an article, which she said she was too tired to write herself, she then changed it all except for one paragraph, only to ring up to say that, having thought further, she'd deleted that too, since, as she told him, she could see that the piece would be better without it.

Byron Cottage was cold (the dame was a fresh air fiend), uncomfortable and wildly disorganized. 'One might,' says Warner Allen, 'have had the feeling that the owner of the house had fallen on evil days and could no longer afford to keep it up in the accomplished style.' Except for her ill-used secretary, Miss Ritchie, her staff at Byron Cottage were constantly leaving her service rather than take her bullying. Even Miss Ritchie used disconsolately to hand in her notice from time to time, though she always withdrew it. The dame's entourage at the *Saturday Review*, however, nearly always forgave her; for her spirit, her commitment to the causes they shared, and her impetuous generosity, both to groups whose predicament troubled her, including impoverished herring fishermen in Scotland and unemployed miners, and to her favoured political causes. To show solidarity with India – by which she meant both the British in India and the native subjects fortunate enough to benefit from their wise and benign overlordship – she funded an expedition to fly over Everest.

When in 1931, the government, shackled by economic constraints, refused to fund a British entry for the Schneider aviation trophy to be produced by Supermarine to designs by R. J. Mitchell, she put up the money herself. Concerned above all by London's defencelessness against a possible threat from the air, she offered the government £200,000 to spend on rearmament. She claimed a uniquely powerful endorsement for this initiative. 'Weary and sore distressed after meditating for many months,' she wrote to the Chancellor, Neville Chamberlain, 'again and again I have prayed to God for advice, and I have asked Him if I am right in fighting in my poor weak fashion for the glory and welfare of England, and always the answer is - "yes, you are right. Fight on."' To her disappointment and rage, Chamberlain refused the offer (on the orders, she deduced, of the traitor MacDonald). 'Please forgive me,' she wrote back to him, 'I evidently have made a mistake – I thought you were a Conservative.'

As editor, Wentworth Day had little choice but to reprint her doggerel, such as this, in honour of the twenty-three-year-old Randolph Churchill, maverick son of Winston, when he fought a by-election at Liverpool Wavertree against the official, Baldwin-supporting, Conservative:

> When the TRUTH is told to Wavertree,
>   Wavertree will set INDIA free
> And Socialist Mac will be up a tree
>   We shall see what we shall see.
>
> Our India kinsfolk over the sea
>   Are crying to thee
> To save them from horrors you cannot see.
>   YOU AND RANDOLPH can set them free.
>
> For Randolph is brave and Randolph has youth
>   And is boldly determined to tell you the truth.

Pitt was premier at twenty-three.

Why not he?

Week by week their correspondence columns bulged with tributes to Lady Houston. Room had to be found not just for her appeals to the women of Britain ('Beware Socialism!' was the rule they ought to adopt) but even her views on music. ('The very name Bach is repellent to me, and I always enjoy the story of the man who answered the question of the lady, "Is Bach still composing?" "Madam, I should think that Bach is by this time decomposing."') He had to repeat week after week tirades by Lady Houston DBE that had given their author particular satisfaction, while throughout the winter space had to be found for Lady Houston's Cold Cure – a concoction in which castor oil played a significant part – accompanied on occasion by tributes from grateful readers who had never been troubled by colds once they'd discovered her remedy.

In the end even he could take no more of her, and in the final months of 1935 he resigned. Yet he had no reservations when he came to write his memoir of her in declaring that here was a truly great lady: the woman who, by taking the interest she did in the Schneider Trophy had helped bring about the design of the Spitfire, and for this and other reasons, 'the woman who won the war and shamed a government that time and again had declined to protect its people'.

But precisely from what and from whom were these vital air defences needed to protect Britain (or, as she more often said, England)? Even her readers must sometimes have been a little perplexed. That Soviet Communism constituted the great threat to civilization in the whole of our island story was taken as read. But what about Germany? She and her confrères were not against Fascist dictators. They shared her boundless admiration for Mussolini (she even gave the name Benito to her griffon dog). In September 1935 she sent him a telegram:

Il Duce Mussolini, Rome

English patriots present their homage to Mussolini, the greatest patriot in the World – for his aim for Italy is to build up and achieve
– while the British politician's aim is to drag down and destroy the
British Empire. English patriots hope Mussolini will stand fast and
damn the League of Nations – WHICH ONLY EXISTS TO
ENABLE RUSSIAN BOLSHEVISM TO DESTROY CIVILI-
ZATION. – Lucy Houston, S.Y. *Liberty*.

But Hitler? He, at least at first, was a rather different matter. In May
1933, at the outset of Lucy's dominance, one *Review* contributor
condemned him in strident terms. It was little short of impertinence
to bracket these two leaders together. Fascism, the doctrine of Mussolini, stood for the family, religion and discipline. None of these
made any appeal to the Nazis. The Germans, others warned, were
set on war, and if war came, would bomb London. Unlike some of
her viciously anti-Semitic associates, Lady Houston was troubled
by Hitler's treatment of Jews and his attitude to religion. Still,
Moscow troubled her more, and by 1935, her admiration for Hitler
had blossomed. The turning point arrived in March 1936 when the
cover of the *Review*, as ever designed by Lady Houston DBE, bore
the message: 'Heil Hitler!' alongside the Führer's portrait. 'No happier event could happen,' the magazine inelegantly pronounced,
'than a pact between Germany, France, England, Italy and Japan.
This would ensure the peace of the world. – Lucy Houston.'

When Hitler took his troops back into the Rhineland, everything
fell into place. On 14 March, 'Kim' (the catastrophist Comyns
Beaumont) ran a piece headed: 'What a Man!' Hitler's 'symbolical'
remilitarization of the Rhineland, it argued, had justifiably broken
the chains with which Germany had been shackled by the Treaty
of Versailles at the end of the First World War. A few pages on, in a
piece titled 'Hitler – The Man of Destiny', Meriel Buchanan wrote:
'It is the penalty of every great man that during his lifetime he is
criticized, misjudged and hated, as well as being admired. Never has
this been more the case than with Adolf Hitler...' The villains in
future would be the French, standing out against that longed-for

alliance, which, by uniting Britain and Germany, would render Hitler's Luftwaffe no kind of a threat from then on.

The *Review* had acquired a new writer who called himself Ignatius Phayre (his real name was William George Fitzgerald) and he caught the new mood to perfection. Despatched by *Homes and Gardens* magazine to write a descriptive feature about Hitler's eyrie at Berchtesgaden, he knocked off a piece for Houston as well:

> Most of his writing is done in the sun-verandah. Thus occupied, no one ever dares to interrupt the German leader in his close labour. Yet it will happen that adorers from Berchtesgaden and the villages down below will prowl around the barbed-wire fences, hoping to get a glimpse of him and a salute in response to their own 'Heil Hitler!' Sometimes, too one of their children may find a way to break in; so that the tense and silent scribe hears a piping cry – 'Oh, Führer – Ein autogramm!' [autograph]. Having written 'perhaps for an hour or full ninety minutes by the study clock, he will declaim his great oration with no hearers save an awed and respectful servant or two...

There was, however, still one thing adrift in the *Review*'s position. Stanley Baldwin's government, with the 'warmonger' Eden installed in the foreign office and taking his orders direct from Litvinoff, was incapable of promoting friendship with Hitler and thus assuring the nation's deliverance. But the dame and her associates found a solution there too. 'Mussolini,' wrote 'Kim', 'is a man of action. So is Hitler. Both these dictators have left the little manikins of democracy gasping for breath.' In Britain's present deplorable state, patriots must conclude that we needed the kind of leader that the happy Italians and Germans already enjoyed. On 2 May 1936, 'Kim' and 'Historicus' heralded the new theme. 'Kim' first:

> Hitler and Mussolini are dictators who, as such, are able to govern for the benefit of their nations and defy the proletariat vote for which Mr Baldwin is always angling but never hooks... What we want above all things in this country is an English dictator who will

aim to place Britain at the top of the nations in warfare and commerce. Such a dictator would throw off the League of Nations like accursed chains. We want a strong man, a pro-British patriot, who will rule with an iron fist. Round such a man, the whole nation would rally without doubt.

Then 'Historicus':

Let us compare the great prestige to which Hitler and Mussolini have raised their countries with the universal distrust and execration to which our fatuous trio of misleading leaders have dragged down our own country, and there is but one conclusion.

What Britain needs is a Benevolent Dictator.

But Our triumvirate of trickers are Baldwin, the Blunderer: MacDonald of Moscow, and Pretty Polly Eden.

There is in Britain to-day one man to whom the whole of the Imperial peoples look with love and confidence, a man tried in statecraft and in battle, a man truly benevolent at heart but strong of will. Our twisted constitution has surrounded him with "advisers" in whom he can have no faith. They have left his Kingdom unarmed at a time when their Moscow-policy has succeeded in antagonizing the most powerfully armed states in Europe...

Who should be chosen as Britain's dictator? She had sometimes been tempted by Oswald Mosley, and at one time, until deterred, had thought of giving him money. On the other hand, Sir Oswald, as she had written, wore a black shirt, whereas hers was red, white and blue. And all chance of accommodation was in any case ruined when one of Mosley's lieutenants wrote an unkind assessment of her, mocking her grammar, her punctuation, her handling of the *Review*, and even her patriotism, while suggesting even more brutally that the dame was old enough to know better. Lloyd George, who was sympathetic to Germany, was another possibility, but not one that convinced her.

Some readers of the *Review* thought the solution was Lucy herself: we don't need a Hitler, one wrote; we have got one already, in the person of Lady Houston.

It was left to the lady herself to specifically name the chosen candidate, one the *Review* had frequently praised for his interest in the armed services and the merchant navy, and even – which might have surprised his friends – for his 'rigid self-denial and self-sacrifice', and one whom Lady Houston both knew and adored: the former Prince of Wales – since January 1936, the king.

So now Lucy, once Poppy Radmall, daughter of a Camberwell boxmaker almost eighty years before, instructed her monarch direct in the pages of the *Review*.

> YOUR MAJESTY
> YOU ARE A GREAT AND MIGHTY MONARCH, BUT, YOU
> ARE **MUCH MORE** THAN THAT, A DEARLY LOVED KING
> WHO REIGNS BY LOVE IN THE HEARTS OF HIS PEOPLE;
> AND I AM WRITING THE THOUGHTS OF MILLIONS
> WHO LOOK TO YOU, THEIR KING, IN THIS TERRIBLE
> TIME OF STRESS TO DELIVER THEM…
>
> Italy has her Mussolini: he is *her* Man of Destiny… Germany has
> her Hitler… he is Germany's Man of Destiny… EVEN AS THE
> DUCE HAS RAISED ITALY TO THE UTMOST PINNACLE
> AND THE FUHRER HAS MADE GERMANY INVINCIBLE,
> WE WHO LOVE YOU LOOK TO **YOU**, OUR BELOVED
> KING, TO BE OUR LEADER, THE ONLY LEADER WE CAN
> TRUST TO SAVE US – AND WE IMPLORE YOU TO DO
> FOR YOUR EMPIRE AND FOR ENGLAND WHAT THESE
> TWO MEN HAVE DONE FOR THEIR COUNTRY.
>
> Lead us, Oh! My King, and we are ready to follow you *to the death*…

And of course this historic moment required a verse:

> That England soon may cease TO BE
> All the world can see – with glee.
> But we who love her must set her free.
> And that's the task for you and – **ME**.

'Kim' and 'Historicus' had already given Edward his orders. There was nothing in the constitution, they insisted, that required him to accept uncritically, or even at all, the advice of his rotten ministers. 'Does the King,' asked 'Historicus', 'yet know the most vital thing about his realm – that ever since the ascendancy of Ramsay Mac-Donald Britain has been virtually ruled to a Russian plan? Does the King know that at Geneva Anthony Eden is regarded as the protégé of M. Litvinoff (né Finkelstein) and that Litvinoff knows him for the protégé of MacDonald, who in 1917 called on the King's subjects to follow Russia into Bolshevism? The King knows how heartily the nation has approved his visit to Wales. Does he know how heartily the nation would welcome a similar practical leadership in all departments of the community's life?' Ministers, he concluded, must be made to give place to a man who could and would save his country. 'There is such a man and there is a need for him. Does the King know?'

It may well have been suspected at the *Saturday Review* that this was advice that the king might be happy to hear. There had certainly been suspicions at Westminster that Edward would not be adverse to the chance of exercising direct power. There were even more widespread suspicions that he was dangerously sympathetic to Hitler. As Richard Griffiths shows in his excellent book, *Fellow Travellers of the Right: British Enthusiasts for Nazi Germany 1933–39*, when Prince of Wales he had been rebuked by the King for making a speech wide open to exploitation by Nazi propagandists. He had argued that Germany's treatment of its Jews was a matter for them alone and not for the rest of the world. He was known after his accession to have been angered by the preference of the war minister Duff Cooper for friendship with France rather than friendship with Germany. The backbench Tory MP and diarist 'Chips' Channon feared the king was 'going the dictator way' and suspected he fancied being 'a mild dictator' himself.

As was to be expected, the *Saturday Review* reported that Lady Houston's article had 'stirred the country'. But what eager respondents to Lady Houston's petition would not have known, so effectively had the story been suppressed in Britain, was that even the king's present position was now under threat because of his wish to marry his American mistress, Wallis Simpson. That the *Review* repeated its demands for the king to take over only sparingly during the autumn suggests it was well aware of the possibly fatal threat to Edward. 'The King's wonderful personality and immense popularity,' 'Historicus' warned on 5 December, 'is frightening the ministers, who, behind the camouflage of the Constitution, in order to keep us tethered to Russian Bolshevism have kept us weak, when their duty was to make us strong.' For the issue of 12 December, Lady Houston, who never believed that the king would surrender, designed a front page with a romantic picture of Wallis, captioned 'The Queen of His HEART' and wrote: 'The plot to get rid of the King has failed – as it was bound to do... TO-DAY THE KING REIGNS GREATER AND MORE FIRMLY THAN EVER IN THE HEARTS OF HIS PEOPLE.' It was too late: rather than give up Mrs Simpson, Edward had announced his decision to leave the throne on the day before these words appeared.

The patriots of the *Saturday Review* knew straightaway who was to blame for this disaster. 'This,' wrote Meriel Buchanan on 19 December, 'is the work of Russia.'

The next edition, on Boxing Day, carried a letter from Lucy written to George VI, the brother who had succeeded her hero, which she described as 'a heart-to-heart talk with a friend'. The *Review*, she explained, had been trying for months to persuade Edward to sack his ministers and proclaim himself dictator. 'The fact that Mr Baldwin's government is most surely working for the Bolshevists via Mr Anthony Eden,' she told the new monarch, 'all who read between the lines must plainly see – and in this festive season sinister underhand work against England is being secretly pushed forward.'

Even now, in the midst of its grief, the *Review* did not forbear to reissue her cold cure. It could, however, offer no cure for a broken heart, and Lucy's faithful old heart, the friends around her feared, was broken; not just by the loss of the king she adored and the loss too, as she saw it, of England's saviour, but the fact that this work had been wrought by a man who had long been her principal enemy – Baldwin. 'When she learned of the abdication,' Collin Brooks wrote on 9 January, 'she raged as some Greek fury would have raged. Her daemonic energy during that week was frightening in its intensity. It killed her ... Sleepless, unable to take nourishment, she drove her mind without mercy, without rest – and saw her cause go down.'

Lucy Houston survived the abdication by a mere eighteen days. She died, entirely exhausted, on 29 December. As Wentworth Day records in his life of his heroine, Lord Horder, who had been Lucy's saviour in Jersey after the death of her husband, visited her that morning, finding all the windows open and the wind and rain driving in. He closed them. She reopened them as soon as he'd gone.

Unprepared for her death, the *Review*'s edition of 2 January had more about the lost king than about its lost editor. That was put right the following week when it reprinted tributes from newspapers across the land, along with valedictory assesments from its own writers, ranging from 'She Lived for England', by Meriel Buchanan, to 'Lady Houston's racehorses', by the racing correspondent, and 'Lady Houston and the Navy', by 'Periscope'. Her faithful worshipping readers must have expected still more tributes in the following week. Astonishingly, there was nothing. Instead the *Review* announced, with unconcealed relief, that the Houston era was over, while putting the price up from twopence, where she'd held it for several months, to its former sixpence. 'Today,' it stated, bizarrely – cruelly, even, '...the dictatorship... is over, and we return to constitutional government...'

Not one letter lauding the fallen warrior was included in the correspondence columns that had long been so loud in her praise. Her cherished writers had vanished with her; from now, readers of the *Review* would be left to find their own cold cures. There was one last event to set North End throwing up its windows and hoping to catch some sight of celebrities: the departure of the body of Lady Houston DBE on her final journey to East Finchley. The new king reigned regardless of her advice; and on 3 September 1939, defying all she had taught it, the nation went to war with Hitler. Before long Lucy Houston was as lost to much of the British public, whose deepest aspirations she had always believed she exemplified, as was Poppy Radmall before her.

24

TROWELL,
NOTTINGHAMSHIRE

ARTHUR SCOTT–PIGGOTT BRINGS UNEXPECTED
FAME TO A RATHER SLATTERNLY BEAUTY AND
THE HARD FIST OF TOIL UNADORNED.

🔖

*Trowell did not seek to be chosen as Britain's Festival
Village, 'nor did it expect that it would thereby become
the target for one of the most lamentable spates of
spite which a gall-filled fountain pen could squirt
in its direction…'*

THOUGH PLEASED AND HONOURED to have been
chosen, the people of Trowell did not try to conceal their
surprise. The rector, the Reverend Mr John Angles Barber,
seemed still to be rubbing his eyes as he summed up his feelings in
his *Trowell Newsletter*: 'We live our life against the background of
the great Stanton ironworks and there you have it! Stanton sends a
lot of money to Trowell and quite a lot of dirt as well, but again that
is how the twentieth century likes it.' 'Surely,' he concluded, 'the
point is that visitors can be directed to the Cotswolds, to Sussex and
to Devon and be told that this is what England was like in 1851.
Now come to places like Trowell and see what a hundred years have
done! That is what happens when the village grows and gets all its
"mod con". Some may see it as a true festival place. Others may
take it as a warning.'

And incomprehension must have been stronger the further you
got from Trowell. When in February 1951, three months before the
Festival of Britain was due to open, the announcement was made

that Trowell on the Nottinghamshire-Derbyshire border had been singled out to be Britain's Festival Village, the reaction outside its borders was one of bafflement lightly seasoned with mirth. Few had ever heard of the place, and even those who had were mostly unsure where it was. Indeed, when the occasion was over, the official history of the Festival located it in Northamptonshire.

Alfriston, Bibury, Finchingfield, Hutton-le-Hole, Thornton Dale – somewhere where visitors came to gasp at the prettiness of the place before enjoying afternoon tea – would have been readily understood. But why pick out this obscure little village of some 1,500 predominantly working-class people somewhere in the charmless east Midlands? There's a standard picture of Trowell that appeared in most of the newspapers when this astonishing news was announced. In the foreground is the sturdy fifteenth-century tower of the church of St Helen; beyond, through a miry industrial haze, the great grim outline of the Stanton ironworks, then the biggest in Britain, employing 8,500 people from Trowell and its environs (and nationalized, as it happened, just five days before the designation as Festival Village was proclaimed). There's a little hill just perceptible to the left of the works: it's a slag heap.

Then as now, Trowell liked to pride itself on being a sociable place with a wealth of village activity. It could not claim then, and does not claim now, to be pretty. Or at least, not 'conventionally pretty'; those who defended the choice liked to argue that the concept of beauty should not be simply defined as the kind of sunny serenity so common across the Cotswolds. Trowell had no village green on which it could dance round a maypole or stage summer fetes and cricket matches. In those days it still had a railway station to bring visitors curious to see what it was that had caught the eye of the festival planners, but what it conspicuously hadn't got – and this was generally agreed to make its selection even more odd – was a pub. There had once been three, perhaps four, but as one old inhabitant explained to visiting journalists, the last had been closed after a brawl that followed a skittles match with a visiting team from the nearby village of Stapleford. 'There were lots of heads cracked that day,' he remembered with unconcealed joy.

The village's own brochure for the festival was commendably blunt about Trowell. There was still, it said, a measure of natural beauty here; half a dozen farms, swans on the canal, the scent of hay in summer, the lovely old church… But modernity had caught up with the place. 'Gone are the old thatched cottages, and, except for a handful of the old dwellings, they have been replaced with small modern villas with all modern conveniences. Ribbon building, slag tips and open-cast workings with other unattractive features of industrial areas have laid a heavy hand on what was once a sleepy old English village.' The great works at Stanton with their blast furnaces and slag tips and haze of smoke, so impressive a sight by day, furnished a veritable pyrotechnical display by night. 'This,' the brochure instructed visitors, 'is the England of 1951, and this is what you have come to see.'

Why precisely Trowell was singled out from among the hundreds of villages considered for this appointment remained, even so, a mystery that a series of official statements failed to resolve. Herbert Morrison, the Labour minister who had taken charge of the project, with the hope, as he put it, of 'making the people sing' – an aspiration unlikely to have been voiced by his predecessor as festival supremo, the famously austere Stafford Cripps – seemed less than certain what the deciding factor had been when he came to the House of Commons on 19 February to answer questions from dissatisfied and envious MPs. As *Hansard* records:

Mr Driberg (Lab, Maldon, Essex,) asked the Lord President of the Council the reasons which have led the Festival of Britain authorities to select the village of Trowell, Nottinghamshire, for special commendation to Festival visitors; and if consideration will be given to the possibility of similarly commending other villages and small towns, in other parts of the country, which have, like Trowell, shown enterprise in planning their Festival programmes but are also, in their physical aspect, more conventionally beautiful.

The Lord President of the Council (Mr Herbert Morrison): Trowell has been chosen as a village whose effort to produce a worthy contribution to the Festival typifies the spirit of such endeavours. The object of this selection is to encourage places which are not conventionally beautiful to seize the opportunity of Festival year and to have a go at improving their amenities. In reply to the second part of the Question, I think it is for villages and small towns to put on the best show they can and for public opinion to judge the results at the time.

Mr Driberg: Is my right hon. Friend aware – with all respect to Trowell, which, I gather, is a delightful as well as a typical industrial village – that the basic industry with which most of our villages and small towns are associated is agriculture? Is he aware that many such places as Finchingfield or Coggeshall, or even places outside Essex, have an equal claim with Trowell to special commendation by the Festival authorities? That is the point.

Mr Morrison: I appreciate that every hon. Member will have quite a list of villages which he can suggest. This one was not picked out on the basis of urging people to go there as against other villages. It is an ancient village; the first mention of it was in 802; its motto is 'Independence and self-help' – [*Hon. members*: 'Hear, hear.'] – I thought that that might revive the earlier doctrines of the Opposition – and, in the words of the rector, it is the type of English village where the old rural life is passing away and where an industrial community has been superimposed… My information is that it is a good example of a case where the parish council is struggling with an industrial superimposition to prevent the village from being spoiled. It was chosen merely as an example of modern social problems in a village.

Earl Winterton (Con, Horsham): Arising out of the right hon. Gentleman's speech, might I ask him whether he could, for the benefit of my constituents and others having rural constituencies, explain the meaning of the term 'conventionally beautiful', so that in his eloquent words they may 'have a go'?

Mr Cocks (Lab, Broxtowe – the local MP): Is it not a fact that this village combines the strength of modern industry with the peaceful beauty of the English countryside, and is, therefore, typical of England today?

Mr Morrison: I understand that that is so.

Mr Oliver (Lab, Ilkeston – a neighbouring constituency): May I ask my right hon. Friend whether conventional beauty or the fact of its being a typical English village was the criterion on which the selection of this village was based? May I also ask him whether my hon. Friend the Member for Maldon (Mr Driberg) had been to see it before he put down this Question?

Mr Morrison: I do not suppose that for a moment.

Mr Driberg: Nor had the Festival people when they picked it.

Mr Driberg, as it transpired, was right about that.

So: a place with an exemplary Festival programme? An example of how to 'Have a Go' (the name of a popular radio quiz programme of the day, in which Wilfred Pickles asked questions and when the right answers were offered told his producer Barney Colehan; 'give 'em the money, Barney'); the scene of a typical conflict between urban and rural values? A nexus of social problems? Take your pick.

A further reason for choosing Trowell was suggested. People in the village will tell you today that one key to its success was its location in the very heart of the land. In a book published in 1976, based on an exhibition staged at the Victoria and Albert Museum to commemorate the 25th anniversary of the festival, the writer Mary Banham says one reason for the choice was that it was 'as near the middle of England, geographically, as could be managed': a statement that seems especially surprising since she places the village in Buckinghamshire. Whether Trowell is close to the centre of England is a matter for argument; but as people in Scotland and Wales might have been quick to note, this was supposed to be the Festival not of England alone but of Britain.

Still, we can at least be sure about the various ingredients in Trowell's exemplary festival programme. Fifteen weeks of events began with a church parade and service on 27 May. On 30 May, the parish council played the church council at cricket. On 2 June, there were displays of folk dancing; on the 6th, centre stage was taken by 'The Frolics – Trowell's own concert party', with repeat performances over the following weeks. More cricket ensued, including a match in Victorian costume between the parish council team and Ye Olde Trowelle Cricket Club. Visiting choirs gave concerts; village children staged a pageant called 'Trowell Through the Ages'; there were instrumental recitals, flower shows, sports days, a fire service display and performances of *As You Like It* and 'an old English comedy', *The Dumb Wife of Cheapside*. For a final flourish in early September, the Nottingham St Cecilia choir came to sing Haydn's *Creation*; there was a Festival of Britain fancy dress ball, and an epilogue service was held at St Helen's, which was floodlit for the occasion.

This programme was flavoured with a distinctly richer dose of nostalgia than the stated themes of the national festival sought to encourage; but certainly, for a village of 1,500 people, it seemed to reflect a commendable amount of endeavour. Yet none of this saved the choice from being met by a chorus of disbelief and disdain. Having ascertained where it was, the national press descended on Trowell, and not for the most part with friendly intent. 'Britain's festival village today,' wrote the kindly man from the *Manchester Guardian*, 'has been entertained by the sight of newspaper cameramen perched in balletic attitudes on the parapet of its bridge. They have been trying to focus in one view the fifteenth-century tower of St Helen's church with the rickyard behind it, a slag-heap or two, the swans drifting across the placid surface of the canal, a new housing estate, a thatched cottage, and the plumed giant chimneys of the Stanton ironworks a mile away...' For himself he discerned in the scene 'a rather slatternly beauty.'

Lord Beaverbrook's newspapers, the *Express* and the *Evening*

Standard in London, sniped as they always did at the Festival; Lord Beaverbrook was against it, so they had to be too. Yet the harshest assault came from the *Daily Mirror*, a Labour supporting paper, which in general backed the Festival. The *Mirror* subjected poor Trowell to a two-pronged attack. A reporter called Eric Wainwright had been to the village and uncovered (he proudly claimed) squalor and discontent. 'Even the 2,000 inhabitants' [the true figure, as the 1951 census shows, was just over 1,500] 'of this small place are surprised', he wrote. '"Why pick on us?" they ask. "There are hundreds of prettier places in t' country."... Slag heaps are its background, smoke rolls like an endless sea across its skies, and the fifteenth-century church tower is stained with soot. This is Britain with the hard fist of toil unadorned.'

Wainwright had been to see the households who lived in an area called the Forge, 'down a broken road, deep in mud'. 'Black-haired, forty-year old Mrs Booth,' he reported, 'bangs the kitchen table angrily. "Festival village? They're plain daft. Look at the conditions we live in down here. Let them do something about THAT."' The twenty-four gaunt brick houses at the Forge were part of the old Trowell, built seventy or eighty years ago, with one outside tap between four houses, twelve outside lavatories shared by everyone, open at the sides, and sometimes not emptied for three months. The rector 'rocked doubtfully on his heels' and ran 'nervous fingers through his black hair' when confronted by Wainwright. 'I agree that Trowell represents the spirit of 1951 better than some old-world village in the Cotswolds,' the Revd Mr Barber told him. 'But what are we to do with visitors if they come? We have no pub, no teashop, not even a village green where they can sit.'

Meanwhile in London his colleague Douglas Howell was naming the guilty men. The decision to pick out Trowell had been made, he'd discovered, not by Herbert Morrison, not even by the Festival director Gerald Barry (he, in fact, as Elain Harwood says in the Twentieth-Century Society's history of the Festival, confessed to a friend that he did not like the choice either, but thought they would have to live with it) but by a committee of four, all complete strangers to Trowell, headed by a man called Arthur Scott-Piggott. 'We had 500 villages on our books,' Scott-Piggott (44) explained to the *Mirror*'s man in his well-filled office overlooking the Strand. 'We chose Trowell out of the hat, you might say. In the first place it has got a very amusing name, and secondly, it is a real British industrial village in the heart of the country.' Mr Scott-Piggott, the *Mirror*'s sleuth reported, buttoned his double-breasted blue blazer and said: 'Are the sanitary conditions bad in Trowell? But they have got a wonderful housing scheme, and you find poor sanitary conditions everywhere.' Nothing here, one may note, about the excellent Festival programme, or the example the village had set in having a go; even the mixture of urban and rural is confessed to come second, in the estimation of the man who was chiefly responsible for taking the decision, to that oh so hilarious name.

The gritty down-to-earth people of Trowell were not in a mood to take such metropolitan snootiness meekly. The parish council called a special meeting to consider the *Mirror*'s attack. And across the county boundary in Ilkeston, the *Pioneer* newspaper summoned its star feature writer and ordered him over the top. He responded with a piece that they published on 16 February. In the view of the *Manchester Guardian* man, it compared with the best of eighteenth-century polemic. It said:

> 'Britain with the hard fist of toil unadorned'
> WHAT A SONG OF HATE
> Bitter attack on Trowell
> Festival village slur
> A reply by LEWIS RICHMOND

> Even the most ardent Southerner must be ashamed of the spiteful and malignant attack made in Wednesday's *Daily Mirror* upon Trowell, whose only offence is that it has been chosen as 'a typical English village' to be featured in the official souvenir programme of the Festival of Britain.

Trowell did not seek the honour, nor did it expect that it would thereby become the target for one of the most lamentable spates of spite which a gall-filled fountain pen could squirt in its direction.

We read: Trowell is five miles from Nottingham, on the borders of Derbyshire. It is built on coal in the shadow of Stanton Ironworks. Slag heaps are its background, smoke rolls like an endless sea across its skies and the 15th century church is stained with soot. This is Britain with the hard fist of toil unadorned...

This is, thank God, not typical British journalism; it is produced by Envy out of Malignancy... Trowell's offence is that it is situated in the heart of an industrial area, far away from the commercialized 'beauty' of the Cotswolds and the tourist agencies of the Metropolitan area... Many cottages in our 'recognised' show villages are not only unsanitary by modern standards but possess extremely bad record in deaths from consumption and other wasting diseases. Even the *Mirror's* venomous critic quotes 88 year-old John Else ('frail and gentle'), Trowell's oldest inhabitant, and describes him as 'sitting by the fire, a grandfather clock ticking in the corner, and a bird twittering in the garden.' Trowell's health and the longevity of its residents is almost a by-word.

...The alleged soot on the grey church tower is nothing to be compared with the dirt and grime that corrodes the spires and the towers of London... As for Stanton's slag heaps, they are fully a mile distant, and distance often lends enchantment, merging them into the foothills of Derbyshire and expressing with Stanton's massive array of furnaces, the mighty power that is Britain...

Taken as a whole, the Festival authorities have done well, very well indeed, to choose such a village for Festival presentation... Overseas visitors will get a far more realistic view of Britain and take away with them a far deeper impression of British life and character than if they were sent to a pretty, pretty picture postcard, pseudo Tudor village, replete with 'tea gardens', souvenir gift shops and half-timbered hostelries.

It was, Richmond admitted, a sad fact that Trowell had no pub; yet when the time came, Ilkeston's many cafés would not be found wanting.

The guns fell silent. The village's exemplary programme ran through the summer almost as planned. The festival left one lasting mark behind it. A pub was at last provided, which the owners had intended to call the Stuart Arms but which now became, as it still is, the Festival Inn. The Reverend Mr Barber was rewarded for his labours with an MBE in the New Year Honours, though local pleasure in that may have been mildly dimmed by the news that Mr Scott-Piggott ('We chose Trowell out of the hat, you might say') was appointed to the superior rank of OBE. Histories of the 1951 Festival give hardly more than a paragraph to the role of Trowell. The much-envied Festival Village faded out of the national consciousness leaving scarcely a mark behind it.

Yet fate had not finished with Trowell. Some time in the 1960s, Ministry of Transport planners drew lines on a map which would put the M1 motorway slap through the village. It was built deep down in a cutting, so it does not bifurcate the place as badly as the villagers must have feared, but local people say the noise is intrusive. At any rate, for outsiders now, Trowell is merely the motorway service station you come across if you're driving north between Donington Park and Tibshelf. This was once an exotic affair. 'Mecca's Trowell services on the M1 near Sherwood Forest (or near enough),' writes Joe Moran in his book *On Roads: A hidden history*, 'had a Robin Hood-themed Sheriff's Restaurant and Marian's Pantry, with a fibreglass greenwood, medieval banqueting hall and a 3D mosaic of jousting outlaws in the foyer. Mecca promoted Trowell as "an oasis in a concrete strip".' All that has now gone, and although the scourge of motorway catering, Egon Ronay, once issued a rare commendation in Trowell's case, when it later changed hands, he withdrew it.

And sadly, the people of Trowell never got to meet and to thank their champion and defender Herbert Morrison. The Festival brochure had promised that the gymkhana would be opened on behalf of the Festival authorities by the Rt Hon. Lord Morrison, which may have quickened expectations that the Lord President of the Council and unofficial Lord Festival would shortly be moving among them. They did indeed get Lord Morrison – but this was not the eminent figure who had helped to precipitate Trowell into its unexpected moment of fame, since he in those days was still plain Mr Herbert. Instead there was despatched to them a junior whip in the Lords called Lord Morrison; a figure in parliamentary terms, one might say, of an almost Trowellite obscurity.

25

HORSHAM, SUSSEX

*The very next week, however, would see the theatre
experiencing the direst night in its history. It could hardly
have been more ill-fated had the cast gathered together
at the rehearsal and chanted some theatrically fatal
word such as 'Macbeth'.*

O N   T H E   E A S T E R N   S I D E of the Carfax, the main
square of the old market town of Horsham in Sussex,
alongside a pub called the Stout House, there's a beauty
salon called Scissor Sisters, housed in an unremarkable building
where only the fanciful diamond-shaped window above the fascia
might hint to the passer-by that, years ago, the merchandise offered
here was laughter, excitement, and dreams.

Number 28 Carfax, into which the Sisters have expanded from
the building next door, began in 1911 as a cinema tucked away behind an outfitter's shop, but in 1917 two local entrepreneurs bought
the outfitter's to give the place a frontage on the square, renaming
it the Carfax Theatre. And theatre gradually superseded cinema, as
was still the case when in the spring of 1953 an actor-manager called
Alwyn D. Fox brought his company to Horsham in the hope of
bringing a sense of permanence to that insubstantial pageant – 'such
stuff as dreams are made on' as Prospero says in *The Tempest* – which
was the town's repertory theatre.

Fox was one of those stalwarts of repertory who appeared on

innumerable stages almost always outside the West End. 'He did seasons,' the profession's journal, *The Stage,* said of him when he died, 'in Crook, Dunoon, Dundee, West Bromwich, Bristol, Felixstowe, Halifax, Southport, Henley, Perth, Blackpool, Maidstone, Mundesley and Horsham. He was in the West End in "Vintage Wine" and was manager of the International Ballet for a time.' He was not an immediately likeable figure. 'A small, rather grisly man of about fifty,' his most subsequently famous recruit at Horsham would later call him. 'A pugnacious Scotsman whom I disliked on sight,' June Wyndham Davies, one of his young Horsham stars remembers (though in fact he was born in Hull). 'However it was obvious he knew the business inside out.' June would later establish herself as one of the key producers of the inspired Granada TV series of Sherlock Holmes stories with Jeremy Brett as the great detective. In retirement she moved to Spain, from where she sent me this account of the origins of Alwyn D. Fox's Westminster Repertory Company:

> The company came about because John Ruck Keene, Edgar Gray, George Cormack, Nada Beall and I were all in a touring production of *Rookery Nook.* We became close friends and had many laughs and were not looking forward to the day when the tour would finish. Edgar told us that he had a great friend, Alwyn Fox, who had a lot of experience running repertory companies and was looking for a theatre to start a new company. Some weeks later Edgar told us that the Theatre Royal Horsham was about to become free and asked if we would be interested in forming a company there. Horsham was close to London and we all decided that it might be possible to get agents, managers etc. to come and see us working. So we agreed to meet Alwyn and went to his flat at Westminster.

If you can get the theatre, they told him, we will all come and work with you. But one problem was the cost of acquiring the lease: a then daunting £100. Which of them could possibly muster that kind of money? According to June, 'As it happened I had just received a hundred from my grandfather. Looking at the anxious faces around me it was obvious where it was needed most. I gave it to Alwyn, who of course promised to return it when we were up and running and naturally I was a partner. Naturally I never saw it again.'

Most of the company were fresh young and burstingly eager to get on a professional stage and show the world what they could do. They must have known that the life they had chosen was by its nature precarious, but perhaps only Fox could have understood the hazards they faced in taking on Horsham. The theatre was empty because two previous companies had despaired of making it work. As normal life began again after the Second World War, an actor-manager called John Gordon Ash had found it in use as a dance hall and reopened it as a theatre, at first for three days a week and then for six. He mixed sure-fire farces and comedies and Agatha Christie thrillers with the occasional Ibsen and even Sartre, and did so with some distinction: in 1950, a production of *Journey's End* transferred to the Gateway Theatre in Notting Hill and then to the West End.

Yet, like all such small local theatres, and especially those prepared to risk the occasional Ibsen, the Court Royal, Horsham, as it called itself at that time, needed a successful pantomine to fill the coffers for the rest of the year and stave off any possible role for real-life brokers' men. In the 1952 Christmas season, that life-sustaining injection failed to materialize. Which was why, as Ash told the *West Sussex County Times*, the final performance of *Too Young to Marry* on 24 January 1953 would ring down his company's final curtain. 'For Mondays and Fridays,' *The Stage* reported him as saying, 'attendances have fallen off so much that on many occasions we have played to no more than a handful of people. Under such circumstances it has become obvious that it would be folly to continue.'

Did Horsham, a town of some 17,000 in the 1950s, want a theatre? Did it deserve a theatre? The *County Times* was confident on both counts, and in February it was reporting loud and prolonged applause for a young and talented company headed by Frank Dunlop (who would one day become a National Theatre director and impresario of the Edinburgh Festival) as it followed Shaw's *Arms and the Man* with André Roussin's comedy *Figure of Fun*, which Dunlop himself produced and in which he appeared as a 'chirpy French radio commentator'. His New London Theatre Company, the *County Times* critic A. S. D. F. enthused, was bringing a new level of drama to Horsham. Yet on 13 March, Dunlop was telling the paper that he did not think the place could work as a repertory theatre if the standard of plays and productions was kept at this level. The only future that he could see was to stage plays with impossibly tiny casts, or to switch to 'leg shows, pure and simple'. Where Ash had lasted six years, Dunlop had lasted three weeks.

Lights down again at the Carfax. Yet the very next week the Westminster Repertory Company was wowing an audience 'helpless with laughter' with a farce called *Love's a Luxury*. The *County Times* quoted Alwyn Fox thanking 'Monday's ecstatic audience'. 'It all depends on you,' he told them. The company soon settled down to a largely safe menu of popular thrillers and comedies – some of the latter written by Fox with scope for the broad North country roles in which he was said to excel.

As must always have been the case for such companies in small towns, it was a demanding regime, learning and rehearsing the play advertised for the following week while still playing this one's, especially when one might be *Charley's Aunt* and the other *King Lear*. Casting these shows could be a trial. The actress Elizabeth Spriggs, who died in 2008, recalled a comparable predicament. While still a green young actress, she had to play the mother of her sixty-year-old actor-manager. Fox's castings were, unavoidably, sometimes almost as bizarre, though A. S. D. F., a supportive though not an over-indulgent critic, thought the actors somehow carried them off. 'To play an eighteen-year-old schoolboy in a farcical comedy one week and the stern, middle-aged Rochester in Charlotte Brontë's strong drama *Jane Eyre* the next,' he, or she, wrote, '– that must be a repertory company actor's nightmare.' Yet Edgar Gray had achieved this with 'a performance of astonishing power and depth in one so youthful and physically unsuited to the role of the tragic master of Thornfield Hall... There is something of a young Olivier about his bearing.' All the more to be praised, he added, since apart from June Wyndham Davies, who 'fulfilled all hopes', the supporting roles were disappointingly played.

Unsurprisingly, performances did not always work out according to plan. 'Nada Beall,' Wyndham Davies recalls, 'had a very revealing role in *While Parents Sleep*. She had to do a scene in black bra and French knickers... Imagine her surprise when a man appeared from the audience, went up the centre footlights and took out his wallet, then threw twenty pounds on to the stage. When Nada ignored this gesture he threw the wallet as well. Fortunately the curtain came down. The wallet and the money were returned to him by the stage manager and he was escorted off the premises. Another time we were rehearsing the next week's play and a five-tread was in the middle of the stage representing the staircase. Suddenly a woman of about fifty wearing a white mackintosh appeared from the wings, walked to the top of the tread, paused, then asked: "which is the way to the Turkish baths?" Luckily it was only a rehearsal.'

On stage and off it, the young actors were having the time of their lives. The one problem was that too few Horsham theatre-goers were doing the same. One possible flicker of hope came with the arrival of a would-be actor called Michael Scott (his real name was Maurice Micklewhite, but he thought that too cumbersome for a stage career). Spotting an ad in *The Stage* for an assistant stage manager with a chance to play small parts, he wrote off to Horsham and was summoned for an interview by Alwyn Fox. 'When I arrived,' the actor writes in his autobiography, 'I was ushered into the theatre by a person of indeterminate sex and introduced to the boss. He was a small rather grisly man of about fifty and the minute he spoke I realised that he was a homosexual.' After looking Scott over, he summoned 'a man even smaller than Mr Fox and very slender indeed. He reminded me of Leonide Massine, the ballet dancer. Another poof, I thought.' This was Edgar Gray. He suggested to Fox that the newcomer might be suitable 'for those small butch parts like policemen that we have so much difficulty with'. 'You start on Monday,' they told him. And that was the beginning of the acting career of the man who became Michael Caine.

In his memoirs, inevitably titled *What's It All About?*, Caine pictures himself as naive and blundering, and regularly needing to be rescued from mishaps by June Wyndham Davies – 'always patient, gentle and kind – virtues that are not, you may be surprised to hear, abundant in the hearts of most leading actresses'. But the files of the *West Sussex County Times* tell a different story. Though it found his initial bit-part performances unconvincing, in July it commended Scott's best appearance so far as the drunken Hindley Earnshaw in *Wuthering Heights*. (Caine himself describes this event as something of a fiasco, in that he, six foot two and weighing over twelve stone, was required to be beaten up by the elfin Gray.) In August, A.S.D.F. was finding Scott's performance as a hypocritically sanctimonious butler 'a grand piece of comic contrast', while the following week in an Agatha Christie, he was turning in a performance 'that is astonishingly good... Mr Scott switches alarmingly from quiet charm to maniacal frenzy in a manner which certainly promoted a succession of spinal shivers in the idolizing bevy of High School beauty which surrounded your critic on Monday'. Idolizing bevies of High School beauty were just what the company needed to keep it alive. So it must have been a blow when after a number of further approving notices Scott was taken ill with a recurrence of the malaria he had contracted on national service in Korea. When his health improved, he wrote to Fox saying he would like to return. But unfortunately by then the Westminster Repertory Company had already succumbed to the curse of the Carfax.

The always optimistic *County Times* had said in November 1953 that Fox and his company had recently been getting some of the best houses since they arrived. And that was before the revenue boost expected from the pantomime, which that year was *Mother Goose*, written by Fox, who was taking the role of the dame. This time audiences lived up to expectations. The goose, even so, was cooked. On 1 January 1954, the *County Times* broke the news that the house would be going dark again. Yet when, still arrayed in his Mother Goose costume, Fox said goodbye to his last evening audience, he held out the hope that Horsham had not seen the last of his players. The company was taking a break, but would reassemble: 'I am sure it will not be long before we are with you again.'

Into their place in March came a company headed by Audrey Binham who, said *The Stage,* brought with her considerable experience in repertory at Halifax, Sheerness, Cleethorpes, Colne and the Channel Islands, in addition to seasons in New York and the West End. Again the *County Times* had high hopes: the company's performance of *A Lady Mislaid*, wrote its critic, was the best seen in Horsham for many a day, and their *Honeymoon Beds*, in March, produced 'gales of laughter'. But they had signed up only until June, and they saw no cause to continue.

Yet hope in this profession regularly outdistances cold calculation and again the vacancy did not last long. On 28 August the *County Times* reported that a new company called the Venturers – made up, as *The Stage* explained, mainly of young people only just out of the Central School of Speech and Drama – would be reopening the theatre under director John Clotworthy. The aspiring young troupe he brought with him were happy enough to play *See How They Run* when they were also in with a chance of appearing in Shaw's *Candida,* or even more daringly, *The Glass Menagerie* by Tennessee Williams. 'The company surpassed themselves,' *The Stage* wrote of this production.

But again, too few of Horsham's inhabitants had come to see them. On 21 January, under the heading 'Theatre producer has "lost £1,500"; Curtains in the Carfax?' the *County Times* sounded its death knell: 'The Venturers, who end their winter season at Horsham's Theatre Royal this week, have ventured as far as they are able without increased support. "Unless something extraordinary happens in the way of a guaranteed increase in the size of the audience, we shall not be able to resume," Mr John Clotworthy, leader of the company, told the *West Sussex County Times* on Monday… "And it's not the result of paying terrific salaries to star names," he added. "Expenses have been kept to the bone. No, the sole reason is lack of public support."'

He had known before coming to Horsham that he was on a 'sticky wicket'. The actors' union Equity, always anxious to protect young actors from the ill-effects of playing to near-empty houses, had been reluctant to allow him to establish his company in Horsham. [But] 'I couldn't believe that it was as appallingly bad as I have since found it to be.' The theatre, the paper said, might now become a warehouse. Happily, all but one of Clotworthy's company had found other work and Mr Clotworthy himself thought of returning to teaching, or he might go into business, as his father had always wished him to do.

No doubt the father of William Cook had nursed similar sensible aspirations for his son. But that didn't stop young Mr Cook from becoming the latest wide-eyed dreamer to try to save theatre in Horsham. On 14 June 1955, his Phoenix Players opened their programme with *A Horse, a Horse!,* a farcical comedy by L. du Garde Peach. This time, the *County Times* combined its usual kindly optimism with a dose of piquant realism; first audience reactions had been encouraging for this 'ill-fated playhouse in the Carfax'. On the Monday of their second week, however, a placard was attached to the front of the theatre that read: 'Unless you support us, we will close down on Saturday.' But audiences on Tuesday and Wednesday were even more meagre than Monday's, and on 1 June, the *Times* had to report: 'The theatre is empty again. The Phoenix Players have left… On Friday three people turned up for their performance of *Trial and Error*, they were given their money back and there was no performance.'

Yet once again, hope was on hand, as a familiar diminutive figure rode to the rescue of what was now the Theatre Royal. Alwyn D. Fox was back in Horsham again, with plans for a grand reopening. His hopes of one day returning with much of his former company had inevitably been disappointed; those left without work by the previous closure had gone to find it elsewhere. John Ruck Keene, a great audience favourite, had gone, and so had June Wyndham Davies, now installed as leading lady at the Margate Theatre Royal. But Fox himself and his partner Edgar Gray were in place, and the *County Times* was as hopeful as ever: 'There was no doubt about it,' it told its readers on 29 July, 'Horsham's theatre-going public welcomed back the Westminster Repertory Company on Monday, if not literally with open arms, with a spontaneous friendliness which permeated the theatre and made itself felt on the stage.'

The opening weeks, this being the summer holiday period, were sticky; but by mid-August the place was 'almost full' for *Why Not Tonight*? September brought a 'record' Monday audience for *Rebecca*, and for *Tons of Money*, which included a 'vintage' part for Alwyn D. Fox, 'the theatre was fuller than I have seen it for quite a long time'. In November there came more good news: Fox would be bringing some of the actors from his other company at Eastbourne to play on the Horsham stage. The very next week, however, would see the theatre experiencing the direst night in its history. It could hardly have been more ill-fated had the cast gathered together at the rehearsal and chanted some theatrically fatal word such as 'Macbeth'.

The play they had chosen was *Affairs of State* by Louis Verneuil. It was, said B. E. D., now the *County Times*'s regular reviewer, a night the company would want to forget. One of the players had 'fluffed' to such a degree that the rest of the cast had been unable to cope. Additionally, the programmes had failed to arrive, leaving the audience (whose size was not specified) to guess who was who. The plot hinged on a scene in which an American statesman offered his wife's lover a job in government. Unfortunately the actor who was due to proffer this promise had lost his way so entirely that he forgot to make it, leaving others in the cast to improvise material to restore some sense to the play.

At the risk of being accused of intruding into personal grief, B.E.D. called at the theatre next morning. The main reason for the fiasco, he was informed, was that the company was simultaneously staging *Lady Hamilton* at Eastbourne. Alwyn Fox, the listed producer for Horsham, had gone down to Eastbourne, leaving the Horsham production to Gray – yet Gray was playing Nelson at Eastbourne. So few of the company were left at Horsham, the paper noted, that at the end of the show one actor, Robert Savery, took one curtain call while his fellow actor John Barrabelle operated the curtain, after which Savery managed the curtain and Barrabelle took the bow.

And that was the last time the curtain fell in the ill-fated Carfax theatre. No word of Shaw or Ibsen, Ben Travers or Philip King, Dorothy L. Sayers or Agatha Christie would be heard in these precincts again. For a time Alwyn Fox maintained his operation at Eastbourne and continued thereafter to surface in a great range of places all over the country, as reported in the columns of *The Stage*. His final appearance there was in April 1982, when they printed his death notice. One of the last of the old school actor-managers, they called him, and said he was in his mid-seventies. In the death notices, a friend called Patricia Graves described him as 'actor-manager, pro-ducer, playwright' and above the line 'tender memories' quoted the famous speech from *The Tempest*: 'We are such stuff / As dreams are made on; and our little life / is rounded with a sleep.'

In Michael Caine's autobiography (where he says that his time at Horsham changed his previously contemptuous view of homo-sexual people) there's a poignant postscript to his account of his brief association with Alwyn Fox:

> Many years later when I was living in luxury in a big house on the top of a Beverly Hill, I received a letter from a social security in-spector in the London Borough of Hammersmith. He said that there was a very sick old man [he had just turned seventy-six] who was absolutely destitute in one of their hospitals, by the name of Alwyn D. Fox. The letter went on to say that Mr Fox had said that he was once a producer and he had discovered Michael Caine. Nobody be-lieved his story but the inspector said he was writing to me in case it was true and that if it was, could I please send a little money so

that he could buy Mr Fox a few extra luxuries to make what he was sure were the last few weeks of his life a little more comfortable.

I wrote a letter back immediately saying that it was indeed Alwyn Fox who had discovered me and given me my first chance as an actor and I included in the letter a cheque for five thousand dollars. Two weeks later I got another letter from the inspector which contained my uncashed cheque and a note saying that Alwyn had been very happy to receive the letter and had showed it to all the staff to prove that what he had said was true. He then went to sleep and died that same night.

26

RENDLESHAM, SUFFOLK

AN ALIEN DELEGATION ARRIVES TOO LATE TO
INTERVIEW RAEDWALD, GREATEST OF ALL THE
WUFFINGAS.

❦

The popular assumption that the first thing any extra-
terrestrial visitors say in such situations is: 'take me to
your leader' is here stunningly vindicated…

O NE SUNDAY MORNING IN October 1983 the people
of south-east Suffolk awoke to find themselves at the
heart of a high excitement. The *News of the World* had
run a report under the headline: 'UFO Lands in Suffolk – and That's
Official'. Some readers might have been a little surprised to note
that tidings of this sensation had taken almost three years to reach
the ears of the paper's news desk, but even so there was little doubt
from now on that Rendlesham, a few miles out of Woodbridge on
the way to the sea, had taken on a significance denied to it until
this moment for something like twelve centuries.

What seems to have happened was this. In the early hours of
Boxing Day morning, 1980, US servicemen on patrol at Woodbridge airfield, a site hacked out of Rendlesham Forest during the
war as a space for emergency landings, saw a strange object in the
sky – metallic, some thought, with a strange yellow mist about it –
and a brilliant light through the trees. They thought an aircraft had
crashed and alerted the police, who, having searched the area,
thought there was nothing to worry about. The brilliant light, they
were satisfied, came from the lighthouse at Orford Ness. Later that
day the servicemen returned to the site where they found what

they thought were significant imprints and damage to nearby trees. The police were called in again; again they were unimpressed and thought the marks on the ground had been left by animals.

Still convinced that something weird had occurred, the service-men went back to the spot two days later with metal detectors. The deputy base commander, Lt. Col. Charles Halt, investigated the site, noting his impressions on a cassette recorder. Around 2 a.m., flashing lights were seen in the sky, and the tape records the men's reactions. 'There's something very, very strange,' Halt exclaims, and then, 'Here he comes again from the south! He's coming towards us now!' and 'This is unreal!'

As time went on, more evidence was brought forward to attest to disturbing events in Rendlesham Forest. In a book he published in 1993 called *Left at East Gate*, one of the security team at the airfield, Larry Warren, claimed to have seen a senior US officer in conversation with extraterrestrials, and later to have chatted himself to a tiny little ET dressed in a white jumpsuit. In 2002, inspired by reports that the parliamentary ombudsman had censured the Ministry of Defence for failing to release information it held on the incident, Mark Lucas went back to the site for the *Independent* in company with a woman called Brenda Butler – 'a UFO expert', as he described her; her partner Peter Parish; her German shepherd dog, Mason, who, according to Butler, had several times been chased by strange lights that engulfed him; and a hypnopsychotherapist called Marek Sinski. This was someone Lucas had met on his way there and who had asked to be allowed to come along for the ride. At one point Sinski fell into a trance, declaring when he resurfaced that something very important had happened.

Disappointingly, no extraterrestrial clad in a white jumpsuit joined them for the occasion, but as Brenda Butler explained, they came and went as they chose. Sometimes, she said, they had turned aggressive; her hair had been pulled and her partner had been hit on the back with a stick – but they'd had a good laugh about that with the aliens afterwards. Butler, a former clairvoyant who disclosed that she herself had been abducted on several occasions by small grey aliens, believed the visitors came through a portal, on interdimensional energy. Asked if people found her accounts bizarre, she replied that she didn't care what they thought. Going out on these expeditions, she insisted, was better than sitting at home drinking coffee and watching the television.

Senior US serving officers, though, are not always known for their fanciful imaginations and what Lt. Col. Halt had to report steers nearer to credibility. The journalist and writer Ian Ridpath accommodates much of the evidence for and against the Rendlesham visitation on his website, where he suggests an explanation that seems to account for much of what witnesses saw on these nights after Christmas. Halt gave the wrong dates for his investigation, and once Ridpath had reallocated them to the correct day, much more became clear. Dr John Mason, who collected reports of unusual sightings for the British Astronomical Association, established that an exceptionally brilliant meteor had appeared in the sky in the early hours of Boxing Day morning, while Ridpath himself confirmed that the intervals between flashes of light reported by Halt corresponded exactly with those of the Orford lighthouse.

In a piece that the *Guardian* published on 5 January 1985, Ridpath wrote: 'If it seems surprising that a colonel in the US Air Force should identify a star as a UFO, consider the alternatives. Is it likely that a bright, flashing UFO should hover over southern England for three hours without being spotted by anyone other than a group of excited airmen?… UFO hunters will continue to believe that an alien spaceship landed in Rendlesham Forest that night. But I know that the first sighting coincided with the burn-up in the atmosphere of an exceptionally bright meteor, and that the airmen who saw the flashing UFO between the pine trees were looking straight at the Orford Ness lighthouse. The rest of the case is a marvellous product of human imagination.'

Yet Nick Pope, who ran the UFO desk at the MoD – set up, the department claimed, perhaps a shade sheepishly, because they had a duty to monitor all possible threats to national security, and shut down in cash-strapped 2009 as an unnecessary use of public money – is unconvinced by that explanation. And believers note that a former Chief of the Defence Staff, Lord Hill-Norton, was one of their number. Perhaps the wisest reaction to this and all other UFO sightings is to adopt a default position of scepticism, but tempered with the famous advice of Hamlet: 'There are more things in heaven and earth, Horatio, than are dreamt of in your philosophy.' That being so, there's a necessary question here that seems to have been neglected by Ufologists, one which Brenda Butler seems not to have asked her unearthly interlocutors – or which, perhaps, the man from the *Independent* failed to ask her about. It is this: why should these aliens, having discovered their portal, have chosen out of all England, all Britain, all Europe, indeed the whole world, Rendlesham, in Suffolk?

I took a bus out of Ipswich that said Rendlesham on the front. Having skirted Woodbridge, it took me down the A1152 towards Tunstall and Snape before turning left on to a side road. From here it proceeded down what might be called an urban spine road, except that the spine was gently curved, thus relieving the general monotony of a procession of houses, mostly detached, some semis, in various shades of red, brown and cream, but all relentlessly recent. This seemed odd, as my *Shell Guide to Suffolk* had promised something quite different: a church with a lofty nave and chancel and a fourteenth-century window, a fine old rectory, and two lodges – all that remained of the old Rendlesham House.

After five minutes or so we came to the end of the houses and appeared to rejoin the main road. 'Excuse me,' I said to the driver, 'but when do we come to the centre of Rendlesham – the church, the pubs, the shops, the school, the fine old rectory, that kind of thing?' He treated me to one of those weary, pitying looks that people on public service so often deploy when they find themselves confronted by an undoubted dolt. 'You've just been through it,' he said.

Clearly, in 1980 the extraterrestrials could not have been aiming to land in this Rendlesham, since it did not then exist. The land it occupies was then still part of a second air base used at the end of the war by the Americans: Bentwaters, whose purpose was proudly stated on a sign displayed near the main entrance: 'Peace through Superior Firepower'. But the Cold War ended, and the judgement was reached that superior firepower no longer needed to be deployed in this quarter of Suffolk. So the last Americans left in 1993, and the local government had to decide what to do with the place. Some in the area favoured a civil airport, but the nearness of Stansted, Norwich and Cambridge airports precluded that. A university for yoga flying was unsuccessfully mooted. In the end, the decision went to modern housing estates, privately built and sold. The result is as much a concocted modern community as the Prince of Wales's at Poundbury, though the effect is not quite so markedly one of pastiche.

There is, however, another Rendlesham, though you'd hardly know that today unless you had been tipped off about it, or had read about it in history books. About a mile before the bus turns off the main road into the modern Rendlesham, there's a narrow country lane whose signpost offers St Gregory's church and Campsey Ash. When I came here first, it still said Rendlesham, but that has been changed, presumably since it had caused confusion among drivers in search of its more compelling late twentieth-century neighbour. At the top of this road you will find the imposing church (kept locked, but keys can be obtained nearby) and the fine old rectory, not occupied for a good many years I suspect by any old rectors.

There must have been some consideration for putting a link road in between these two Rendleshams, but in fact no attempt has been made to associate the two places. Old Rendlesham has lived through many years of decline. An 1868 gazetteer said of it: 'the village, which is small and irregularly built, was once a small market town… the church… is an ancient structure, with a tower… There is a free school, chiefly supported by Lord Rendlesham, who is lord of the manor. Rendlesham Hall is the principal residence.' Now it is not even deemed worth a signpost.

Yet here, I think, we come to what UFO believers should surely by now have identified as the key to this whole mysterious business. For this now almost airbrushed-out Rendlesham was once a place of great consequence, described by Bede as 'a kingly town'. This was indisputably the home of the mighty Wuffingas, descendants of Offa and kings of East Anglia. The greatest of these, who by defeating the king of Northumbria in a battle close to the river Idle near Bawtry, Yorkshire, became the supreme king in all England, was the seventh-century king Raedwald. His connection with Rendlesham used to be stated in terms of unwavering certainty. 'At Rendlesham in this county,' wrote John Wodderspoon is his *Historic Sites and Other Remarkable and Interesting Places in the County of Suffolk*, published in 1839, 'it is recorded that Redwald, a King of the East Angles, built a magnificent palace for the residence of himself and his court, and occupied the building as his seat of government. The place where once stood this ancient building is near the spot now occupied by Rendlesham House, the seat of the present Lord Rendlesham.'

When, in one of the most astonishing archaeological discoveries of the twentieth century, the burial ship at Sutton Hoo, some four miles from Rendlesham, was uncovered in 1939, it was thought, not least because of its grandeur, that the man buried within it could very well have been Raedwald. 'Nothing has yet been found which can produce a decisive identification,' wrote H. M. Chadwick, Professor of Anglo-Saxon in the University of Cambridge from 1912 to 1941. 'There is no reason for doubting that he was a wealthy East Anglian king... All probability is in favour of the great and wealthy high-king Raedwald, who seems to have died about 624–5.' Reviewing the available evidence in an instructive book called *The Reckoning of King Raedwald*, the Suffolk-based historian Sam Newton concludes that from all that we know so far, 'Raedwald is the most likely of the Wuffing lords to have lain in state in the great ship berthed beneath Mound One at Sutton Hoo.'

Bede, almost the only source for what we know about Raedwald, is not a total admirer. The king, he says, having earlier been a subordinate of King Ethelbert of Kent, followed him in embracing Christianity, but influenced by his wife and 'certain perverse advisers', apostasized from the true faith, trying to serve both Christ and the ancient gods, and having within his temple two altars, one dedicated to Christ and the other 'on which victims were offered to devils'. This made him 'a man of noble descent but ignoble in his actions.' Bede, of course, was a churchman, Raedwald a politician – no doubt settling in this instance for what later generations would call an each-way bet.

So here at last is a reason why strange little people in natty white jumpsuits might have picked out this airfield site close to Rendlesham and even closer to Sutton Hoo, as their likeliest destination. The popular assumption that the first thing any extraterrestrial visitors say in such situations is 'Take me to your leader' is here stunningly vindicated. They were hoping by coming here to meet the most powerful man in the land. Unhappily, their intelligence seems to have been out of date, by something like twelve centuries; but no doubt across such vast distances news travels slowly. This would also explain why most Ufologists – though not Brenda Butler, who told the man from the *Independent* that she still encountered these creatures quite regularly – assume they have never returned.

The Forestry Commission has established a UFO trail through Rendlesham Forest, which takes you by an irregular route to the edge of the now largely derelict Woodbridge Airfield. When I went there the information kiosk was shut and there wasn't much guidance along the way as to what exactly one ought to be looking for. But it makes for a pleasant stroll through woods that, because of the extensive damage in the great storm of 1987, have been largely replanted since the aliens allegedly came here. True, on the day I came, part of the airfield was in ear-splitting use for some kind of motor cycle event; the decibel level for such occasions is said in instructions to participants to be fixed at 103 *dba* at 0.5 metres from each exhaust (and ABSOLUTELY NO REVVING OF ENGINES BEFORE 10 a.m. please), but when such events are on you would hardly go to the forest for peace and reflection. Even so, one might say, concurring on this count at least with Brenda Butler, wandering through this territory is better than sitting at home drinking coffee and watching the television.

AFTERWORD

⁊⧫

There's never any shortage of reasons for visiting Shropshire. Handsome historic Shrewsbury, the county town; glorious Ludlow, with its castle, church and irreplaceable streets; Bridgnorth on its perch high above the Severn, less admired than Ludlow but pleasingly less self-conscious; calm, stately Much Wenlock, with its sixteenth-century Guildhall and ruined twelfth-century priory which revived the Olympic Games well before the rest of the world got round to it; then smaller towns like Bishops Castle, tucked just inside the Welsh border, with its amiable High Street climbing up from the church to its eccentric town hall, Church Stretton, beneath the Long Mynd, Cleobury Mortimer… And beyond, Ironbridge, recreated birthplace of the Industrial Revolution, and the villages that A. E. Housman commemorated as the quietest under the sun: Clunton and Clunbury, Clungunford and Clun; together with treasures to be sought out deep in the countryside, like Llanyblodwel and Upton Cressett.

It's a long and alluring list, which would not, on most calculations, find a place for the railway junction town that was named, there being little else to name it for, after a hotel called the Craven Arms. The railway company, perhaps having calculated that few would wish to visit Craven Arms except to change trains (the minor lines to Bishops Castle and to Wenlock, Coalbrookdale, Wellington and Shifnal went long ago, but the Heart of Wales line, mysteriously saved from every railway 'rationalization', still potters at intervals through Knighton, Llandrindod Wells and Llandeilo to Swansea) originally called its station Craven Arms and Stokesay, invoking a fortified manor house, long the home of the Craven family, and then, as now, very much on the tourist trail, a mile or two down the road. But Craven Arms? Before the railway came in the middle nineteenth century there was nothing here but a tiny village called Newton. You can savour the wooded hills around it, but the town itself seems at first glance to have little or nothing to offer.

But now, down one of these drab grid pattern streets, in the old market hall, there's been added to its etiolated list of attractions a place called Stella Mitchell's Land of Lost Content. It's the fruit of some forty years of obsessive collecting of overlooked everyday objects, which began when the young Stella Brain was an art student in Birmingham. She decided to make them the basis of a permanent show, and in time with her husband Dave Mitchell set up in a disused church in East Wittering near Chichester, calling their project Rejectamenta. Their shift to Shropshire in 2003 enabled them to find a new name for the operation in the pages of that great celebrator of Shropshire, A. E. Housman: 'That is the land of lost content, / I see it shining plain. / The happy highways where I went / And cannot come again.' They might equally well have called it 'The Way We Lived Then'. And a further plangent, insistent subtext keeps cropping up as you wander through the collection: those were the days; fings ain't wot they used t' be.

It's a kind of anthology of the twentieth century, built on items resurrected from such humble sources as car boot sales and skips, re-enlivening the treasures, preoccupations, everyday artefacts, distractions and general baggage of household and high street life. For those who have lived through half or more of the twentieth century, the main emotion here is nostalgia – nostalgia above all for the acquisitions that seemed at the time so thrilling and now look so demeaningly obsolete: the clunking wireless sets, the tiny televisions, a 1980s Commodore computer; though less so perhaps for the primitive electric heaters, which seem to have 'lethal' written all over them, or the drills with which your dentist attacked you, pedalling away with his foot.

Yet these rooms must also be fascinating for any intelligent child.

Was it really like that? Did you really go out dancing in a dress like that, Grandma? Did your family really sit in the evenings playing Escalado, the thrilling action race game, while that soupy music crooned away on your Dansette record player? Did you really all rock with hilarity when Mother fetched from the cupboard a game called Impertinent Questions, The Mirth Maker That Sets the World Laughing (with a picture on the box of the globe, close to splitting its sides)? Did the week's washing really involve an object that looks like a tank with a mangle attached to the top of it? Indeed it did.

Stella Mitchell attaches to her exhibits sharp, evocative, sometimes caustic comments, reminding the visitor of pleasures and values embodied in her domestic scenes which the subsequent years have forgotten or disregarded. 'In honour,' says one, 'of all those who went before; who lived much harder lives than the children of today can ever imagine and yet seem to have known a "content" that we have lost along the way somewhere.' When, after a couple of years, I went back there for a second visit I noticed not only new acquisitions (Harry Potter is here now, of course, and I don't remember seeing before the Sinclair C5 hanging upside down from a ceiling) but also – what had not at all struck me before – the expressions on the faces of the dummy figures around whom some of the scenes are built. They are, of course, nothing but waxworks, yet there seemed on almost all of their faces – discounting one who's asleep in his chair with the *Chichester Observer*, bearing the headline: 'City Centre Cars Ban Likely by 1973', draped over his face – a look of mute disappointed reproach. Respect us, they seem to be saying. We were once as real as you.

That put me in mind of another beautiful Housman poem, where he reflects on the past that is buried beneath and within the present:

> On Wenlock Edge the wood's in trouble;
> His forest fleece the Wrekin heaves;
> The gale, it plies the saplings double,

And thick on Severn snow the leaves.

'Twould blow like this through holt and hanger
When Uricon the city stood:
'Tis the old wind in the old anger,
But then it threshed another wood.

Then, 'twas before my time, the Roman
At yonder heaving hill would stare:
The blood that warms an English yeoman,
The thoughts that hurt him, they were there.

There, like the wind through woods in riot,
Through him the gale of life blew high;
The tree of man was never quiet:
Then 'twas the Roman, now 'tis I.

The gale, it plies the saplings double,
It blows so hard, 'twill soon be gone:
To-day the Roman and his trouble
Are ashes under Uricon.

And oddly, the most potent effect of Stella Mitchell's museum, outdistancing even the persistent theme that for all its privations the past was a more contented time than today, comes at the moment you leave it. After this hour locked away in the past, the drab, utilitarian grid-patterned streets with their routine late-Victorian cottages, the lettering of the names on the shop fronts, the decorated delivery van outside the florists', seem suddenly full of colour and life. The Land of Lost Content teaches you to treasure the everyday, the unremarked upon, the taken for granted.

The past, says L. P. Hartley in the endlessly quoted line from *The Go-Between*, is 'a foreign country: they do things differently there'. Yet navigating the narrow stairs through Stella Mitchell's collection; walking the South London streets where the crowds jostled and stretched in the hope of seeing Garibaldi; standing quietly in the churchyard at Llandeilo where the rowdy and drunken Carmarthenshire election of 1802 reached its climax; wandering the streets where people observed the dogged rough-suited progress of Hugh Miller through Cromarty; or perched on the edge of Hampstead Heath where Lucy Houston used to appear with her cornucopian handbag, looking for wantful persons on whom to bestow her benevolence, Hartley's unconditional claim no longer feels true. The past illuminates and serves to explain our present: our present predicts the future. We wonder at the survivals in Stella Mitchell's collection now; coming generations will wonder in much the same way at that which surrounds us today. We smile at their Commodore computers – how could it have been so exciting to acquire something so simple and clumsy? Yet without them we would not today have the rampant, endlessly multiplying technologies without which our twenty-first-century lives would seem hopelessly incomplete; technologies that in such a museum in fifty years' time will seem just as quaint and sentimentally pitiable as the ones that our forerunners marvelled at.

Then 'twas the Roman, now 'tis I.

SOURCES AND
FURTHER READING

A constant companion throughout has been the *Oxford Dictionary of National Biography*, augmented on occasion by *Who Was Who* and the *Annual Register*. To discover how people and events were seen through local eyes, I have made extensive use of the local daily and weekly press, as cited chapter by chapter.

Additional chapters not included in this book, together with a much longer account of the decline and fall of the Peels, can be found at www.brightparticular.info

I LOWER LYDBROOK, GLOUCESTERSHIRE

For explorations of the Wye: William Gilpin, *Observations on the River Wye, and several parts of South Wales, &c. relative chiefly to Picturesque Beauty; made in the summer of the year 1770 by William Gilpin, M.A.* (London, 1782); Charles Heath, *The Excursion Down the Wye. From Ross to Monmouth, including Historical and Descriptive Accounts of Wilton and Goodrich Castles; also of Court Field, etc.* (Monmouth, 1808); Thomas Whately, *Observations on Modern Gardening* (London, 1770); M. Willett, *The strangers' guide to the banks of the Wye: including Chepstow, Piercefield, Windcliff, Tintern Abbey, Raglan Castle, and other parts of the Welsh borders: with historical, topographical, and antiquarian remarks* (Bristol, 1845); and William Wordsworth, 'Lines composed a few miles above Tintern Abbey, on revisiting the banks of the Wye during a tour' in *Poetical Works of William Wordsworth* (London, 1842). For an ingenious examination of where Wordsworth was when these feelings came over him, see David S. Miall, *Locating Wordsworth: 'Tintern Abbey' and the Community with Nature* <http://www.erudit.org/revue/ron/2000/v/n20/005949ar.html> For mockery of Gilpin: William Combe, *Dr Syntax's Three Tours: In Search of the Picturesque, of Consolation, and of a Wife*, Illustrations by T. Rowlandson (London, 1809).

For modern assessments of Wye Valley industry: S. D. Coates, *The Water Powered Industries of the Lower Wye Valley: the River Wye from Tintern to Redbrook* (Monmouth Borough Museums Service, Monmouth, 1992); and of the valley's romantic appeal: C. S. Matheson, *Enchanting Ruin: Tintern Abbey and Romantic Tourism in Wales* (University of Michigan, 2007).

2 LLANDEILO, CARMARTHENSHIRE

The quotation from Edwin Poole is taken from Arthur Mee (ed), *Carmarthenshire Notes, Antiquarian, Topographical and Curious, vol. 1* (Llanelli, 1889–91). This is not the Arthur Mee of the King's England books but an earlier one, Scottish-born but a journalist in Wales. The quotation from Anne Beale is taken from Eirwen Jones, *Concise History of Llandeilo* (Llandeilo, 1984).

For a compendious collection of electoral wrong-doings, see T. H. B. Oldfield, *The Representative History of Great Britain and Ireland: Being a History of the House of Commons, and of the Counties, Cities, and Boroughs of the United Kingdom, from the earliest period. In six volumes* (London, 1816). Also, Cornelius O'Leary, *The Elimination of Corrupt Practices in British Elections 1868–1911* (Oxford, 1962).

3 BISHOPS CANNINGS, WILTSHIRE

For the village of Bishops Cannings, see Ida Gandy, *Round About the Little Steeple: The Story of a Downland village and its Parson in the Seventeenth Century* (London, 1960) (the drum is on p. 22). Also the same writer's *A Wiltshire Childhood* (London, 1929). For comparable events elsewhere in the county, Alfred Williams, *A Wiltshire Village* (London, 1920). For the village church, Simon Jenkins, *England's Thousand Best Churches* (London, 1999).

For the history of friendly societies, P. H. J. H. Gosden, *The Friendly Societies in England 1815–1875* (Manchester, 1961). For Lloyd George's disillusion with them, A. G. Gardiner, *The Pillars of Society* (London, 1913). Friendly society records cited here are held in the archives at the Wiltshire and Swindon History Centre, Chippenham.

4 TIDESWELL, DERBYSHIRE

For Blincoe as told to Brown: John Brown, *A memoir of Robert Blincoe, an orphan boy: sent from the workhouse of St Pancras, London, at seven years of age, to endure the horrors of a cotton-mill, through his infancy and youth: with a minute detail of his sufferings, being the first memoir of the kind published* (London, Manchester, 1832). For an echoing testimony, Revd J. R. Stephens, *Orphan John at Litton Mill* (from *Ashton Chronicle*, May 1849), in *Orphan Child Factory Workers at Litton and Cressbrook Mills: the Dark Satanic Mills, re-edited by Martin Hulbert*, no publisher stated, available at St John the Baptist church, Tideswell. For a mildly sceptical account of these events, Canon J. M. J. Fletcher, *Tideswell in the Days of Parson Brown 1780–1836* (Tideswell, 1929); republished with additions (Tideswell, 1986). For a deeply sceptical one, Stanley D. Chapman, *The Early Factory Masters: the Transition to the Factory in the Midlands Textile Industry* (Newton Abbot, 1967). For a modern retelling of Blincoe's story, John Waller, *The Real Oliver Twist. Robert Blincoe – A Life That Illuminates a Violent Age* (Thriplow, 2005).

5 CRANE COURT, LONDON

The Satirist newspaper is held at the British Library Newspaper Reading Room, Colindale.

On the early days of Crane Court and surroundings, John Timbs, *Curiosities of London: Exhibiting the Most Remarkable Objects of Interest in the Metropolis, with Nearly Fifty Years' Personal Recollections* (London, 1855).

On events in the theatres, W. J. Linton, *Memoirs* (London, 1895; first published as *Three Score and Ten Years*, New York, 1894).

6 BIRMINGHAM

On the nature of G. F. Muntz, see Eliezer Edwards, *Personal Recollections of Birmingham and Birmingham Men* (Birmingham, 1877).

On Muntz's and other political beards, David W. Bartlett, *What I saw in London: or, Men and things in the great metropolis* (Auburn, 1852); William White, *The Inner Life of the House of Commons, with new introduction by E. J. Feuchtwanger* (Richmond, Surrey, 1973); Andrew Roberts, *Salisbury, Victorian Titan* (London, 1999).

On beards in general, William Andrews, *At the Sign of the Barber's Pole; Studies in Hirsute History* (Cottingham, 1904); Reginald Reynolds, *Beards: Their Social Standing, Religious Involvements, Decorative Possibilities, and Value in Offence and Defence Through the Ages* (London, 1949).

7 KILWINNING, AYRSHIRE

The main source for this chapter is Revd William Lee Ker, *Kilwinning* (Kilwinning, 1900). See also Ian Anstruther, *The Knight and the Umbrella: An Account of the Eglinton Tournament 1839* (London, 1963). (Because of the rain, one of the knights went into action sporting a large umbrella.) For notable ceremonial fiascos, see David Cannadine, *The Content, Performance and Meaning of Ritual: The British Monarchy and the 'Invention of Tradition', c. 1820–1977*, published in *The Invention of Tradition*, edited by E. J. Hobsbawm and Terence Ranger (Cambridge, 1983).

8 BROADWAY, WORCESTERSHIRE

Much of this chapter is based on Henrietta-Phillipps's diary, as selected and edited by the Shakespeare scholar Marvin Spevack, *A Victorian Chronicle: the diary of Henrietta Halliwell-Phillipps, selected by Marvin Spevack* (Hildesheim, 1999). The essential source for Sir Thomas is A. N. L. Munby, *Portrait of an Obsession. The Life of Sir Thomas Phillipps, the World's Greatest Book Collector, adapted by Nicolas Barker from the five volumes of 'Phillipps studies'* (London, 1967).

9 CHELTENHAM, GLOUCESTERSHIRE

Contemporary accounts used in this chapter were chiefly George Jacob Holyoake, *Sixty Years of an Agitator's Life*, 2 volumes (London, 1892), and *Occasional Sermons Preached in the Parish Church of Cheltenham by the Rev. F. Close, M.A., Incumbent* (London and Cheltenham, 1844), available on Google Books. Also three Cheltenham newspapers: the *Chronicle*, the *Examiner* and the *Free Press*. Recent accounts are chiefly Owen Ashton, *Clerical Control and Radical Responses in Cheltenham Spa 1838–1848*, in Midland History 8 (Birmingham, 1983); also Gwen Hart, *A History of Cheltenham* (Leicester, 1965).

10 AUSTREY, WARWICKSHIRE

The two main sources here are available on Google Books. They are: *The trial of Lawrence, Earl Ferrers, for the murder of John Johnson: before the Right Honourable the House of Peers in Westminster-Hall in full Parliament, on Wednesday the 16th, Thursday the 17th, and Friday the 18th of April, 1760: on the last of which days, judgment for murder was given* (London, 1760) and *Proceedings Upon the Trial of the Action Brought by Mary Elizabeth Smith against the Right Hon. Washington Sewallis Shirley Earl Ferrers for Breach of Promise of Marriage; Damages Laid at £20,000; before Mr Justice Wightman and a Special Jury on the 14th 16th 17th and 18th of February 1846 in the Queen's Bench Westminster Hall* (London, 1846).

The *Britannia* newspaper is held in the British Newspaper Library, Colindale.

11 CROMARTY

Books by Hugh Miller include: *Poems, written in the Leisure Hours of a Journeyman Mason* (Inverness, 1829); *Letters on the Herring Fishing in the Moray Frith, by the author of 'Poems, written in the Leisure Hours of a Journeyman Mason* (Inverness, 1829); *Scenes and Legends of the North of Scotland; or, The Traditional History of Cromarty* (London, 1850)*; My Schools and Schoolmasters; or the Story of My Education* (Edinburgh, 1860); *The Old Red Sandstone; or, New Walks in Old Fields* (London, 1906)*; The Cruise of the Betsey; or, A Summer Ramble among the Fossiliferous Deposits of the Hebrides, with, Rambles of a Geologist* (Edinburgh, 1858); *First Impressions of England and its People* (Edinburgh, *c.* 1861).

Books about Hugh Miller: Peter Bayne, *The Life and Letters of Hugh Miller* (2 volumes), (London, 1871); George Rosie, *Hugh Miller, Outrage and Order; a biography and selected writings, with an introduction by Neal Ascherson* (Edinburgh, 1981); Michael A. Taylor, *Hugh Miller, Stonemason, Geologist, Writer; foreword by Marian Allardyce McKenzie Johnston, preface by David Alston* (Edinburgh, 2007).

12 HARTLEPOOL

The main source for this chapter is Eric Waggott, *Jackson's Town: The Story of the Creation of West Hartlepool and the Success and Downfall of its Founder,*

Ralph Ward Jackson, Including the Battle for Christ Church (Hartlepool, 1980). There are also Robert Martin, *Historical Notes and Personal Recollections of West Hartlepool and its Founder (Ralph Ward Jackson)* (West Hartlepool, 1924); Robert Wood, *West Hartlepool: the Rise and Development of a Victorian New Town* (West Hartlepool, 1967).

13 NINE ELMS, LONDON

The main source for this chapter is the local press in London and Southampton. There are many lives of Garibaldi: see, for instance, Jasper Ridley, *Garibaldi* (London, 1974); Lucy Riall, *Garibaldi: Invention of a Hero* (New Haven and London, *c.* 2007). The McGonagall poem was the first he wrote: he slipped it through the letter box of the *Dundee Weekly News*, which published it. See his 'brief autobiography' in *Poetic Gems selected from the works of William McGonagall, poet and tragedian* (Dundee and London, 1969), p. 7.

14 BLOOMSBURY, LONDON

For Procter's writings: Adelaide Anne Procter (ed.), *The Victoria Regia. Original Contributions in Poetry and Prose* (London, 1861); *Legends and Lyrics* (London, 1879); *A Chaplet of Verses* (London, 1862); *The Poems of Adelaide A. Procter* (Boston, Mass., 1863). For assessments of her writings: Margaret Drabble and Jenny Stringer (eds), *The Concise Oxford Companion to English Literature* (Oxford, 1987); Gill Gregory, *The Life and Work of Adelaide Procter: Poetry, Feminism and Fathers* (Aldershot, *c.*1998).

15 BLACKBURN

For a Blackburn view, see Graham Phythian, *Shooting Stars: the Brief and Glorious History of Blackburn Olympic F.C., 1878–1888* (Nottingham, 2007). Also local newspapers as cited. For an Old Etonian view, see *Eton College Chronicle*, held at Eton College library; Shane Leslie, *Men Were Different: Five Studies in Late Victorian Biography* (London, 1937).

16 GILLINGHAM, KENT

The main source for this chapter is P. G. Rogers, *The Sixth Trumpeter. The Story of Jezreel and his Tower* (London, 1963). There is much useful material on the sect at the Medway Archives and Local Studies Centre, Civic Centre, Strood, Kent. For an account of the tower as Gillingham's one conspicuous landmark, see Pennethorne Hughes, *Kent – a Shell Guide* (London, 1969).

17 SPITALFIELDS, LONDON

The main sources for this chapter were Anne J. Kershen, *Strangers, Aliens and Asians: Huguenots, Jews and Bangladeshis in Spitalfields 1660–2000* (London, 2005), and Kershen (ed.), *London, the Promised Land? The Migrant Experience in a Capital City* (Aldershot, c. 1997); Dr Gerry Black, *J. F. S., The History of the Jews' Free School, London, since 1732* (London, 1998). Israel Zangwill, *Children of the Ghetto: a Study of a Peculiar People* (London, 1893) is a matchless evocation of Jewish Spitalfields. See also Ed Glinert, *The London Compendium: A Street-by-street Exploration of the Hidden Metropolis* (London, 2003); Lisa Picard, *Victorian London* (London, 2005); John G. Bennett, *A Journey Through Whitechapel and Spitalfields* (Nottingham, 2009); and Monica Ali, *Brick Lane* (London, 2003).

For a vivid account of Money Moses's malpractices, see Camden Pelham (pseudonym), *The Chronicles of Crime, or, the New Newgate Calendar, being a Series of Memoirs and Anecdotes of Notorious Characters who have Outraged the Laws of Great Britain from the Earliest Period to the Present Time* (London, 1891), available on Google Books.

18 CRADLEY HEATH, STAFFORDSHIRE

For Mary Macarthur, see Mary Agnes Hamilton, *Mary Macarthur: A Biographical Sketch* (London, 1925); Margaret Cole, *Women of Today* (London, 1938). For Galsworthy's visit to Cradley Heath, John Galsworthy, *The Inn of Tranquillity: Studies and Essays* (London, 1912). See also Robert H. Sherard, *The White Slaves of England* (London, 1897); *Women Chain Makers. Be Anvil or Hammer!* (Dudley, 2009).

333

19 SHOREHAM BEACH, SUSSEX

N. E. B. Wolters, *Bungalow Town: Theatre and Film Colony* (Shoreham, 1985) and the Marlipins Museum exemplify the value of a dedicated local historian to a community such as this one. Dennis Hardy and Colin Ward, *Arcadia for All: The Legacy of a Makeshift Landscape* (Nottingham, 2004) is a wonderful guide to this as to many other improvised off-beat places.

20 EYNSFORD, KENT

Reliable sources for Warlock: Barry Smith, *Peter Warlock: The Life of Philip Heseltine* (Oxford, 1994); Gwen McIntyre, *Peter Warlock 1894–1930: The Eynsford Years* (pamphlet for Farningham and Eynsford Local History Society, Farningham, 1996). Less reliable sources: Cecil Gray, *Peter Warlock: A Memoir of Philip Heseltine, with contributions by Sir Richard Terry and Robert Nichols; foreword by Augustus John* (London, 1934). Far from entirely reliable, though extremely vivid: Nina Hamnett, *Is She a Lady? A Problem in Autobiography* (London, 1955).

21 DRAYTON MANOR, STAFFORDSHIRE

Much of this chapter is based on press reports, particularly those of *The Times* and above all the *Tamworth Herald*. There are two standard biographies of the great Sir Robert: Norman Gash, *Mr Secretary Peel: The Life of Sir Robert Peel to 1830* (London, 1961) and *Sir Robert Peel: The Life of Sir Robert Peel after 1830* (London, 1986); Douglas Hurd, *Robert Peel: a Biography* (London, 2007). The first Peel biography, quoted here, was, as published in English, F. P. G. Guizot, *Memoirs of Sir Robert Peel* (London, 1857).

For the third baronet: William White, *The Inner Life of the House of Commons with new introduction by E. J. Feuchtwanger* (Richmond, Surrey, 1973); Edward Stanley, 15th Earl of Derby, *A Selection from the Diaries of Edward Henry Stanley, 15th Earl of Derby, edited by John Vincent,* Camden 5th Series, vol. 4 (London, 1994). There is more material, most of it unflattering, on this Sir Robert as Chief Secretary to Ireland, in *The Journal of John Wodehouse, First Earl of Kimberley, for 1862–1902, edited by Angus Hawkins and John Powell,* Camden 5th Series, vol. 9 (London, 1997).

The fourth baronet published two novels: *An Engagement* (London, 1896); and *A Bit of a Fool* (London, 1897).

For the fifth baronet, see Beatrice Lillie, *Every Other Inch a Lady: An Autobiography by Beatrice Lillie aided and abetted by John Philip, written with James Brough* (New York, 1972) and Joseph Hunter, *My Memories of Fazeley and the Peels of Drayton Manor* (Fazeley, n.d.).

For the subsequent fate of Drayton Manor, see Fred Bromwich, *Drayton Manor: George and Vera Bryan's Memories of a Family Fun Park* (Tamworth, 2006).

22 BOOSBECK, CLEVELAND

Michael Tippett, *Those Twentieth Century Blues: an Autobiography* (London, 1991).

Mark Whyman, *The Last Pennymans of Ormesby, vol. 1, 1883–1944: The Lives of Jim and Ruth Pennyman; edited with additional text by Mark Whyman* (Richmond, North Yorkshire, 2008).

Malcolm Chase and Mark Whyman, *Heartbreak Hill, a Response to Unemployment in East Cleveland in the 1930s* (Cleveland, 1991).

23 NORTH END, HAMPSTEAD

The *Saturday Review* is held at the British Library Newspaper Reading Room, Colindale, and at the London Library. For the lady observed at close quarters: J. Wentworth Day, *Lady Houston, D.B.E; the Woman Who Won the War* (London, 1958); H. Warner Allen, *Lucy Houston, D.B.E: 'One of the Few'; a Memoir* (London, 1947); Collin Brooks, *Fleet Street, Press Barons and Politics: the Journals of Collin Brooks, 1932–1940. Edited by N. J. Crowson*. Camden 5th Series, vol. 11 (Cambridge, 1998). For Nesta Webster, see especially Nesta H. Webster, *Secret Societies and Subversive Movements* (London, 1924); *The Surrender of an Empire* (London, 1931). For a wider account of the tendency of which these people formed part, see Richard Griffiths, *Fellow Travellers of the Right: British Enthusiasts for Nazi Germany 1933–9* (London, 1980).

In *Spitfire, the Biography* (London, 2006), Jonathan Glancey argues that Houston made a genuinely significant contribution to the development of the plane and therefore to the war effort.

24 TROWELL, NOTTINGHAMSHIRE

The main source for this chapter has been national and local newspapers. But see also Mary Banham and Bevis Hillier (eds), *A Tonic to the Nation: the Festival of Britain 1951, with a prologue by Roy Strong* (London, 1976); and Elain Harwood and Alan Powers (eds), *Festival of Britain* (London, 2001). The record of Commons exchanges is taken from House of Commons Hansard, vol. 484, 1950–51, pp. 881–3. For the motorway and its contribution to the fame of Trowell, see Joe Moran, *On Roads: A Hidden History* (London, 2009).

25 HORSHAM, SUSSEX

The main sources here are the *West Sussex County Times* and June Wyndham Davies; together with Michael Caine, *What's It All about? The Autobiography* (London, 1992).

26 RENDLESHAM, SUFFOLK

For a determined claim that it really happened, see Larry Warren and Peter Robbins, *Left at East Gate: a First-hand Account of the Bentwaters–Woodbridge U.F.O. incident, its cover-up and investigation* (London, 1997). For a firm assertion that it was all an illusion, see Ian Ridpath, <http://www.ianridpath.com/ufo/rendlesham1a.htm>. For earlier activities at Rendlesham, see Bede, *Ecclesiastical History of the English People*, edited by Bertram Colgrave and R. A. B. Mynors (Oxford, 1991); John Wodderspoon, *Historic Sites and Other Remarkable and Interesting Places in the County of Suffolk* (London and Ipswich, 1839); and Sam Newton, *The Reckoning of King Raedwald – The Story of the King linked to the Sutton Hoo ship-burial* (Colchester, 2003).

AFTERWORD

L. P. Hartley, *The Go-between* (London, 1953).
A. E. Housman, *Collected Poems of A. E. Housman* (London, 1939).

INDEX

❦